GCE **AS Level** Single Award

D1081343

DISCARD

AS Level for Edexcel

Health &
Social Care

Series editor:
Neil Moonie

www.heinemann.co.uk
✓ Free online support
✓ Useful weblinks
✓ 24 hour online ordering

01865 888058

Heinemann is an imprint of Pearson Education Limited, a company incorporated in England and Wales, having its registered office at Edinburgh Gate, Harlow, Essex, CM20 2JE. Registered company number: 872828

Heinemann is a registered trademark of Pearson Education Limited

Text © Neil Moonie, Anne Bates, Beryl Stretch 2005

First published 2005

10 09
10 9 8 7 6 5 4 3

British Library Cataloguing in Publication Data is available from the British Library on request.

ISBN 978 0 435 45371 8

Edited by Neil Moonie
Designed by Lorraine Inglis
Typeset by TechType, Abingdon, Oxon

Original illustrations © Harcourt Education Limited, 2005

Illustrated by TechType, Abingdon, Oxon

Cover design by Wooden Ark Studio

Printed by Scotprint

Cover photo: © Getty Images

Picture research by Ginny Stroud-Lewis and Ruth Blair

Acknowledgements
Every effort has been made to contact copyright holders of material reproduced in this book. Any omissions will be rectified in subsequent printings if notice is given to the publishers.

Websites
There are links to relevant websites in this book. In order to ensure that the links are up to date, that the links work, and that the sites are not inadvertently linked to sites that could be considered offensive, we have made the links available on the Heinemann website at www.heinemann.co.uk/hotlinks. When you access the site the express code is 3718S.

Please note that the examples of websites suggested in this book were up to date at the time of writing. It is essential for tutors to preview each site before using it to ensure that the URL is still accurate and the content is appropriate. We suggest that tutors bookmark useful sites and consider enabling students to access them through the school or college intranet.

Contents

Introduction

This book has been written to support students who are studying for the single award AS level GCE using the course structure designed by Edexcel. The book is designed to support the three AS level units:

Unit 1   Human Growth and Development (externally assessed)

Unit 2   Communication and Values (internally assessed)

Unit 3   Positive Care Environments (internally assessed)

This book has been organised to cover each of these units in detail. Headings are designed to make it easy to follow the content of each unit and to find the information needed to achieve a high grade. As well as providing information, each unit is designed to stimulate the development of the thinking skills needed to achieve an Advanced level award.

Assessment

Each unit will be assessed by coursework or by an external test set and marked by Edexcel. Detailed guidance for coursework assessment and external test requirements can be found in the unit specifications and at Edexcel's website: for access to this webite go to www.heinemann.co.uk/hotlinks webite and enter the express code 3718S. This book has been designed to support students to achieve high grades as set out in the guidance from Edexcel available during 2004/2005.

Special features of this book

Throughout the text there are a number of features that are designed to encourage reflection and to help students make links between theory and practice. In particular this book has been designed to encourage a depth of learning and understanding and to encourage students to go beyond a surface level of descriptive writing.

The special features of this book include:

Think it over   Think it over...

This feature is designed to provide thought provoking questions that will encourage reflective thinking, or possibly reflection involving discussion with others.

Did you know?   ✱ DID YOU KNOW?

Interesting facts or snippets of information included to encourage reflective thinking.

Scenario   SCENARIO

The term 'scenario' is used in place of the more traditional term 'case study' because the idea of people being perceived as 'cases' does not fit easily with the notion of empowerment - a key value highlighted by government policy and by Edexcel standards. Scenarios are presented throughout the units to help explain the significance of theoretical ideas to Health, Social Care and Early Years settings.

Consider this

A 'Consider this' feature is provided at the end of each subsection of each unit. Each 'Consider this' involves a brief scenario followed by a series of questions. The first questions ask you to identify issues; if you can do this then you are likely to be able to describe key issues. The next questions ask you to go into greater depth and analyse using theory. These questions are designed to challenge your thinking skills beyond a simple memory for information. Finally, there are questions that ask you to evaluate. At this level you are being challenged to access a wider range of learning in order to make an appropriate judgment or evaluation about an issue. The ability to evaluate is the 'thinking skill' that will enable students to achieve an A grade at Advanced level.

Key concept

Because the development of analytic and evaluative skills requires the ability to use concepts, the authors have identified key concepts and offered a brief explanation of how these terms might be used.

Assessment guidance

At the end of each unit there is a 'How you will be assessed' section that either provides sample test material for externally assessed units, or outlines guidance and ideas designed to help students achieve the highest grades when preparing internally-assessed coursework.

Glossary

This book contains a useful glossary to provide fast reference for key terms and concepts used within the units. Glossary terms are highlighted in **bold** throughout the book.

References

At the end of each unit there is a full list of references and further reading used within that unit together with a list of useful websites.

Author details

Neil Moonie, former Deputy Director of the Department of Social Services, Health and Education in a College of Further and Higher Education. Chartered Psychologist, part-time lecturer and contributor to a wide range of textbooks and learning resources in the field of health and social care. Editor of Heinemann's GNVQ Intermediate and Advanced textbooks on health and social care since 1993 and editor of the 2000 Standards AVCE textbook.

Beryl Stretch, former Head of Health and Social Care in a large College of Further Education. Currently part of the senior examining team for Edexcel, GCE and GCSE Health and Social Care. Former external and internal verifier for VCE, GNVQ, NVQ programmes and examiner for GCSE Human Biology. Contributor to several bestselling textbooks on health and social care at all levels.

Anne Bates has worked in statutory social work since 1977 in a range of settings including child care, mental health, adult services and inspection and monitoring of day care services with under 5's. Anne is currently working part-time as a social services team manager with a community dementia team and also as a lecturer and tutor on a social work degree programme in outer London.

UNIT 1

Human Growth and Development

This unit covers the following sections:

1.1 Life stages and aspects of human growth and development

1.2 Factors affecting growth and development

1.3 Promoting health and well-being

Introduction

Every health and social care practitioner needs to acquire a working knowledge of the ways in which people grow and develop between conception and later adulthood. Key periods (or life stages) are characterised by distinctive patterns of growth and the development of a range of skills and abilities. The rate of growth and development in individuals is influenced by a range of factors including their genetic inheritance, environmental factors and lifestyle choices. This unit focuses on human growth and development across the whole lifespan and includes an exploration of the influence of different factors and health experiences.

How you will be assessed

This unit is externally assessed through a written examination.

1.1 Life stages and aspects of human growth and development

Life stages

It is traditional to see human lives as involving certain definite periods of development. Terms like infant, child, adolescent and adult have been used for centuries to classify the age-related status of individuals. One individual might believe that an 18-month-old girl is an infant whereas another might say she is a child; so agreeing the chronological boundaries for life stages is an important first step in studying this unit.

FIGURE 1.1 *Identifying life stages from appearance can be difficult*

In fact, they are infant and adolescent, but it is difficult to tell from appearance alone.

You should understand, however, that other workers and researchers in this field, and other qualification specifications and their associated text references, might not use exactly the same age boundaries or titles for life stages as those given in this unit (see Figure 1.2).

LIFE STAGE	CHRONOLOGICAL AGE BOUNDARIES IN YEARS
Infancy	0–2
Childhood	2–8
Adolescence	9–18
Early adulthood	18–45
Middle adulthood	46–65
Late adulthood	65+

FIGURE 1.2 *Chronological age boundaries for life stages*

During the last century, it was common to assume that there was a universal pattern to both physical and social development. From infancy through childhood to **adolescence**, a person would grow physically and learn the knowledge and skills needed for a working life. Adulthood was a time when people would work, marry and bring up their own families. Children would be grown up when their parents reached middle age, and rearing their own families when their parents became retired in old age.

An American theorist has described the developmental tasks of the different life stages and some examples are given in Figure 1.3.

Later theorists argue that life has changed so much that the notion of life tasks fitting into specific life stages is no longer relevant for many people. We now live in a rapidly changing world in which, increasingly, it is the norm for many people to choose their own style of living and

INFANCY AND EARLY CHILDHOOD	MIDDLE CHILDHOOD	ADOLESCENCE
Learning to take solid foods Learning to walk Learning to talk Learning bowel and bladder control Learning sex differences and sexual modesty	Learning physical skills necessary for ordinary games Learning to get along with peers Learning appropriate gender role Developing basic skills in reading, writing and numeracy Developing concepts necessary for daily living Developing conscience, morality and a scale of values	Achieving new and more mature relationships with peers of both sexes Achieving a masculine or feminine role Accepting one's physique and using the body effectively Achieving emotional independence of parents and other adults Preparing for marriage and family life Preparing for an economic career

EARLY ADULTHOOD	MIDDLE AGE	LATER MATURITY
Selecting a mate Learning to live with a marriage partner Starting a family Rearing children Managing a home Getting started in an occupation	Assisting teenage children to become happy and responsible adults Reaching and maintaining satisfactory performance in one's occupation/career Relating to one's spouse as a person Accepting and adjusting to the physiological changes of middle age Adjusting to ageing parents	Adjusting to decreasing physical strength Adjusting to retirement and reduced income Adjusting to the death of one's spouse Establishing satisfactory physical living arrangements

FIGURE 1.3 *Developmental tasks ascribed to life stages by Havinghurst (1972)*

plan social roles, families and careers with less reference to age. There are, however, still some generalisations about social, biological and emotional development that will help care workers to understand their service users' needs.

Principles of growth and development

Every individual has a unique pattern of growth and development because of his or her genetic

Think it over...

Discuss the relevance of the developmental tasks listed by Havighurst for early adulthood, middle age and later maturity to adults living in the twenty-first century.

For example, it is not unusual for adolescents and people in their forties (and older) to start families in or out of marriage.

inheritance and the large number of other environmental factors influencing his or her progress.

After the mother's ovum is fertilised by the father's sperm the resulting zygote undergoes many divisions to form the new human being, the placenta (to supply nourishment) and the coverings such as the amnion. During the first 8 weeks of life in the uterus, the **zygote** becomes the **embryo** and all major organs are formed by the end of this period. For many of these weeks, the female may not be aware of the pregnancy so exposure to harmful substances can damage the formation of major organs, resulting in reduced health experience. For the remainder of the pregnancy (about 32 weeks) the embryo becomes the **foetus** and although major organs are formed, their further growth and development can also be affected by many factors, such as smoking.

✱ DID YOU KNOW?

If a pregnant mother catches Rubella (German measles) in the first 3 months of pregnancy, the foetus may be aborted, stillborn or have defects of the nervous system, particularly affecting vision and hearing.

There is, however, a great deal of controversy over the time when a foetus is said to be a human being and this is largely fuelled by the debate around legal abortion.

In Britain, the Abortion Act (1967) allowed termination of pregnancy up to the 28th week of gestation (the period of the pregnancy); in 1990, the time limit dropped to the 24th week of gestation. But advances in medical technology and images from a revolutionary new ultrasound scan showing a foetus 'walking' after just 12 weeks in the womb have re-ignited the debate about abortion. Most people now feel that there is a need to update Abortion Act legislation. There is now a one-in-five chance of survival for babies born at 23 weeks and this doubles for those born one week later. However, such babies could legally be aborted under the current laws.

Some religious and pressure groups (such as Life) as well as many individuals consider that all abortion is wrong and that human life is sacred from the date of fertilisation.

Think it over...

Discuss the pros and cons for having abortion legislation. What change, if any, would you propose to the time limit for abortion?

A newborn infant, often called a **neonate**, is a helpless individual needing the care and protection of parents or carers to survive. The nervous system, which coordinates many bodily functions, is immature and needs time to develop. The digestive system is not able to take and/or absorb food that is not in an easily digestible form, such as that found in breast milk. There is no control over bladder and bowel function and locomotion is purposeless or based on automatic reflexes. The circulatory and respiratory systems have undergone major changes at birth due to physical separation from the mother and air breathing for the first time. The neonate can be susceptible to hypothermia because of an immature temperature-regulating system and because a reproductive capacity is totally lacking.

Patterns of development

Development, despite being a continuous sequential process, is also an uneven one that affects parts of the body differently. The upper part of the body, chiefly the head and brain, grows and develops rapidly compared to the rest of the body, particularly the lower limbs. This is known as **cephalo-caudal development**, which really means head to tail. Similarly, the organs in the mid-line of the body progress faster than the arms and legs at the extremities. The reason for this is not hard to find, as the vital organs are controlled by the brain and protected by the head and trunk. Limbs are not vital at this stage, as the neonate is dependent on the mother for nourishment and protection (see Figure 1.4).

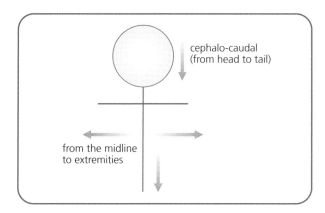

cephalo-caudal
(from head to tail)

from the midline
to extremities

FIGURE 1.4 *The sequence of development*

There are characteristic patterns of development in the different life stages; for example, gross motor skills progress most rapidly in infancy than in any other life stage, and **social development** starts slowly in infancy but continues through all other life stages.

The rate of growth throughout the remaining life stages is never as rapid as that of the embryo and foetus. The average neonate comes out of the womb weighing around 3.5 kg and is approximately 50 cm in length. By the child's second birthday his or her height/length has nearly doubled and this is mainly due to the increasing length of long bones in the limbs.

During the remainder of childhood, there is a steady growth rate with boys just 2–3 cm taller than girls. Adolescence begins 2–4 years earlier in girls than boys, so for a short period their adolescent growth spurt makes them taller and heavier. The boys soon recover and overtake the girls once their **puberty** kicks in and they remain taller and heavier for the rest of their lives.

Key concept

Adolescence: This incorporates all the social, emotional, intellectual and physical changes associated with this life stage. Puberty refers only to the physical changes associated with sexual maturation.

Growth in bone takes place from plates of cartilage (known as epiphyses) sandwiched between the ends of bones and the shaft. When the epiphyses of differently named bones turn into bone (ossification), further growth is impossible and these dates can be useful in determining the age of an individual when this is unknown. They are visible as clear areas on X-ray.

Consider this

Using the figures given in the table below, plot growth curves for boys and girls on graph paper.

AGE IN YEARS	AVERAGE HEIGHT IN CM	
	BOYS	GIRLS
0	51	50
2	95	92
4	104	103
6	117	115
8	130	128
10	140	138
12	149	151
14	162	159
16	171	162
18	174	162

FIGURE 1.5 *Increase in height of boys and girls up to 18 years*

Write explanatory notes comparing the growth curves of boys and girls.

Mass (or weight) follows similar patterns of general increase in childhood and adolescence to that of growth. There is also increased weight gain during the adolescent spurt.

Although growth curves reflect the growth of the trunk and the limbs, not all parts of the body grow at the same rate in childhood. The graph overleaf (see Figure 1.7) shows the rapid expansion of the head and brain, which is almost full adult size by the age of 8 or 9 years.

The different rates of growth between the head and the torso from infancy to adulthood produce marked proportionate changes in growth profiles (see Figure 1.6). The figures are sketched to the same height to demonstrate the change in proportions. You will notice how small the head of an adult is in comparison with the newborn

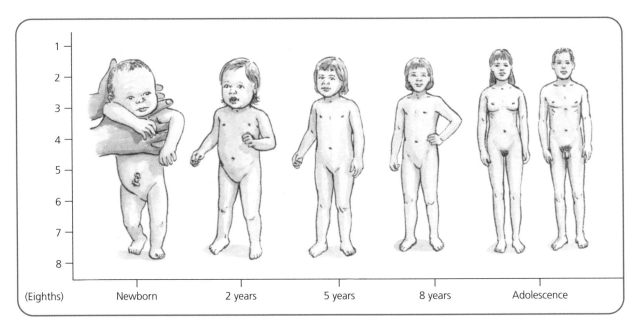

FIGURE 1.6 *Growth profiles from birth to the end of adolescence*

and, conversely, how long the length of the lower limbs of an adult are compared to those of the newborn. The intermediate age figures demonstrate the gradual shift in proportions.

By contrast, the reproductive organs remain small and undeveloped until adolescence, when there is a massive increase to adult size over a 4–5 year period. An endocrine gland called the thymus gland (not shown), located in the upper chest and lower neck, is large in infancy and continues to grow to a maximum at puberty, after which it declines slowly. It is associated with the immune system (see Figure 1.7).

Growth in height ceases in early adulthood but some individuals can increase in mass as they progress through adulthood. This is largely due to both increases in the number of fat cells and the volume of fat contained in each cell.

In early and middle adulthood there is no change in height as the skeleton has completely ossified. However, in later adulthood there is often some height reduction because the cartilaginous discs between the vertebrae of the spine become compressed over time.

Frequently, weight does change and middle-age spread is a well-recognised phenomenon, although there is no physiological reason for an increase in weight at this time. It is probably the result of maintaining the same pattern of eating

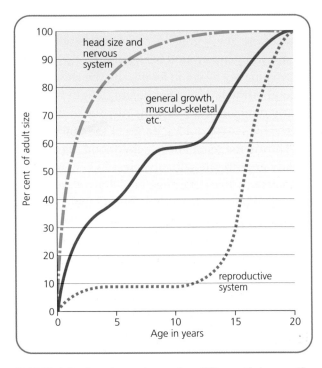

FIGURE 1.7 *Graph to show the differential growth of different body parts*

from early adulthood with reduced levels of activity.

Although some individuals remain large in later adulthood, many become thinner possibly due to reduced appetite and less efficient absorption of food from the digestive tract.

Key concept

Control of growth: This is largely due to inherited characteristics, hormones, dietary patterns and health experience.

There are a large number of factors causing variations in the patterns of growth described above and you will find further information about some of these in Section 1.2.

✱ DID YOU KNOW?

The tallest man in the world was an American (who died in 1940) who was 2.62 m tall. The smallest is Chinese (still living) at a mere 0.70 m!

Development of physical skills

Infancy (0–2 years)

The neonate (newborn infant) is uncoordinated in movement and only **primitive reflexes** are present. Reflexes are automatic responses to stimuli and the most important are the rooting, suckling, grasp, Moro (startle) and walking reflexes.

✱ DID YOU KNOW?

The **paediatrician** Ernst Moro (1874 –1951) was the first to describe the defensive reflex seen in babies in the first six months of life.

Primitive reflexes disappear in the early months of life and are replaced some time later by voluntary movements. Some theorists believe that any reflex that persists longer than its allotted span interferes with learning at a later date.

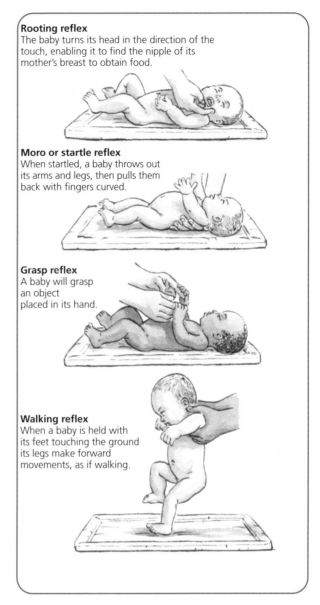

Rooting reflex
The baby turns its head in the direction of the touch, enabling it to find the nipple of its mother's breast to obtain food.

Moro or startle reflex
When startled, a baby throws out its arms and legs, then pulls them back with fingers curved.

Grasp reflex
A baby will grasp an object placed in its hand.

Walking reflex
When a baby is held with its feet touching the ground its legs make forward movements, as if walking.

FIGURE 1.8 *Primitive reflexes*

Neonates can also smell, taste and hear as well as automatically blink their eyes.

NAME OF REFLEX	STIMULUS	RESPONSE
Rooting	Touch on cheek	Turns head towards breast and nipple
Suckling	Touch on the mouth	Starts to suck
Moro (startle)	Sudden noise or movement	Arms flung outwards and legs straightened, often with a cry. Limbs bend inwards as if trying to catch hold of something.
Grasp	Object placed in palm of hand	Strong grasp of object
Walking	When held upright with feet	Forward movements by legs, mimicking walking

FIGURE 1.9 *Primitive reflexes of the neonate*

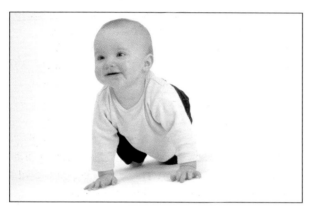

FIGURE 1.10 *Using gross motor skills*

Not surprisingly (see 'Patterns of development' on page 4) head control begins first. When the newborn infant is held in a sitting position, his or her head falls forward, but towards the end of the first month an infant can lift his or her chin for a few seconds. At 2 months of age an infant can hold

his or her head up, and at 4–5 months will support and control his or her head when pulled to the sitting position. At age 3 months, infants will turn their heads to follow an adult, reach out for things, grasp a rattle for a few moments only and become fascinated by their own hands.

Infants can sit supported at 4–5 months of age, but around 6–7 months they can sit without support.

FIGURE 1.11 *Sitting without support*

Around 2 months of age, babies lie flat or prone on the floor with their legs extended and can raise their head for only a second or two. By 3 months of age, they can lift their head for much longer and support their body weight on their forearms. Gradually, infants learn to tuck their knees under the body and turn over, such that by 9 or 10 months of age they can crawl quickly. Some infants never crawl but instead use their arms to bump the bottom around in a rapid 'shuffling' movement.

Around 6 months of age, babies can support their weight if held upright and by 10 months they can stand without support but holding onto furniture. Baby's first birthday is always an important occasion and he or she can celebrate by walking whilst holding onto an adult's two hands, gradually becoming steadier and needing only one hand. Between 13–15 months of age, an infant takes the important first steps alone without support, gradually increasing in confidence to carry toys around and climb steps.

Infants usually go up stairs in a crawling mode and come down backwards on their tummies.

For most infants, their walking has progressed so well by 18 months of age that running and kicking a ball are possible by their second birthday. Infants fall down regularly and this is part of the learning process; however, safety gates, guard rails, safety locks and fireguards should be used by parents or carers to ensure that no serious falls or escapes take place.

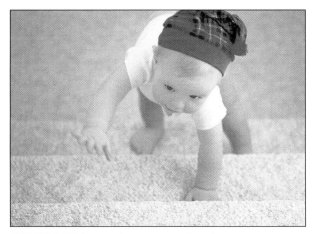
FIGURE 1.12 *Becoming more adventurous*

Fine motor skills are more pronounced after the age of 6 months, beginning with transferring objects from one hand to the other and picking up dropped toys. From the age of 9–12 months the 'pincer' movement develops, i.e. using the thumb and forefinger to pick up small objects; this is also the time for great fun for infants as they drop and throw toys from their buggy or high chair.

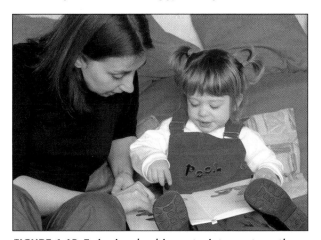
FIGURE 1.13 *Enjoying looking at pictures together*

Between 18 months and 2 years of age, the infant learns to hold small objects such as chubby crayons for drawing and a spoon for eating. At this stage, infants love action songs like pat-a-cake, turning the pages of books and building towers of blocks up to six blocks high.

Early childhood (2–8 years)

Children are now very mobile, with the ability to run, climb, kick a ball and go up and down stairs, placing one foot at a time on each step. A sense of balance develops and a child may take great pleasure in skipping, jumping, standing on tiptoes, balancing on one leg, using climbing frames, slides and roundabouts and riding (first a tricycle and then a bicycle). Fine motor skills have also progressed to threading beads, picking flowers for making a 'chain', drawing and painting, copying shapes and using scissors. Fastening shoelaces and buttons can still be challenging for a child at school entry, but by 6 or 7 years of age a child is usually competent at these tasks. School children become increasingly coordinated in their physical activities and by the end of this life stage they enjoy playing games of tennis, football, netball and other sports.

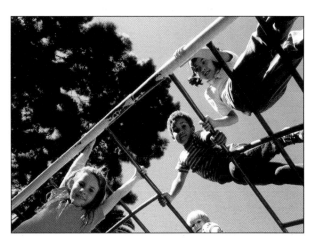
FIGURE 1.14 *Becoming competent with motor skills*

Growth in height and weight still increase steadily but not as rapidly as in infancy.

Both boys and girls are usually in control of complete bowel and bladder function during the day and night by the time they start school at 5 years of age.

Adolescence (9–18 years)

Anytime from 8 years old, a girl's breasts start to enlarge; this occurs well before the start of menstruation (called the **menarche**) and is usually the first outward sign of adolescence. Girls show major changes associated with puberty between 10–13 years of age, with boys following about 2 years later.

> **Key concept**
>
> *Hormones:* The pituitary gland at the base of the brain secretes hormones (gonadotrophins – follicle stimulating hormone (FSH) and luteinising hormone (LH) that stimulate the production of oestrogen and testosterone (the sex hormones) from the ovaries and testes respectively.

These sex hormones cause the growth of body hair, genital organs, the skeleton and muscles, and secondary sexual organs. They also cause the onset of menstruation, ovulation (about one year later) and sperm production.

Figure 1.15 lists the major physical changes associated with adolescence.

Early adulthood (18–45 years)

At the beginning of this life stage, people are said to be at the peak of their physical powers and considerably fertile. Towards the end, however, many people have begun to thicken around the waistline and become less physically active. Head hair in males starts to thin and recede, and hair colour in both sexes begins to fade as grey or white hairs appear. The ability to fine focus deteriorates, so many people need reading glasses

PART OF BODY	IN MALES	IN FEMALES
Breasts		Start to enlarge becoming glandular after ovulation has started
Body hair grows	Underarm (axillary) hair Pubic hair Chest hair Facial hair	Underarm (axillary) hair Pubic hair
Primary genital organs grow and become productive	Testes and scrotum enlarge and begin to produce sperm	Ovaries get larger and ovulation starts
Secondary sexual organs grow	Penis and accessory glands grow and start to secrete – giving rise to 'wet dreams'	Uterus, vagina and associated glands enlarge Menstruation becomes established
Skeleton	Growth spurt in height and weight Shoulders widen, hips remain slim	Growth spurt in height and weight Hips widen causing body shape to alter and a different walk with swinging gait
Voice changes	Rapid growth of voice box or larynx causes voice to change and become deeper in pitch	Voices tend to become less shrill, but not usually considered a significant change
Shape alters due to changes in soft tissues	Significant muscle development	Fat deposited under the skin and around the breasts leads to a curvaceous shape
Tonsils, adenoids, thymus and other lymphatic tissues	Having grown rapidly during childhood, they begin to shrink	Having grown rapidly during childhood, they begin to shrink

FIGURE 1.15 *Physical changes in males and females during adolescence*

as they become increasingly long-sighted (presbyopic). This is due to the eye lens becoming less elastic through age. A few wrinkles may appear as the elastic fibres in the skin begin to age.

Women still menstruate at this stage and increasingly, more women are having babies in their forties. Males produce sperm and can father children.

Middle adulthood (46–65 years)

People in this life stage do not think of themselves as middle-aged or old as they lead independent, fulfilling lives. The ageing process is subtle and the changes so tiny at first that they usually occur without notice.

The main physical event occurring in this life stage is the **menopause** for females. This is the gradual cessation of menstruation and may take between 1–2 years to complete. Because there are no more viable eggs left in the ovaries, the gonadotrophins are produced in greater quantities as they try to stimulate egg production. The high levels of these hormones causes symptoms such as irritability, night sweats and hot flushes. With the consequent decline in oestrogen and progesterone from the ovaries, the primary and secondary organs of the reproductive system shrink and become less glandular. In some women, this is accompanied by a loss of interest in sexual intercourse and some emotional turbulence.

Other symptoms that begin in the forties and continue throughout this phase include further loss of hair in males, long-sightedness, reduced skin elasticity and possibly early difficulties with mobility as a result of wear and tear on the joints.

Some people may experience further decline in the senses: their balance may not be as good, they may not hear high-pitched sounds as well as they once did, and their sense of smell may also decline.

Later adulthood (65+ years)

People in the early stages of later adulthood still do not think of themselves as old. Most live healthy and fulfilling lives and, with the right support and help, their quality of life can be good. People live longer than they used to, particularly women, and many are physically active until their late seventies and eighties.

FIGURE 1.16 *Many people in late adulthood are physically active*

> ### Key concept
>
> *Ageing:* Reduced functions of most organs takes place as a result of the ageing process, leading to the characteristic traits of later adulthood, although many service users may suffer from one or two effects only.

CHARACTERISTIC TRAITS OF LATER ADULTHOOD	
Skin	Thinner and less elastic so more wrinkled in appearance and acquires blemishes; less sensitive to temperature fluctuations so more likely to develop hypothermia in cold weather
Bones	Less dense therefore more likely to fracture, particularly in females
Muscles	Weaker therefore less power
Joints	Stiffer, reduced range of movements; may be painful; ligaments weaker
Height	Shrinks due to disc compression; spine may become rounded

CHARACTERISTIC TRAITS OF LATER ADULTHOOD	
Balance	Impaired, particularly when turning around
Heart	Less efficient at delivering and draining blood from tissues, so functions less well
Blood pressure	Rises with age due to reduced elasticity of vessel walls and calcium deposits; more risk of stroke or haemorrhage, particularly in brain
Breathing	Less efficient as muscles are weaker; gaseous exchange affected due to decline of elasticity in alveolar walls
Hormone production	Reduces due to ageing cells and resistance; lack of insulin gives rise to diabetes; lack of thyroxine leads to lowered metabolism
Alimentary canal	Muscles controlling peristalsis are weaker so constipation more likely; nutrients in food not absorbed so well, so anaemia and other deficiency diseases occur more often

FIGURE 1.17 *Effects of the ageing process*

It is also worth remembering that while the list of declining physical faculties shown in Figure 1.17 seems long and awesome, it can be counteracted by the acquisition of wisdom and peace of mind, especially when there is a support network of family and friends.

Development of intellectual skills

Infancy (0–2 years)

Soon after birth, infants appear to be ready to form relationships with parents and carers; they show interest in human faces and voices from a few weeks old and soon recognise their mother by sound and appearance.

Language development

Between the age of 6–9 months, infants respond to certain vocal instructions such as 'wave bye-bye' and 'clap hands', although they cannot yet say words. Babbling sounds that may seem like words are common around one year of age and some children will manage about three whole words; other children will be able to use sounds, facial and eye movements to communicate their needs to carers. Nearly all 2-year-old infants can put two words together such as 'Jane garden' or 'Sam milk'.

Thinking or cognitive development

Many psychologists have studied cognitive development and **Piaget** is one of the best known. Piaget believed that thinking was at first limited to repeating actions. The teat of the breast or bottle was placed in the mouth so the baby placed a rattle in his or her mouth. Young infants rely on in-built mental patterns for sucking, crawling and watching. Later, babies explore further by sucking toys, fingers, and clothes, for example, to develop an understanding of objects. The tongue contains thousands of sensory receptors and the baby uses these to explore texture, shape, hardness, and so on.

Piaget thought that up to the age of 18 months or 2 years an infant could not understand that his or her mother existed once she had left the room if the infant remained there. Piaget called this the **sensori-motor** stage of development and it ended when the infant could understand the existence of objects and people even when they could not be seen, heard, smelled or touched. Many people now believe that this stage is much shorter (probably 8–9 months) and infants are more capable than Piaget believed.

> ✱ DID YOU KNOW?
>
> The psychologist Jean Piaget (1896–1980) studied the development of thought processes in children.

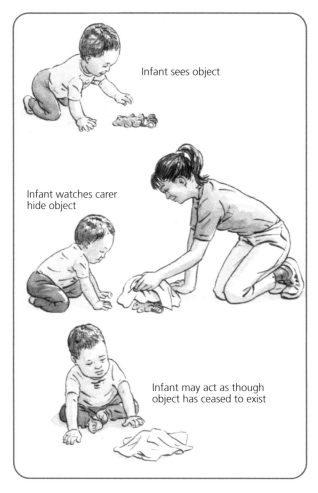

Infant sees object

Infant watches carer hide object

Infant may act as though object has ceased to exist

FIGURE 1.18 *The sensori-motor stage*

Early childhood (2–8 years)

Language
As children progress through childhood, they use their own pattern of language communication.

STAGE	NATURE OF STAGE	EXAMPLE
First (around two years)	Two-word statements	John comed
Second	Short phrases	John come play
Third	Being able to ask questions	Where John go?
Fourth	Using sentences	John come play and Sally come play
Fifth (around five or six years)	Adult sentences and fair vocabulary	John and Sally have come to play with me
Sixth (eight years and upwards)	Understanding and use of speech together with increasing vocabulary	John and Sally have come to play with me today and I will be delighted to go to their house tomorrow

FIGURE 1.20 *Development of language*

Young children do not use adult language and are best left uncorrected. The probable list of stages after 2 years of age is given in Figure 1.20

Thinking skills
Children in this stage still tend to base their thinking on what things look like rather than the logic of newly acquired counting skills. They also learn to weigh things but may believe that a large

FIGURE 1.19 *Understanding the concept of **object permanence** (18 months)*

pile of feathers will weigh more than one iron bar. Piaget called this stage the '**pre-operational**' period, meaning pre-logical.

Children may begin to use logic before 8 years of age providing that they can see things to help them.

Adolescence (9–18 years)

Piaget described the next stage as the 'concrete operational' period, extending from 7–12 years of age, in which children and adolescents can work out problems logically, providing that they have images, graphics or real life situations to assist them. From 12 years of age onwards, Piaget moved to the '**formal operational**' (or formal logical) stage, in which adolescents can imagine and think about things that they have never seen or done before. They are able to imagine and plan for future achievements and can solve problems in the same way as adults, although a lack of experience may not produce the right decisions. Decision-making skills are something that we acquire throughout the course of our entire lives.

Early adulthood (18–45 years)

Intellectual skills and abilities will increase during adulthood providing that the opportunities exist to exercise those skills.

Middle adulthood (46–65 years)

Older adults may be slightly slower in working out logical problems, but this reduction in speed may be compensated for by increased knowledge. Using knowledge gained from many years of experience helps people to make better decisions and judgements than those with more limited experience. As a consequence, they are often said to be wise or learned.

Later adulthood (65+ years)

Older people who stimulate their minds and enjoy good health can continue to develop their store of knowledge and wisdom even if they take longer to respond to situations.

Some people may suffer from ill health that interferes with mental activities, particularly illnesses that result in poor oxygenation of brain

> ✳ **DID YOU KNOW?**
>
> In the UK 1 per cent of adults over 60 years of age are afflicted with **dementia** and the rate doubles every 5 years after 60. The most common form of dementia is Alzheimer's disease.

tissues such as respiratory and circulatory difficulties. This may result in confusion, poor decision-making, memory loss and difficulties in solving problems.

The main signs and symptoms of dementia are:

✳ difficulty in communication, expressing thoughts and understanding other people

✳ reduced ability to control emotions

✳ difficulties in recognising people, places and things, coupled with loss of memory

✳ being unaware of where you are and what is going on around you

✳ problems with daily living, such as personal hygiene and dressing.

It is important to remember that most people in later adulthood do not suffer from dementia although they may have periods of confusion and difficulties with daily activities. The causes of dementia are not fully known and are probably multi-factorial (i.e. many influences may be involved). Causes of dementia will include genetic inheritance and environmental factors such as heavy smoking, alcoholism and infections such as HIV.

Emotional development

Emotional development considers how people develop a sense of themselves and how they develop feelings towards others.

> ✳ **DID YOU KNOW?**
>
> **Self-concept** is said to be part **self-esteem** and part **self-image**. Self-esteem is how you value (or feel about) yourself and self-image is how you see yourself.

Infancy (0–2 years)

It seems that infants enter the world with an in-built ability to recognise and react to basic feelings in other people. Infants use this ability to attract attention and build emotional attachments with their parents and carers. By one year of age, infants can recognise and react to emotional expressions of happiness, distress and anger, and be guided by the emotions shown by their parents and carers.

Young infants probably do not have a sense of being an 'individual' but by 2 years of age, they have become aware of 'self' with a fixed gender.

During the first 18 months of life, the infant forms a loving bond that ties him or herself emotionally to parents or the main carers. There is general agreement among theorists that if the bonding process fails to develop, then a child's social and emotional development will be impaired.

Early childhood (2–8 years)

Children who have been able to bond well now start to feel safe in getting to know other children and adults, although starting school or playgroup may still be a daunting prospect even at the age of 5 years. From two and a half years onwards, children can use their imagination, particularly in copying what others do. As imagination develops in play with dolls, watching characters on TV, interaction with parents and others, so children come to understand who they are and have an idea of 'self'. Children need to feel valuable to family and friends and build up their self-esteem or self-worth in order to grow up feeling emotionally secure.

Children as young as 3 years will describe themselves as small or big, tall or short, but they can progress to a much fuller picture that includes hair and eye colour, school, family, and so on, by the time they are aged 8.

Adolescence (9–18 years)

Towards the end of their primary school life, adolescents can describe their self-worth in terms of what makes them happy. They will say, for example, what makes school good or bad, or which friends they like and why. A year or so later, they start to compare themselves with others. For example, 'Holly is better at Maths than I am, but Sally is better than both of us'. As they grow older, friends gradually take the place of family in being the major influence on self-concept.

As the sex hormones 'kick in' during the teens, the adolescent experiences huge physical, emotional and social changes. Adolescents are renowned for being 'touchy' with rapid mood swings, rebelliousness and anger, and their friends become the main emotional support rather than parents. Many suffer from depression, lack of **self-confidence** and low self-esteem as they struggle to come to terms with so many changes at a time of important educational and life decisions.

During this period, people will have to acquire a concept of themselves that guides them through leaving home, obtaining work and learning to live with a partner of their choice. These life events can cause a loss of self-esteem, conflict and stress.

Adolescents often develop a strong sense of self in terms of beliefs such as vegetarianism, religion, animal rights or other things seen as right or wrong; this has been termed the idealistic phase and it merges into developing an adult self-concept that helps to build confidence for future life changes.

Key concept

Self-concept: The understanding that we have of ourselves. A learned idea of how we are distinct from other people.

✱ DID YOU KNOW?

Self-concept is said to be positive or negative, not high or low. A person's self-concept can change as he or she progresses through life.

When you have a positive self-concept you are:

✱ self-confident

✱ keen to accept new challenges

✱ more likely to be successful

✱ motivated to do things

✱ good at mixing with other people

✱ happy in your life.

Early adulthood (18–45 years) and middle adulthood (46–65 years)

Our self-concept does not usually settle down until we are ready to undertake full-time work or leave home and live with a sexual partner. Such adult commitments may perhaps force us into making decisions about ourselves. A clear sense of what you are like and what you are good at may be necessary to be happy, confident and successful in work and in love; such clarity is more likely to be achieved in an individual's early twenties.

Research has suggested that many adults feel more satisfied with the quality of their lives in their thirties and forties than in their twenties. Young adults can experience a lot of stress in trying to establish a satisfactory lifestyle for themselves.

Adults can explain how they see themselves and the quality of their lives in much greater depth and detail than when they were adolescents. Adults will be aware that their sense of self can be influenced by events that happen in their lives.

You may hear an adult say, ' I became a stronger person after I lost my job' or 'I had to make all the decisions after Ted died'. Equally, a person's self-concept can be changed negatively after a life event, such as 'I lost all confidence after losing my job' or 'I felt that I was never the same person after that'.

Some people are able to change their self-concept as they get older. Success in an occupation or business career, having children, and gaining professional qualifications and experience are all likely to enhance self-concepts positively.

Think it over...

Think of circumstances that might change a person's self-concept negatively.

Some theorists have suggested that older adults may lose interest in other people and socialising once their families have grown up and left home; they become very settled in their ways – in a 'rut'.

The menopause, with the consequent hormone reduction, can cause emotional problems for some women, who may become depressed, tearful (often with rapid mood swings) and irritable, also affecting the males who are their partners. Some women feel 'down' because the menopause marks the end of the child-bearing years; they feel less feminine and unwanted as their children have grown up and left home. This is often called the 'empty nest' syndrome.

Successful ageing, therefore, might be regarded as the ability to remain socially engaged with people in an emotionally satisfying way.

✱ DID YOU KNOW?

Loss of skills and abilities resulting from trauma such as a stroke or accident can lead to feelings similar to those experienced in bereavement – namely fear, anxiety, frustration, anger, sadness and grief. In time, acceptance may follow, allowing the individual to undergo rehabilitation to achieve the best possible quality of life and independence.

Later adulthood (65+ years)

Older people can develop problems with their health which can affect their self-concept in a negative way; confusion, depression and loss of self-confidence are relatively more common in elderly people. As well as coping with their health problems, they also have to cope with the way in which society treats older people. Stereotyping of people in later adulthood is common. Others tend to treat older people as being less able than they actually are, causing their self-esteem and self-image to reduce.

Some theorists have suggested that the main challenge of later adulthood is to retain a strong sense of one's own self-esteem despite the problems that can arise with age. Some older adults may have more self-knowledge than during early adult life and show 'wisdom' in the way they explain their self-concept.

Development of social skills

Key concept

Social skills: These include the ability to communicate and make relationships with others; they are closely allied to and overlapped by emotional development, particularly in the early life stages.

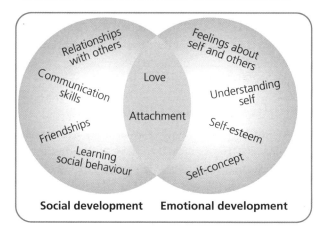

FIGURE 1.21 *Social and emotional development overlap*

Infants (0–2 years)

It seems that babies come into the world prepared to make relationships and learn about others because they are able to:

✱ follow a moving person with their eyes during their first month of life

✱ start to smile at human faces and may recognise their mother at age 2 months

✱ at 3 months of age, smile and make a noise when an adult or child goes by

✱ at 5 months of age, distinguish between familiar and unfamiliar people

✱ smile at a mirror image by age 6 months.

Infants may have an in-built need to form a close emotional relationship or bond with their primary carer. 'Bonding' was originally emphasised by Bowlby (1953), who felt that separation of a baby from its mother at a critical period would produce psychological damage. Later researchers have doubted that separations, such as going to work or into hospital, cause very much damage and they feel that it is making the bond of love that is important, not whether temporary separation occurs. As the infant gets older, the bonds forged with parents are less intense but still important; bonds with siblings, grandparents and other members of the extended family follow closely behind.

Early childhood (2–8 years)

Children begin to be interested in other children from the age of 2 years. Initially, they are content to play by themselves alongside another child (called **parallel play**). Then one or two years later, the children actually play together (**cooperative play**).

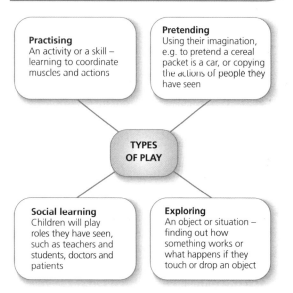

FIGURE 1.22 *Different types of play*

Children aged 3–4 years prefer to be with their parents than with friends, but by age 7 years this preference is reversed. Older children seek friendships based on trust rather than on the availability of others to play, and this continues through life. Up to the ages of 7 and 8 years, children's social groups are likely to be of mixed gender, but after this age they tend to be of the same gender. They will also choose friends with similar attitudes and values.

Relationships in the family setting provide opportunities for children to learn from others by copying what they do. They learn attitudes, behaviours and beliefs from parents, siblings and relatives in a process called **primary socialisation**. Families and other social groups develop attitudes about the right things to do, or norms. Some families have their evening meal together while sitting at a table; others would be surprised at this and eat from a plate on their lap while sat in front of the TV – both are norms for those families.

Adolescence (9–18 years)

Friendship groups now become more important than family groups and this is known as **secondary socialisation**. Adolescents (12+ years) explore relationships and sexual behaviour and begin to take on job responsibilities in the home, such as washing up and cleaning the family's car. Taking on adult responsibilities and trying to achieve more independence tends to cause most adolescents to become rebellious, bringing them into conflict with their parents.

Early adulthood (18–45 years)

Networks of personal friends become more extensive and most young adults experience sexual encounters and more or less permanent partnerships. Some plan to concentrate on gaining qualifications and career progression, putting ideas of marriage and family on hold.

Many people find coping with a partner, being a parent and an employee extremely stressful, and if they are experiencing financial problems as well, this can create emotional and social problems at home. Some older adults may find it difficult to support their grown up children at university, both socially and emotionally, or to help with accommodation costs once they have left home. As well as the effect on the family finances, they may feel that they have lost part of their social purpose because their children are no longer living with them.

Middle adulthood (46–65 years)

Many adults in this stage have smaller groups of long-lasting friendships that have stood the test of time and difficulties. New friendships can be made often as a result of holiday meetings, but they tend to fade away with time. Just as their children begin to start their own lives, new pressures appear as support for their own parents in later adulthood is required. Increasingly, grandparents take on the burden of childcare at some point in the week, so that their children can acquire and enjoy the luxuries of life without extra costs.

Later adulthood (65+ years)

In their sixties and early seventies, many adults lead varied and interesting lives. Long-distance travel, often to see siblings and other relatives, and new leisure pursuits such as painting and writing are common. The opportunities for older people to meet new friends can be extensive when their health is good and they have sufficient money. There are, however, many older people who find it difficult to make ends meet and tend to withdraw from socialising, due to feelings of shame. In addition there are those who suffer from ill-health and impairments, which results in their social isolation. A network of family and friends can provide vital and practical support, physically, socially and emotionally.

Summary of Section 1.1

The following key areas of theory have been considered in this section:

Infancy	Physical skills
Early childhood	Intellectual ability
Adolescence	Growth and development
Early adulthood	Emotional development
Middle adulthood	Social skills
Later adulthood	

1.2 Factors affecting growth and development

Genetic inheritance

The nucleus of every cell in the human body contains 23 pairs of chromosomes and each chromosome, made of DNA (deoxyribonucleic acid), carries units of inheritance known as genes.

Key concept

Genes: Genes control the chemical reactions in the cells and, therefore, inherited characteristics such as gender, hair and eye colour, height, skin colour and much more. Although scientists have made enormous advances in genetics in the last 20 years, each person is still a product of the genetic inheritance from his or her parents.

The mother donates one of each pair of chromosomes to the fertilised egg and the remainder comes from the father's sperm. It is the father's donation of the Y chromosome in the 23rd pair (called the sex chromosomes) that determines the sex of the child. For a person to have a genetic disorder, the abnormal genetic material must be present in every cell of the body, meaning that it must have been present in the egg cell or the sperm cell (known as gametes) or both. For this to happen, either one or both of the parents must have the faulty genetic material, or the fault initiates during one of the many cell divisions that preceded the formation of the gametes (the most likely) – this is known as a mutation.

Chromosome abnormalities

About one in 200 babies born alive has chromosome abnormalities, but there is a much higher incidence in spontaneous abortions (about one in two) suggesting that babies with such conditions are less likely to survive.

✱ DID YOU KNOW?

The physician Longdon Down (1828–1896) linked certain learning disabilities with a particular genetic disorder where three chromosomes (trisomy) appear at pair 21.

Abnormalities of chromosomes can and do occur, the best known being Down's syndrome (or trisomy 21); the name derives from the presence of three chromosomes instead of two at pair 21. This results in striking changes in the development and health of a person who happens to receive this extra chromosome. The incidence of Down's syndrome (about one in 650 babies born) increases with rising maternal age and pregnant women in their late-thirties and forties are offered screening tests to detect this and other genetic abnormalities. The invasive tests of sampling foetal cells from amniotic fluid (**amniocentesis**) or **chorionic villus sampling** carry risks to both mother and foetus and follow indicative blood tests.

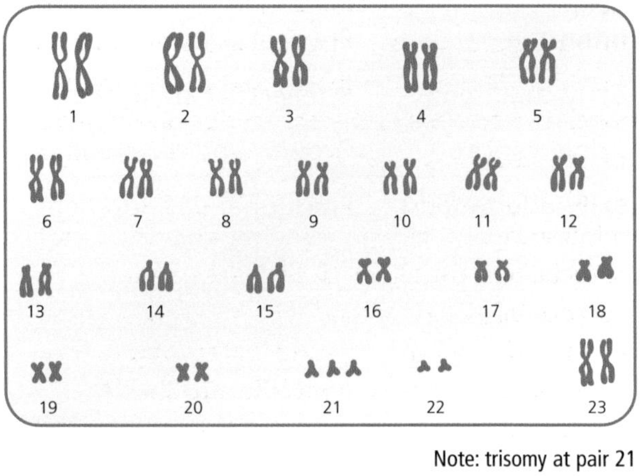

Note: trisomy at pair 21

FIGURE 1.23 *Karyogram depicting a chromosomal abnormality*

However, conclusive blood tests are currently being implemented throughout the UK that can provide results as early as 11 weeks of gestation without invasive investigations. Parents are offered counselling and the possibility of termination if the test is positive for Down's syndrome. Most people with Down's syndrome have distinctive small facial features with eyes that slope upwards at the outer corners and skin folds covering the nasal corners. Their hands are short and broad with unusual palm creases and the back of the head is flat. The tongue is large and often protruding. Many service users with Down's syndrome choose to have cosmetic surgery to alter their facial features.

Down's syndrome children are loving, cheerful and friendly, and they mix well with other children and adults.

FIGURE 1.24 *Young people with Down's syndrome enjoying life*

People with this condition have varying degrees of learning disability, but all are capable of some learning. Many individuals hold down useful jobs, live independently and have a good quality of life. Less than a generation ago, many Down's syndrome children did not live beyond adolescence or early adulthood because of the associated multiplicity of birth defects and susceptibility to infection. However, with advanced medical and surgical techniques, life expectancy has risen to middle adulthood.

Birth defects associated with Down's syndrome are:

✷ congenital heart disease

✷ congenital deafness and susceptibility to ear infections

✷ narrowing of intestines

✷ increased risk of atherosclerosis (narrowing of arteries by plaques of fatty tissue)

✷ general increased risk of infections.

✷ some neck joint problems.

Clearly, growth and development as well as the health experience for children and adults with trisomy 21 can be fraught with difficulties.

Other trisomies are rare, causing multiple physical defects and early death; but other abnormalities including missing or extra parts of chromosomes are more common. Abnormalities of the 22 pairs of 'ordinary' chromosomes are called *autosomal abnormalities* but those of the sex chromosomes are referred to as *sex chromosome abnormalities*; the former are slightly less common and are associated with physical defects and learning disabilities. The latter, not surprisingly, are linked to defective sexual development and infertility.

> ✷ **DID YOU KNOW?**
>
> A syndrome is a group of signs and symptoms that occur together and characterise a particular medical abnormality.
>
> When the genetic faults lie with genes rather than chromosomes, they may be unifactorial or multifactorial disorders.

Unifactorial disorders

These cause considerable disability. They result from one defective gene controlling a particular protein production and, therefore, forming the start of a metabolic error. They can be divided into autosomal and sex-linked disorders, nearly always associated with the X chromosome.

Autosomal disorders

In each cell there are 23 pairs of chromosomes. The gene controlling a particular factor is composed of two units called alleles, each one of which is on a single chromosome. Put more

AUTOSOMAL ABNORMALITIES	SEX CHROMOSOME ABNORMALITIES
Down's syndrome or trisomy 21 – presence of three chromosomes (i.e. an extra chromosome) at pair 21	*Turners's syndrome* – affects 1 in 2,500 females; one X chromosome instead of two; do not have proper ovarian development; typically short height
Cri du chat syndrome – part of chromosome missing results in severe birth defects, small head and brain, small larynx with a cat-like cry	*Klinefelter's syndrome* – affects 1 in 500 males; one or more extra X-chromosomes along with Y; affects learning disability is common

FIGURE 1.25 *Chromosome abnormalities*

simply, a gene consists of two alleles controlling a particular factor, each allele originating from one parent. It follows then, if there are two different alternative forms of alleles, usually indicated by letters, there are three variations that can occur.

For example, in the case of the gene for black hair, indicated by the letter B or b (two alternative forms), the gene could be composed of 2 alleles BB, bb or Bb (bB is the same effect):

✱ BB indicates alleles for black hair received from both parents

✱ bb indicates alleles from neither parent for black hair so the recipient will be fair-haired

✱ Bb (or bB) signifies one allele from each parent, only one of which is for black hair.

The recipient of the Bb inheritance is also black haired indicating the *dominance of the black-haired allele*, traditionally written with a capital letter. The allele B is said to be the **dominant** allele and allele b is the recessive allele for hair colour.

Autosomal disorders are also caused by dominant and recessive alleles, just as for hair colour. Only one parent has to possess and pass on a dominant allele for a disorder, but two parents must pass on two recessive alleles for an affected child, the normal allele being dominant and absent. Many of us carry recessive alleles for characteristics and disorders and are totally unaware of their existence because normal genes dominate them. We are said to be carriers of the conditions. When two carriers have children, there is a one in four chance of producing a child with an autosomal recessive condition and this may come as a complete surprise to the family. Autosomal disorders tend to affect both sexes in equal proportions.

Figure 1.27 shows some autosomal dominant and recessive genetic disorders affecting growth and development.

Sex-linked genetic disorders

In these genetic disorders, the faulty recessive gene is on the X-chromosome; a female has two X-chromosomes so the normal X dominates the affected allele and the female is normal, although

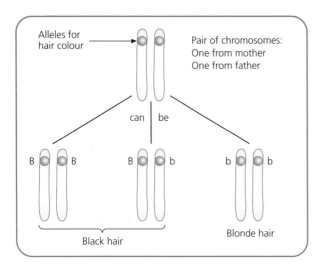

FIGURE 1.26 *Genetic inheritance of hair colour*

AUTOSOMAL DISORDERS	
AUTOSOMAL DOMINANT ALLELES CAUSE:	**AUTOSOMAL RECESSIVE ALLELES CAUSE:**
Achondroplasia – short stature	Albinism – lack of pigment in skin, hair and eyes
Familial polyposis – multiple polyps of the bowel eventually becoming cancerous	Cystic fibrosis – thick sticky mucus that predisposes to chronic lung infections
Huntington's chorea – early onset (age 35–40 years) of **dementia** and rapid jerky movements	Phenylketonuria – blond, blue-eyed babies lacking a vital enzyme that leads to severe learning disabilities unless placed on a special diet
Polycystic kidneys – multiple cysts in both kidneys that destroy kidney tissue	Sickle-cell anaemia – deformed red blood cells leading to severe anaemia, mainly in those of Mediterranean and African origins

FIGURE 1.27 *Examples of autosomal dominant and recessive disorders*

a carrier. When the female carrier has sons, one X-chromosome is passed on together with the normal Y-chromosome from the father and this may be either X. Statistically, 50 per cent of sons are normal and 50 per cent affected, as they do not have the normal dominant X. Similarly, this happens to daughters as well, although in this case there will be a normal X-chromosome from the father to mask the affected allele; 50 per cent of daughters are normal and 50 per cent are carriers. It is theoretically possible for a female carrier to have children with an affected male and produce an affected daughter, but the chances of this happening are very remote.

Probably the two most well known examples of sex-linked inheritance are haemophilia and colour blindness.

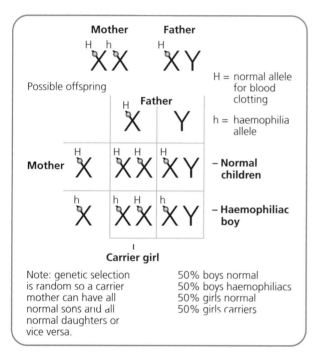

FIGURE 1.28 *Inheritance of haemophilia*

Haemophilia

Haemophilia, almost exclusively a condition of males, is a bleeding disorder due to the lack of a particular protein known as Factor VIII. Sufferers experience severe bleeding into muscles and joints even after very minor injuries. Such bleeding can lead to deformities of knees, ankles and other joints, and painful arthritis. In the past, many haemophiliacs were transfused with unscreened, donated plasma containing

Factor VIII and as a result many clients and their sexual partners became infected with viruses such as HIV and viral hepatitis. Today, genetically engineered Factor VIII is available and it is virus-free. Donated plasma Factor VIII is screened for HIV, but there is still a risk of hepatitis.

Women who are known to be carriers often have brothers who are haemophiliacs and may choose to have termination in the case of male foetuses during early pregnancy rather than give birth to affected sons, although 50 per cent of male foetuses will be normal. (Few women choose to do so). Nowadays, the sex of an unborn child can be determined by ultrasound scanning and the appropriate treatment planned well in advance; if thought inconclusive, more invasive techniques (see page 20) can be employed, although the risks to the mother and baby are more significant.

Colour blindness

This is a sex-linked recessive disorder; however, it would pose very little influence on an individual's growth and development or health experience providing that person was careful in terms of hazards.

Duchenne's muscular dystrophy

Another sex-linked genetic condition is Duchenne's muscular dystrophy, which causes progressive deterioration in muscle fibres. It affects about one in 3,000 boys and there is no effective cure. A blood test looks for the enzymes released from damaged muscles

> **✳ DID YOU KNOW?**
>
> The **physician** Guillaume Duchenne (1806–1875) described a disease of the muscle resulting in dystrophy.

Multifactorial disorders

Large numbers of disorders are caused by the additive effects of certain genes together with various environmental factors, but the actual pattern of inheritance is complex; these are called multifactorial disorders. Asthma, insulin-dependent (Type 1) diabetes mellitus, schizophrenia and some congenital birth defects such as cleft palate are classed as multifactorial disorders.

Generally speaking, genetic faults cause serious effects on growth, development and health experience and the individual can only receive **palliative** treatment of symptoms. Genetic counselling and DNA sampling (through **amniocentesis** or **chorionic villus sampling**) can help in reducing the chances of a child being born with a serious genetic disorder.

Environmental factors influencing growth, development and health experience

There is a large range of environmental factors that impinge on the growth, development and health experience of all humans and research studies constantly supply more evidence of this on a daily basis. Basically, environmental factors can be divided into four groups:

* *lifestyle factors* such as substance abuse, diet, exercise and stress

* *social and community support factors* such as family, friends, health services, social class, cultural beliefs

* *physical environment factors* such as various types of pollution, safe neighbourhoods, access to employment, education and income

* *psychological factors* such as self-esteem, self-concept, relationships with family and partners, and stress.

Lifestyle factors

Diet

The Acheson report (1998) refers to 'food poverty' and notes that people in low socio-economic groups 'spend more on foods rich in energy and high in fat and sugar, which are cheaper per unit of energy, than foods rich in protective nutrients, such as fruit and vegetables' (1998: 65). 'People on low incomes eat less healthily partly because of cost, rather than lack of concern or information. Therefore increased availability of affordable 'healthy' food should lead to improved nutrition in the least well off'. (1988: 66.) The same report found that people in low socio-economic groups:

* consumed more processed food with high levels of salt, sugar and fat, thereby increasing the risk of cardio-vascular disease

* were less likely to breastfeed their babies and thereby protect them from infection

* were more likely to have low birth-weight babies than higher income groups, this being linked to the risk of cardio-vascular disease in later life

* had a greater risk of ill-health, generally due to obesity.

People on low incomes find it more difficult to travel to supermarkets to stock-up on cheaper food and 'special offers' and instead tend to shop on a daily basis at the local 'corner shop' where prices are higher. The Acheson report found that so-called 'healthy' food, therefore poverty may push people into choosing less healthy options.

Recommendations to consume five helpings or pieces of fruit and vegetables each day may have to be ignored when there is only a small amount of money available each week with which to purchase food to feed the family. Processed pies, chips and tinned beans will fill the family's stomach and lead to less complaint. Such a meal once in a while is all right, but day after day with little variation leads to obesity, heart disease, strokes, problems with mobility and, in some cases, cancer.

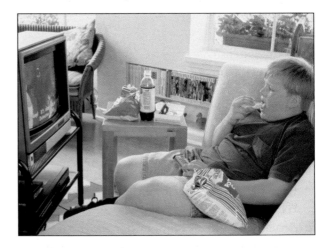

FIGURE 1.29 *Some children are in danger of becoming 'couch potatoes'*

Middle-class families frequently consist of overweight members too; children's sedentary leisure activities such as watching TV and playing computer games have taken the place of football in the park and skipping. Walking to school has been replaced by car journeys and, as increasing numbers of school playing fields are sold off, there is little physical activity in school. In the national press there are daily reports and articles about slimming diets for all, schools' attempts to try different school-meal options, and the poor health practices of multinational food industries. The British public is overwhelmed by food information and yet very little has changed. Overweight children are now suffering from cardiovascular disease. One study in Dundee, Scotland (1999) revealed that one-quarter of Scottish 11–14 year olds were beginning to show signs of heart disease not normally seen until middle age. One study in Glasgow by Reilly (1999) found childhood obesity between 2–15 years had doubled in 10 years: 'We found obesity was much more common than we expected – especially amongst children of a pre-school age'.

In February 2004, the World Heart Federation's World Heart Day had the theme 'Children, Adolescents and Heart Disease'. It noted that, globally, the number of obese adults has reached over 300 million and that about 22 million children under 5 years of age are obese, with and many more overweight. Common descriptions of this situation include phrases such as 'a time-bomb waiting to go off' and 'an epidemic of obesity'. It would seem that finally Western governments are waking up to the certainty that health services will collapse, when today's children reach early and middle adult life because their health problems will be colossal.

Possible actions:

* increase awareness through media activity especially during children's programmes

* develop improved food content information and labelling on packaging and restaurants

* develop and promote physical activity programmes, such as skipping skills

FIGURE 1.30 *Skipping together!*

* have cheap fruits and vegetables more readily available

* replace less healthy foods in vending machines with healthy options

* have healthy options near the cash points in supermarkets

* minimise the sale of fizzy drinks and high calorie foods in schools

* produce more healthy school meals

* increase physical activity by providing more sports facilities

* decrease salt and sugar content in foods and substitute fat

* encourage healthy cooking skills and the consumption of traditional food rather than processed or 'fast food'

* adopt price policies to make healthy foods more affordable and energy-rich foods more expensive, e.g. 'Fat VAT could save lives'

* make healthy choices more easy

* use legislation where voluntary actions fail to deliver.

Clearly, changes like these will not happen in a few months, but collective action is essential to advance public health and reduce the hazards of this global epidemic of obesity.

Exercise

Exercise, or the lack of it, has been mentioned several times in connection with diet since body weight is a balance between the input of food and

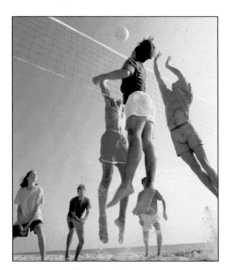

FIGURE 1.31 *Adults enjoying exercise*

the output of energy. This relationship becomes self-perpetuating because the lower the energy output, the more weight the body acquires (assuming food intake remains the same) and the inclination to exercise reduces further and so on.

There are many ways to enjoy physical activity, from simple walking to cycling in the Olympic games, and most also involve intellectual, social and emotional skills. People feel good after exercise and become more relaxed and confident. Exercise helps to combat the effects of stress in our daily lives, assists us to make relationships with others and encourages cooperation between individuals. A lack of exercise leads to a reduction in strength, suppleness and stamina, poor circulation and respiratory functions, and a build-up of fatty deposits in the arterial system. People who exercise regularly in adult life tend to live longer and have a better quality of life.

Stress

There are many occasions in our lives when we experience physical or mental tension and we might say that we are stressed.

Key concept

Stress: A physiological reaction to perceived threat. In other words, if a person believes that he or she is threatened, the stress reaction is set off.

The signs of tension received by the brain cause it to respond by secreting a hormone called adrenaline and increasing the activity of the sympathetic branch of our nervous systems. Both these activities 'switch' on the same actions around our bodies, but the outpouring of adrenaline boosts and sustains the actions more than the increased activity of the nervous system.

Figure 1.32 shows the different actions of adrenaline on the body.

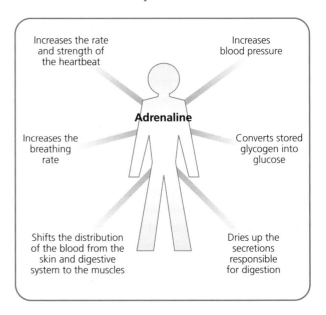

FIGURE 1.32 *The effects of adrenaline during stress or fright*

Large amounts of energy are released almost instantaneously into the blood and, together with increased oxygen, this is pumped rapidly around the body, chiefly to the muscles. From an evolutionary perspective, this response was designed to help an individual run away fast from enemies or stand up and fight. Adrenaline is therefore known as the fright, flight or fight hormone. Whilst some stress can liven up the body and help us to meet new challenges, some people in today's society experience stress on a continuous and long-term basis. The responses that adrenaline produces are often not helpful in the 21st century, as we are unable to run away or physically fight today's stressors, such as pollution, traffic jams, examinations and office hassle, for example. In fact, adrenaline-induced responses in the long-term can be positively harmful as they can lead to high blood pressure and increase the risk of coronary thrombosis, strokes and respiratory problems.

Think it over...

There are many symptoms of stress. The following list contains only a few; try to add more to this list:

Anxiety, heart disease, irritability, sleeplessness, diarrhoea, . . .

Mental and social problems arise with continuous stress, relationships break down, depression is common and suicidal or violent periods occur.

Use of drugs

A single or a mixed course of antibiotics or associated drugs can cure many infections that once might have caused death, disability or long-term illnesses in people. These prescribed drugs have revolutionised medical treatments although we have now reached the situation where scientists are struggling to maintain this supremacy over infections. This is because of the development of 'superbugs' resistant to the standard antibiotics – the infamous MRSA being one such strain.

Think it over...

Find out what words the initials MRSA stand for and their significance.

Surf the Internet to discover the causes and effects of MRSA infection on clients who need care.

An increasing number of drugs can now be bought in a pharmacy or supermarket and these are known as 'over-the-counter' drugs, with those for headache, toothache, coughing, influenza and colds being the most common. These types of drugs help people to avoid pain and other

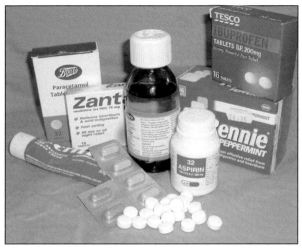

FIGURE 1.33 *Some common over-the-counter drugs*

symptoms almost instantaneously, so have to be mainly good for health and development. On the other hand, such drugs, being easily and widely available, can be a source of harm; all drugs carry the risk of side effects and over-use of most will result in liver and kidney damage, skin rashes, blood disorders and gastro-intestinal problems.

Illegal or controlled drugs are those taken by people to achieve a change in mood or behaviour. Only in a small number of special cases are these substances legally prescribed. Some drugs are called recreational or 'dance' drugs as they are taken to achieve a state of excitement at parties or raves. It is important to understand that many of these drugs arrive from foreign countries in very dubious circumstances, (some are even transported inside the living bodies of individuals) and hardly any are manufactured under safe, controlled laboratories. Before sale, they are often diluted or 'cut' with other materials that are often unsafe. The dose of each drug is not calculated accurately and people react to them in different ways. Taking illegal drugs once only can be dangerous, and taking them regularly can produce addiction. Addiction leads to tolerance whereby a higher dose of the drug is required to achieve the same effect, so the situation becomes more dangerous. As more research studies on the misuse of drugs report, there seem to be an increasingly large number of side effects emerging.

✱ 10 per cent of all those who have tried cannabis develop some form of psychological dependence.

✱ Cannabis remains the most widely taken illegal drug.

✱ Girls experiment with drugs almost as much as boys; young 'middle class' adults take drugs as much as people from poor social backgrounds; rural areas are affected as much as inner cities.

The range of illegal drugs is extensive and the side effects wide-ranging. You will find more specific details in Figure 1.34.

Alcohol

Deciding to drink alcohol can, in moderation and over the short term, confer some benefits such as a feeling of well-being and protection against coronary heart disease (in men and post-menopausal women). Recent research has demonstrated that alcohol raises the level of steroids in the body, which may increase the risk

MISUSED DRUG	APPEARANCE AND USE	EFFECTS OF USE	POSSIBLE RISKS TO HEALTH
Cannabis or hash, grass, marijuana, Black Leb, rocky, weed	Like dried herbs, a dark brown block or sticky and treacle-like; usually smoked but sometimes eaten	Feeling of sickness, hunger or worry More alert and talkative Imagine things (hallucinations)	Bronchitis and damage to lungs Raised pulse rate and blood pressure Inactivity and loss of memory Mental illness
LSD or acid, trips, tabs	Blotters and micro-dots that are swallowed (e.g. impregnated rice paper)	Greater self-awareness Disorientated in time and place Altered hearing, panic Depression and feeling that everyone and everything is against them (paranoia)	Never quite returning to previous normal state and needing more and more to achieve the same effects (tolerance) Flashbacks Anxiety Disorientation and depression
Heroin or H, Henry, smack	White or brown powder that is injected, sniffed up the nose or smoked	Feel sleepy and loved	HIV / AIDS and Hepatitis B when it is injected Thrombosis of veins or abscess at the injection sites Blood infection (septicaemia) Heart and lung disorders Can be fatal if impure
Ecstasy or E, xtc, M25s, lovedoves, Adam	Flat, round tablets that are swallowed	Confidence, calmness and alertness Thirst, anxiety Symptoms of heat stroke Sexual feelings	Nausea, headache and giddiness Raised body temperature with no sweating Muscular cramps Collapse Mental illness including paranoia
Cocaine, coke, snow or Charlie	White powder that is injected or sniffed	Anxiety, thirst and heat stroke symptoms	HIV / AIDS and Hepatitis B when it is injected Thrombosis of veins or abcess at the injection sites
Crack	Crystals that are smoked	Feel on top of the world, could do anything Panic, worry or hostility	Blood infection (septicaemia) Heart and lung disorders Highly addictive Raised body temperature with no sweating, muscular cramps Lack of appetite (anorexia)
Amphetamines or speed, sulph, whizz	White powder in tablets or screws of paper that is swallowed, sniffed or injected	Palpitations (increased force and rate of heart beat), weakness, hunger Lots of energy and confidence Depression and worry	HIV / AIDS and Hepatitis B when it is injected Raised blood pressure and risk of stroke Mental illness Tolerance develops
Solvents or glue, Evo, aerosols, petrol, lighter fluid	Various fluids or sprays that are sniffed	Heightened imagination, depression, happiness or sadness, hostility Fatigue, confusion	Liver and kidney damage Increased risk of accidents during the abuse Heart failure, suffocation, vomiting / choking, death

FIGURE 1.34 *The effects and risks of some commonly misused drugs*

of breast cancer in adult women up to the menopause. Anyone who consumes more than the current alcohol recommendations increases the risks to his or her health.

> ✱ DID YOU KNOW?
>
> In the UK, daily alcohol recommendations are 3 units for women and 4 units for men.
>
> 15 per cent of men and 27 per cent of women drink more than the recommendations.
>
> 1 unit = one half-pint of beer or similar or
> one small glass of wine or
> one measure of spirits

The effects of alcohol consumption are shown in Figure 1.35. Short-term effects will continue until all the alcohol has been broken down by the liver and eliminated through the kidneys. Approximately one unit is metabolised per hour, but this varies from person to person. Women have smaller livers than men so are more susceptible to the effects. Both sexes will also be more prone to accidents as their self-control is impaired; women are less likely to protect themselves against unwanted pregnancies.

Over 10 units of alcohol per day in pregnancy can lead to foetal alcohol syndrome in babies, resulting in facial deformities, stunted growth, heart and joint abnormalities and learning disabilities.

Smoking

Significant changes in social attitudes to smoking have occurred in the last few years and further progress is planned for the near future. Some countries, including Ireland, have already banned smoking in public places and the government in the UK is being urged to follow suit.

The director of the Tobacco Control Resource Centre states that 'tobacco smoke is a potent cocktail of over 4,000 toxins (poisons) – more than 50 of which cause cancer.'

The Acheson report (1998) points out major class differences in smoking behaviour. 2 per cent of men and 16 per cent of women in the professional classes smoke, compared with

EFFECTS OF ALCOHOL CONSUMPTION	
SHORT-TERM EFFECTS	**LONG-TERM EFFECTS**
Increased heart rate	Raised blood pressure
Palpitations	Coronary heart disease
Increased skin temperature	Pancreatitis and cirrhosis of the liver
Diuresis – enhanced urine formation	Weakened immune system
Increased happiness and reduced inhibitions	Decreased sex drive
Slurring of speech	Irregular menstrual cycles, some sterility Foetal alcohol syndrome
Tendency to be argumentative	Increased risk of strokes
More accident prone	Increased risk of some cancers e.g. oesophagus
Muscle weakness	Obesity
Facial flushing	Brain damage and depression

FIGURE 1.35 *Effects of short- and long-term alcohol consumption*

41 per cent of men and 36 per cent of women in the unskilled classes. Other theorists have noted that smoking rates increase with poverty and that women, in particular, find it difficult to give up. Some social groups will say that smoking is the only way to manage the stress of living on a low income and that it is the only luxury they allow themselves.

> **Think it over...**
>
> In groups, consider the arguments you might use in trying to encourage a young single parent on benefits to stop smoking 40 cigarettes a day.

> ✱ DID YOU KNOW?
>
> More than 1,000 people die every year as a result of diseases linked to passive smoking.

The home is now the most common place where children are exposed to tobacco smoke, and some places in the UK are taking part in an initiative called *Smoke-free homes* to tackle this problem. The biggest barrier that prevents people from making their homes smoke-free is the fear of harming important relationships with family and friends who smoke. More than 17,000 children are admitted to hospital each year in the UK because of the effects of inhaling tobacco smoke.

> **✱ DID YOU KNOW?**
>
> In 2000, the EU spent over £650 million on subsidies (i.e. grants of money) to tobacco producers and £1.3 million on smoking prevention! Under the common agricultural policy, tobacco is the most heavily subsidised and the only non-food product to be subsidised.

So, why is smoking so harmful to people? The pattern diagram below (Figure 1.36) shows the most serious effects of smoking.

Social and community support factors

An individual needs social and community support if his or her development is to proceed without problems or difficulties. We need to develop relationships with others to advance our social skills, and emotional development is likely to be affected if there is no one to share our 'highs' and 'lows' with. Intellectual stimulation is often dependent on good social and emotional development as well as the stimulation of exchanging views with others. Growth, development and health in childhood and adolescence are closely dependent on the groups to which we belong.

Family support

> **Key concept**
>
> *Family:* A family is a social group made up of people connected to each other by blood or marriage. Families in Britain usually consist of adults acting as parents or guardians to children.

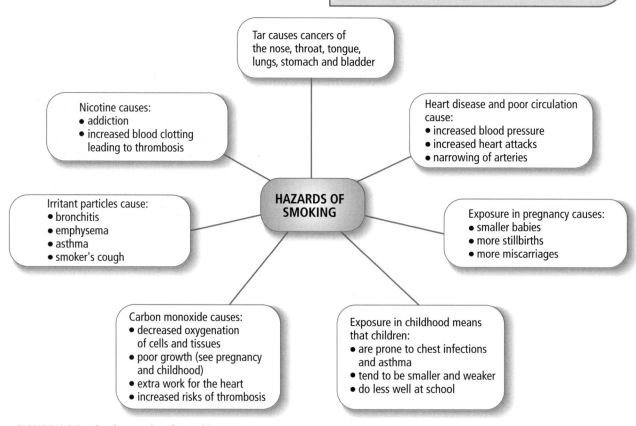

FIGURE 1.36 *The hazards of smoking*

Families usually support each other financially – money is shared

Provides an introduction to social rules – socialisation

Provides the setting where the majority of people will develop a sense of belonging and self-esteem – or fail to develop this

Physical health and mental health is influenced by the family

Should provide setting to meet physical needs for food, shelter and warmth

Relatives provide a network of people who can give support or advice

The family

Contributes to intellectual, social and emotional development of children

Relationships can be a great source of support and satisfaction, or a source of stress

May care for older relatives

FIGURE 1.37 *Advantages of belonging to a family group*

Belonging to a family can have many advantages – such as safe, care settings for children; education and guidance for children and adolescents; and social and emotional support for older people. (See Figure 1.37.)

Sociologists have identified four types of families, which are classified as:

* extended
* reconstituted
* nuclear
* lone-parent.

Extended families

An extended family is where parents, children, grandparents and sometimes aunts and uncles live in close proximity so that they are in constant contact. The extended family provides a network of people who care and financially support each other. Families used to live this way in the 19th century so that everyone could help with feeding animals and working in the fields. However, industrialisation caused many people to travel to cities to work and live in much smaller houses.

Nuclear families

This term is used to describe the smaller family unit of husband, wife and children. In the past, the husband worked to earn money and the wife shopped, cooked, cleaned and looked after the children. In today's society, many families consist of two working parents, with nurseries, child-minders or nannies caring for the children except at weekends. Men and women share more of the household tasks although women still tend to undertake the biggest share.

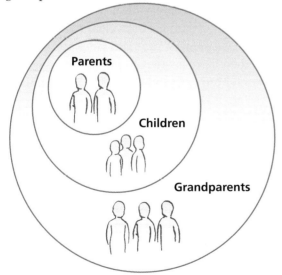

FIGURE 1.38 *The extended family*

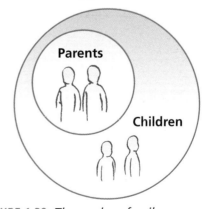

FIGURE 1.39 *The nuclear family*

Reconstituted families

Approximately one marriage in three ends in divorce and more people are now cohabiting than ever before. Some of these couples will eventually marry whilst others will also split up. Around one-quarter of children under the age of 16 will experience their parents divorcing. A reconstituted family is one in which the partners are not both the biological parents of each child in the family.

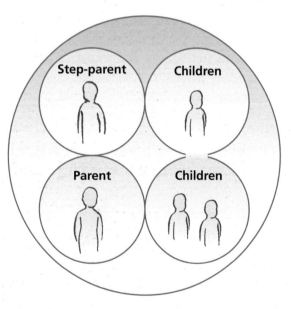

FIGURE 1.40 *The reconstituted family*

Lone-parent families

The proportion of families containing a married or cohabiting couple with dependent children declined from 31 per cent in 1979 to 21 per cent in 2002; by comparison, families headed by a lone parent rose from 4 per cent in 1979 to 7 per cent in 1993. Nearly one-quarter of all families with dependent children are now lone-parent families; most are led by the mother as the lone parent. While some lone-parent families are in satisfactory financial circumstances, most are disadvantaged because they survive on benefits or low incomes.

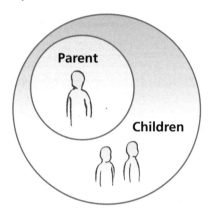

FIGURE 1.41 *The lone-parent family*

Insufficient family support

Insufficient support, however, may arise from dysfunctional, incomplete, undisciplined or over-large families, often as a result of circumstances beyond their immediate control. When there are large numbers of siblings born close together, an over-worked parent or carer, lax rules and low income, then there is often disregard for education, more aggression and slower cognitive progression. It is important to recognise the dangers of stereotyping for there are many entertainers, sports personalities, academics and authors who describe such backgrounds and have performed extremely well. Some wealthy entrepreneurs admit to disinterest in school and education during childhood and adolescence and to fending for themselves in a wider world. It might seem as if 'hunger' would drive some people onwards in a dynamic and exceptional way, but the majority of people lacking appropriate family support and/or income might find life increasingly difficult.

In recent years, we have recognised the importance of family support and instituted **holistic** treatment when an individual finds life difficult. Children and young people with psychological and/or behavioural problems might therefore be treated as part of the family rather than as individuals. Family therapy is becoming increasingly important and regular meetings with a therapist help to expose the feelings between family members. The therapist then works with the family to promote greater understanding and harmony.

Family is the setting in which we first learn social values. This is called primary or first socialisation.

Friends

Key concept

Socialisation: The process by which we learn the norms, values and behaviour that makes us a member of a particular group. Learning to socialise or be a social member of a group.

As childhood advances into adolescence and early adulthood, we find that friendship groups create a process called **secondary socialisation**. This is where friends influence our beliefs and values. A life without friends is likely to be very difficult indeed, for we call upon our friends to assist us in a variety of ways.

The same life-stage friends can be particularly important as experiencing the same or similar joys and difficulties forges a strong bond between people. Individuals from different life stages can also make firm friendships but often of a different nature, the elder listening to the younger person's problems and offering advice in an objective way.

Recent studies have shown, however, that children and adolescents who go about in 'gangs' do less well than those who have a few strong friendships. Gangs tend to move progressively

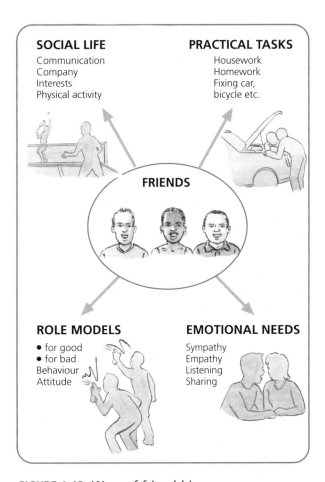

FIGURE 1.42 *Ways of friendship*

towards increasingly risky pastimes and the member who wants to withdraw is subjected to ridicule, bullying and even violence. In many communities, it is much safer to conform and belong to a gang than to be outside it.

FIGURE 1.43 *It is safer to belong to a gang than to be outside it*

Health services

The Acheson report (1998) identified an 'inverse law' in some areas of care. Communities with the greatest need receive the lowest level of service, whilst those with the lowest need receive the highest level of resource. In the field of preventive medicine, communities at the most risk of ill health often experience the least satisfactory access to the full range of preventive services. For example, the lack of a female general practitioner in a practice may deter Asian women from cervical cytology and other essentially female services. Deprived areas have increasing difficulty in recruiting GPs, health visitors and practice nurses. Dentists in the NHS have become extremely scarce in many areas of the country and several local populations, including children, have experienced several years of dental neglect.

New methods of booking appointments to see GPs and telephone consultations have disadvantaged people who do not have a private telephone, dislike using the instrument or have communication difficulties. The proportion of GP consultations at home fell from 22 per cent in 1971 to 5 per cent in 2002, but this coincided with increases in telephone (4 to 9 per cent) and surgery consultations (73 to 86 per cent). Clients in rural districts, who need to travel long distances to see GPs must to some extent appreciate new arrangements for telephone consultations.

Doctors spend more time with middle-class patients (social classes 1 and 2) and there is evidence that NHS expenditure is 40 per cent greater than on those in classes 6 and 7 because the former can manipulate the health systems to their advantage. (See Figure 1.45.)

Community groups

There is a wide range of groups serving different needs in the community. The primary focuses of these groups can be broadly categorised into serving these needs of its members as in Figure 1.44. Members of each group might also serve as friends and intimate relationships can be formed through shared interests.

Emotional needs
- Counselling
- Mother & Baby groups
- Music

Intellectual needs
- Quiz groups
- University of the Third Age
- Bridge clubs
- Whist groups

COMMUNITY GROUPS

Social needs
- Playgroups
- Derby & Joan Clubs
- Age Concern
- British Legion
- Youth Clubs

Physical needs
- Meals on Wheels
- Sports club
- Specialist groups such as Alzheimer's Society
- Dance

FIGURE 1.44 *Community groups*

Think it over...

Some examples of community groups have been added to Figure 1.44. Make a list of community groups in your locality and add them to the relevant branch of a similar diagram.

Social class

In the UK we divide society into different levels according to the degree of wealth and power possessed by individuals. Historically, there was an upper class consisting of aristocrats who did not work for a living; middle classes who were in trade (shopkeepers, wholesalers, businessmen) or professions; and the working classes who worked for the middle and upper classes and generally had to manage on low incomes.

Key concept

Social class: The status given to different types of occupation or work.

Occupations are chosen because they are linked to a level of income, behaviour, lifestyle and standing in a community. The new system of

THE NATIONAL STATISTICS SOCIO-ECONOMIC CLASSIFICATION – ANALYTIC CLASSES	
1	Higher managerial and professional occupations Large employers and higher managerial occupations, e.g. chief executives of major organisations Higher professional occupations, e.g. doctors, lawyers
2	Lower managerial and professional occupations Middle management in bigger organisations, departmental managers, e.g. physiotherapists, teachers, police
3	Intermediate occupations, e.g. clerks, bank workers
4	Small employers and own account workers, e.g. painters, decorators, small manufacturing company owners, taxi drivers
5	Lower supervisory, craft and technical occupations, e.g. plumbers, builders, joiners, train drivers
6	Semi-routine occupations, e.g. shop assistants, hairdressers, labourers
7	Routine occupations, e.g. cleaners, refuse collectors, assembly workers
8	Never worked or long-term unemployed

FIGURE 1.45 *The National Statistics Classification*

classification shown in Figure 1.45 is now used in research into health and social issues.

Countries with the smallest income differences between the classes have the best health status; in the UK, where the income difference between classes is large, there is likewise inequality in health status. Accidental deaths in children are five times greater in the lowest social classes than in the higher classes. Infant mortality, lung cancer, stroke and heart disease rates are all several times greater in the lowest social classes.

Argyle (1987:189) states, 'The lower social classes are affected by most illness, more often, take more days off from work, and die a little sooner because of them (the illnesses). This is

Think it over...

There are over three-and-a-half times more suicides and four times more accidents in social class 7 than in class 1. What possible reasons can you think of for this?

partly due to inequalities in the conditions of life – smaller homes, less heating, larger families, less good food and so on.' Argyle argues that middle-class people make more use of preventive health services such as antenatal clinics, vaccination programmes and cervical screening, than do working class people. There is evidence that social classes 1 and 2 smoke less, weigh less and exercise more than classes 6 and 7.

A study by Blaxter (1990) found that there is a close link between poverty and ill health and that there might be more ill health for the very wealthy than for those who are just well off.

Socialisation

A child learns a great deal from copying the activities of members of its family, but characters on TV, in books, in computer games, on DVDs and on radio also influence him or her. **Primary socialisation** then, occurs from experiences learned at an early age in the home and through the media. Children learn the 'norms' or beliefs of the family. When father goes to work every weekday to earn money to satisfy the needs of the family, this becomes the norm, and a family whose male parent does not work is outside that norm. Similarly, when appointments for clinics, surgeries or hospitals are largely ignored or complained about, the child rapidly picks up that such arrangements are not important and the indifference becomes perpetuated in their families in the future.

Secondary socialisation comes from a wider field of influence when the child becomes older. Between the ages of 11–15 adolescents become very involved with their own group of friends and the influence of the family wanes (but doesn't disappear) while that of the friendship group increases. This is particularly noticeable in music styles, sports enthusiasms, eating and drinking habits, substance abuse and fashions. Popular culture often does not include healthy lifestyles but fortunately, most of these lapses are temporary.

Cultural beliefs

Culture remains a strong influence on individuals during their lifespan. Different people have different beliefs about what is morally right and wrong and these can extend into aspects of care as well as in the home.

Physical environment factors

Air quality

Local authorities control air pollution from about 20,000 small industrial processes and the Environment Agency regulates the release of pollutants from over 2,000 major, more complex industries. The EU is legislating to bring a wider range of processes into regulation. Major sources

POLLUTANT	MAIN SOURCES	MAIN EFFECTS ON HEALTH
Particulate matter	Transport exhausts Burning of fossil fuels	Tiny particles enter and remain in the lungs; may cause inflammation and be a source of allergy and asthma. Can cause ground ozone (with carbon monoxide)
Carbon monoxide	Transport exhausts Burning of fossil fuels Furnace gas	Combines more powerfully with haemoglobin than oxygen so results in less oxygen available to the tissues. Headaches, faintness, nausea and dizziness result. In large quantities will cause brain damage and even death. When combined with soot particles in the presence of sunlight makes smog and ozone at ground level – a lethal mix of gases that causes breathing problems and asthma. Common in some cities in sunny climates, e.g. Los Angeles, Tokyo
Carbon dioxide	All combustion including gas fires, gas central heating	Transmits sunlight but partially resists the outward flow of infrared radiation from Earth to space, resulting in 'the greenhouse effect' and preventing the Earth from cooling at night. Consequently, the Earth's surface is warming up – so-called global warming with freak storms and hurricanes increasing the number of deaths and injuries
Sulphur dioxide	Coal-burning power stations, industrial processes	Causes the finer bronchioles in the lungs to contract making breathing more difficult and irritation of the upper respiratory tract. Largely responsible for 'acid rain'
Nitrogen oxides	Burning of fossil fuels Transport exhaust gases	Also forms 'acid rain' and ground ozone (see carbon monoxide) Damages stratospheric ozone layer, causing increased skin cancer and genetic mutations from extra radiation
CFCs chloro-fluoro-carbons	Chiefly aerosols	Damages the stratospheric ozone layer (see under nitrogen oxides)
Moulds	Decaying organic matter	Spores from moulds can cause allergies, hay fever and asthma

FIGURE 1.46 *Main sources and effects of air pollutants*

of pollution such as transport (chiefly cars) are controlled by a combination of actions at European, national and local levels.

Main pollutants of air are **noxious** gases and small particles (particulate matter PM10). You can check out their main sources and effects in Figure 1.46.

The good news is that levels of air pollutants are falling. However, the fall may not be fast enough to prevent large numbers of people suffering problems with their health.

Falling pollution levels are attributable to:

* regular monitoring of industrial processes and heavy fines for non-compliance with regulations

* catalytic converters fitted to cars

* reduction in coal-fired power stations

* regulations about the sulphur and lead content of fuel

* more 'lean-burn' engines in cars which reduce nitrogen oxide levels.

Water quality

There is sanitation, sewage treatment, waste disposal and water treatment in the UK and most developed countries. Water is sterilised and tested before it is supplied to homes; consequently, tap water is considered very safe. Accidents happen only very rarely when some contaminant enters the water system and correction or shutting down occurs quickly. Most of our sanitation systems are many decades old and modernisation is urgently needed in some parts of the country. Rats are a problem in our sewers and waterways, and if rats bite people there is always the possibility of diseases such as Weil's disease, typhus and plague.

> *** DID YOU KNOW?**
>
> The **physician** Adolf Weil (1848–1916) isolated rats as the cause of a particular disease he had described in humans.

Certain diseases, such as typhoid fever, cholera and viral hepatitis A, can transmit through water, so it is always prudent to boil or otherwise sterilise water in developing countries. Bottled or canned water is usually safe too, although there have been some incidents of too many salts in commercial preparations. Many of the diseases hitherto mentioned are potentially fatal diseases so it is very important to maintain water safety.

Noise pollution

Exposure to a very loud noise such as a jet engine at 30 metres can cause immediate and permanent damage to the ears; but, more commonly, hearing loud noise for a long time results in high-pitched tones becoming lost. Loud music or pneumatic drills can cause pain and temporary deafness, lasting minutes or hours. Regulations exist in workplaces to ensure that noise levels do not rise above certain levels and that those people exposed to loud noises in their occupations wear ear protectors. A common complaint, especially from those living in inner cities, is about traffic noise. Although regulations exist for minimising such noise, it can be extremely stressful, cause sleeplessness and eventually ill health. Similar experiences happen to people who live near busy airports, and night flights are particularly troublesome.

Access to employment

Worthwhile employment is one of the few ways to improve lifestyle, income, housing and health prospects. However, if an individual suffers from ill health and is deemed unreliable by employers, he or she is less likely to retain a job or get good references to obtain a new one. Maternity leave and the care of small children can also disadvantage women of childbearing age. Lone parents find it particularly difficult to find work that allows them to care for school-age children because of school hours and long holidays. Part-time work is usually low-paid and having to combine part-time work, school hours and holidays makes worthwhile employment almost impossible, even if a willing employer can be found. In such circumstances living on benefits becomes more attractive. Such a lifestyle also carries with it the enormous stress of dealing with being punctual, sudden child sickness, or school closures for elections and teacher training days. Many couples paying for childcare, either pre-school or after-school, find that the costs almost equate to one salary or wage packet.

As manufacturing declines in the UK there are fewer social class 7 jobs available, particularly in the North, and the cost of living in the South prohibits people from moving. This leads to frustration, anger, stress and ill health for the long-term unemployed and their families. Unemployment affects the way we treat other people, the treatment we receive from others, the services we are entitled to and our attitude to life generally. Unemployment also contributes to the decline of areas, as people have little money with which to purchase commodities, so shops close down, vandalism is rife and dereliction becomes the norm. People who live in the poorest areas tend to have low self-esteem and this is a significant deterrent to potential employers when being interviewed for all but the lowliest of jobs. Unemployment has a profound effect on self-esteem and motivation; there is no point in working hard to gain qualifications if there are no jobs to apply for.

Unemployment in the UK (measured by the International Labour Organisation, ILO, 2002) is running at 4.7 per cent or just under one and a half million people. This figure relies on the Labour Force Survey of the number of people without employment who have made recent efforts to find it.

There has been marked growth in employment in the UK in the recent past, but most jobs are part-time and low paid. In 1996, just over a quarter of a million people entered employment of which 63 per cent were part-time, and a quarter of employed people earned less than £4 per hour.

People *not* counted as unemployed but who want to work include those:

* who informally care for others – children, elderly or disabled people

* working part-time because they cannot get a full-time job

* young people on training schemes like New Deal and Modern apprentices

* people who have moved on to sickness or disability benefit rather than the 'dole'

* students in full-time education

* adolescents under 18 years who are not allowed to register as unemployed.

The Trades Union Congress (TUC) has reported that as many as two million people not counted as unemployed want full-time work. If these people were added to the 'official' ILO figures, then the UK would have a higher unemployment total than France or Germany.

People most likely to be unemployed are lone parents, disabled people, those without many skills or qualifications, those over 50 years and people from ethnic minorities.

Many people are multi-disadvantaged; for example, a lone parent from an ethnic minority and with low qualifications. If we removed people in these areas of society from the unemployment register, we would have only 4 per cent unemployed.

Unemployment is mainly concentrated in deprived areas where the rate can be many times the national average.

Key concept

Income: Money that an individual or household gets from wages, benefits, investments or other sources.

Many families who are well off tend to have the best of everything, including rich food. Too much of the wrong kind of food, rich in fat and salt content, is harmful to the cardiovascular system and causes obesity, with all its problems. Such families are usually regularly monitored by their physicians and given the correct advice and attention. They can afford designer-wear clothes, to go to private gymnasia or even to have a personal trainer to take them in hand. Many families in the social classes 1 and 2 tend to drink too much alcohol, particularly on holiday, which is the main occasion for so-called 'binge-drinking'. Young adults, particularly females, regularly drink more than the recommended allowance, putting their physiological health at risk, together with possible accidents and unwanted pregnancies.

Despite the Welfare State, the gap continues to widen in life expectancy and health experience between those who are well off and those who are poorer. Several studies have reported on the number of unnecessary deaths, particularly of those under 65 years of age, which take place in the poorest areas of Britain. It has been estimated that if full employment could be achieved some 2,500 deaths would be prevented each year.

The UK has the second highest proportion of full-time workers on low pay of all major economies in the West; only the United States has more. People on low pay are also more vulnerable to unemployment and after losing a job are more likely to be paid even less on re-entering work. The longer someone has been on a low income, the more likely they are to remain so and this especially applies to older workers and women.

Levels of dental decay and rates of infant mortality, teenage pregnancy, and suicide are all increased in deprived areas. Suicides are strongly linked to poverty and depression and are two to three times higher among the unemployed. The suicide rate in Scotland is twice as high as in England and Wales and a serious cause for concern. Teenage pregnancies, linked to poverty and unemployment, in Scotland are the highest in Western Europe.

The lower the income of an individual or family the more risks they suffer throughout all life stages.

Education

Education levels in the poorest areas are lower than for the rest of the country. The government believes the improvement in primary and secondary schools is vital to give people the necessary skills to achieve jobs and careers. Schools in deprived areas suffer more vandalism, rubbish accumulation and lack of resources than more affluent schools. This produces stressful working conditions for staff and pupils, who are less likely to take full advantages of learning opportunities. Children arrive at school hungry, without energy-sustaining breakfasts, tired and minus homework, or even simple writing instruments. The start of the school year is particularly difficult for teachers, as many children may have had to fend for themselves over the long summer break, while parents are at work, or worse, on holiday. Parents who continually hear about the difficulties and behavioural problems of their children soon cease to be interested in parents' evenings or education generally. Stress, depression and social exclusion reduce the interest level even further.

Acheson (1998) reports that education has a link with health in that low levels of educational achievement are associated with poor health in adult life. Poor health and poor educational achievement are caused by **poverty**. It is likely that the combined effects of poor resources, low expectations and the need to earn money often influence young people from low-income families to give education a low priority.

New initiatives from the government to increase participation in higher education are likely to be offset by the student loan debate and the almost certain legacy of incurring a large debt. The effects of maintenance allowances, which aim to encourage students from low income families to achieve university entrance qualifications, are likely to be countered by the pressure from the family to work and provide extra income.

Safe neighbourhoods

The Rowntree Report (1995) drew attention to the fact that some neighbourhoods were particularly stressful to live in because of high levels of poverty, unemployment, crime and vandalism.

The Social Exclusion Unit Paper 'Opportunity for all' (1999) explains that some communities are 'trapped outside mainstream society'. High levels of crime form one of the main problems in such communities; people are afraid to venture out, principally in darkness, as they are afraid of becoming victims of crime. Growing up and living in the most deprived neighbourhoods may greatly restrict an individual's chance of developing his or her full intellectual, social or emotional potential.

Much of the crime on estates is drug-related, as individuals search for money or valuables to pay for their next 'fix'. Gun crime is increasing in the UK and most of this is also drug-related. Innocent people have been gunned down in Liverpool, Manchester, Nottingham and London while carrying out their day-to-day business or leisure activities. High levels of crime also facilitate gang formation, as individuals feel safer in the company of several friends.

Unemployment, low income, poor educational opportunities, high crime levels, poor health, poor services, neglect and abuse of all types 'feed' off each other, creating housing estates that undermine all but the very strongest.

Psychological factors

Health can be strongly influenced by the way individuals feel about things, particularly themselves.

Self-concept is a term used to incorporate both self-esteem and self-image. Self-concept is defined as an understanding of self, gained from how we feel about or value our self and the reactions of others towards us.

> ### Key concept
>
> *Self-esteem:* How highly we value our skills and abilities.
>
> *Self-image:* How we see our self and the reactions of others towards us.

Self-esteem

This is the regard individuals have for themselves, which can influence behaviour and moods. Having a high self-esteem increases self-confidence and makes an individual more able to cope with the difficulties he or she might face. It also might mean that a person is popular with peers and more likely to be successful. A child having high self-esteem is more likely to be content and happy in his or her adult life. It would seem that a close, loving relationship with his or her mother, a fair, constant framework of discipline and the ability to express individuality provides a good foundation for the development of self-esteem through childhood.

Self-esteem and the development of self-concept

As children grow they become socialised into the beliefs, values and norms of their initial family or care-giving group. Later, the beliefs, values and norms of their friends with whom they mix and play will influence them. Children adopt other values and norms in order to be accepted into social groups, to be liked and to be popular. Mead (1934) believed that children learn general social rules and values during childhood. He believed that children might learn to display emotion as expected in their social roles and the cultural context of their home. They do not simply do what others teach them, however; they internalise values from the world around them, built into a sense of self that becomes part of their self-concept and social identity.

This sense of self will guide the individual to exaggerate, suppress or even substitute emotional expression. In some geographical areas and social classes, boys may learn to exaggerate feelings of anger and aggression to achieve social status. In a different social class, boys may learn to express anger in terms of clever verbal behaviour with little hint of emotion. Some girls may learn to hide feelings of distress in order to look in control. Mead's theory explains how social influences work on an individual. It is the idea of 'self' or 'me' that explains how social values influence individual behaviour.

During adolescence this sense of self becomes of central importance. Erikson (1963) believed that biological pressures to become independent would force adolescents into a crisis, which could only be successfully resolved if the individual developed a conscious sense of self or purpose. He wrote, 'In the social jungle of human existence, there is no feeling of being alive without a sense of ego identity.'

Other theorists have regarded the development of the self-concept as more gradual and less centred on biological maturation. A clear sense of self might provide a person with the ability cope with changes in life and lead to a feeling of self-worth.

The psychologist Donaldson (1986) believes that a child can only develop a strong or positive self-concept when he or she feels effective, independent and competent.

The benefits conferred by a positive self-concept can be to:

* make effective social and sexual relationships with others

* cope with decision-making, especially in work environments

* develop self-confidence in social and work settings

* accept new challenges with enthusiasm

* cope with own feelings to arouse motivation

* cope with complex interpersonal situations by using appropriate skills, e.g. assertion.

Consider this

With a good friend to help you, draw up a list of questions to investigate the strength of a person's self-concept. You can use the following phrases to get you started:

* physical attraction

* intelligence or cleverness

* athletic or sporting ability

* popularity

* fitness

* problem-solving

* decision-making.

When you have completed the list, devise a method of scoring, say, from 0–5, where 0 represents no ability at all and 5 represents excellence. If you have 9 questions, then 45 is the top score. You can also devise a means to interpret the score in terms of self-concept – for example, 35–45 is a positive self-concept and 0–20 is a negative self-concept. Some individuals will be positive in some aspects and more negative in others. Try your system out on each other and analyse the results in terms of effectiveness for you.

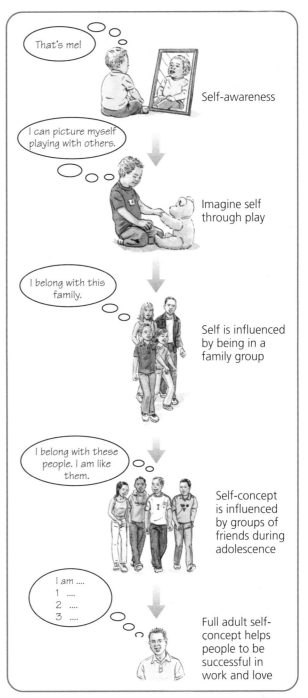

FIGURE 1.47 *The development of self-concept begins with self-awareness*

Think it over...

Using your 'home-made' self-concept from the last exercise, explore the ways in which your self-concept has been influenced by the factors in Figure 1.47. Talk your answers through with the person who previously partnered you.

AGE	STAGE OF DEVELOPMENT
$1\frac{1}{2}$–2 years	Self-awareness develops – children may start to recognise themselves in a mirror
$2\frac{1}{2}$ years	Children can say whether they are a boy or a girl
3–5 years	When asked to say what they are like, children can describe themselves in terms of categories, such as big or small, tall or short, light or heavy
5–8 years	If you ask children who they are, they can often describe themselves in detail. Children will tell you their skin colour, eye colour, about their family and to which school they belong
8–10 years	Children start to show a general sense of 'self-worth', such as describing how happy they are in general, how good life is for them, what is good about their family life, school and friends
10–12 years	Children start to analyse how they compare with others. When asked about their life, children may explain without prompting how they compare with others. For example: 'I'm not as good as Zoe at running, but I'm better than Ali.'
12–16 years	Adolescents may develop a sense of self in terms of beliefs and belonging to groups – being a vegetarian, believing in God, believing certain things are right or wrong
16–25 years	People develop an adult self-concept that helps a great deal as they grow older
25+ years	People's sense of self will be influenced by the things that happen in their lives. Some people may change their self-concept a great deal as they grow older
65+ years	In later life it is important to be able to keep a clear sense of self. People may become withdrawn and depressed, without a clear self-concept

FIGURE 1.48 *Overview of the developmental stages of the self-concept*

General factors influencing self-concept are displayed in Figure 1.48.

An overview of the developmental stages of self-concept might be summarised as in Figure 1.49.

Relationships with family and partners

Blaxter (1990) discovered that stressful life events such as widowhood, bereavement, divorce, unemployment and moving home were associated with increased morbidity (incidence of disease) and mortality (death). She reported that people were protected or 'buffered' against these effects of stress when they had a close social support network of friends, family, partners and/or community links.

As well as protection against stress, support will also maintain self-esteem, self-concept and identity when these may be threatened. Argyle (1987) maintained that the quality of support was important and that both sexes preferred to have meaningful dialogue with females, who are more pleasant and open to self-disclosure than men.

Blaxter (1990) noted that family relationships and close bonds were strongly protective against stress, perhaps through positive effects on self-esteem and feelings of control. The relationship between social networks and health is so strong that it can be used predictively in relation to mortality. People with poor social networks run a greater risk of dying from illness than those with close relationships. In terms of support, marriage

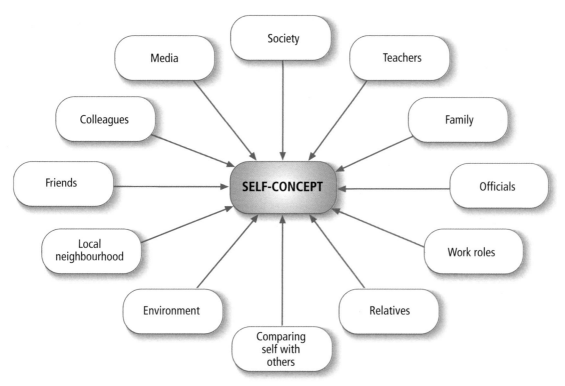

FIGURE 1.49 *Influences on self-concept*

produced the strongest protection, followed by friends and relatives – even more than belonging to church or other organisations.

Argyle further contends that stress impairs the immune system – the natural defence against disease. Social support might restore the immune system by replacing negative emotions such as depression and anxiety with the positive emotions of hope and belief. Those with good relationships are more likely to seek support and help than turn to drinking and smoking.

Blaxter's study (1990) provided evidence that marriage and cohabiting have a more positive relationship on health than being single. This is significant for men generally and older men in particular, as living alone is associated with more illness and poorer psychological and social well-being. Socially isolated people may lack a buffer to protect themselves against anxiety, strain and threat.

Stress

There are many ways to define stress, but one expression that fits life generally is 'any interference that disturbs a person's healthy

mental and physical well-being'. Some people are more susceptible than others to stress-related problems, but most people find the death of a loved one, the birth of a baby, moving house, divorce, violence and conflict, and other significant life events, cause them stress.

The physiological responses to adrenaline and cortisol outpourings produce changes in heart rate, blood pressure, respiratory rate, metabolism and physical activity designed to improve overall performance; however, such responses also reduce the individual's ability to cope. Long-term stress reduces the ability of the immune system to protect against disease, produces depression and anxiety, indigestion, palpitations, hypertension (and resulting heart disease) and muscular aches and pains.

Nature–nurture debate

The debate about inherited and environmental influences on behaviour, health and well-being is sometimes referred to as the nature (inherited influences) or nurture (environmental influences) debate. The argument has been going on between

GOOD RELATIONSHIPS CAN PRODUCE:	POOR RELATIONSHIPS CAN PRODUCE:
Infancy Secure attachment between the infant and parents A rich learning environment A safe, loving environment which meets a child's emotional needs	A failure to make a secure or safe emotional attachment between parents and the child Neglect, rejection of the child
Early childhood A secure home from which to develop slowly Parents who can cope with the stressful behaviour of young children Friendships with other children	A stressful home situation Neglect or rejection of the child Inconsistent attempts to control a child Parents who become angry or depressed because of the child Isolation from other children
Later childhood Membership of a family or care group Socialisation into a culture Friendships with others at school Increasing independence from parents A feeling of being confident and liked by other people A feeling of being good at things	Stress and change if parents fight each other or separate No clear feeling of belonging with a group or culture Limited friendships Feelings of not being liked by others Feelings of not being good at anything or not as good as others
Adolescence Independence but still with the support of the family A network of friends, a sense of belonging with a group of friends A culture shared by friends A positive environment that has opportunities for the future	Conflict and fighting with parents and family Few friends, feeling depressed and rejected No feeling of belonging with other people No clear sense of who you are The feeling that life is not worth much
Adulthood A network of friends and family who help and support you A secure, loving, sexual relationship Good relationships with work colleagues The ability to balance time pressures between work, partner and other family relationships A feeling of being secure and safe, with other people to help you	Feelings of isolation, loneliness, rejection and no feeling of belonging with friends No support Changing relationships No social protection from stress Low self-esteem
Old age A network of family, friends and partner to provide emotional support Control of own life A sense of purpose	Few friends, no social support No social protection from stress Isolation No sense of purpose

FIGURE 1.50 *The effects of personal relationships at different life stages*

theorists for decades – long before genes and chromosomes were discovered.

Bateson, quoted in *The Independent* (18th February 1995) argued that human development is a process like baking a cake: the end result of which is nothing like the ingredients that were used to make it, and the process of mixing and baking produces something quite different. Similarly, the contribution of environmental factors on human growth and development are impossible to separate from the contribution of genetics. Human beings are infinitely more complex than cakes, which become finished products, whereas human learning and development continues until death. A useful conclusion is that neither nature nor nurture can be abstracted from the process of development, but that they both interact throughout the lifespan. At some times, it appears that genetic influences are more dominant and, at others, environmental factors override the inherited component.

Recently, the leader of the private effort to decode the human genome, Venter, said, 'genetic determinism, the idea that a person is controlled by their genes, is a fallacy.' He made his remarks after stating that humans had far fewer genes than expected – only 30,000 – and suggested that environmental influences play a larger role in development than was previously thought.

Researchers predict that soon the data will unlock the secrets of how genes influence behaviour. Other theorists have argued that the (relatively) small number of genes does not indicate the larger role of environmental influences at all. The nature–nurture debate, as old as it is, just will not go away!

Summary of Section 1.2

The following key areas of theory in nature versus nurture have been covered in this section:

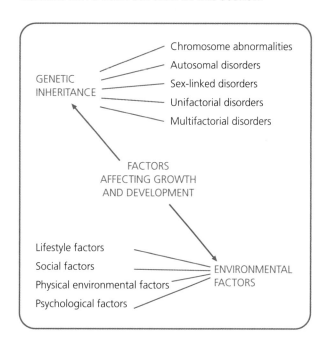

Consider this

Tom's family has a history of coronary heart disease due to a high level of blood cholesterol. Several close members of his family have died in early and middle adulthood, making it necessary for him to have regular checks by the family doctor.

Tom used to be both a heavy smoker and drinker and he works long hours with disadvantaged children. His frail mother now lives with Tom, his wife and four children ranging in age from 4–15 years. The house is fairly crowded and the older two children go out most evenings to their friends. Tom worries that he is losing touch with the teenagers and that they might get into trouble but is anxious to help out with the younger children and his mother, who he feels has not long to live.

Using concepts, can you identify?
1. Genetic factors that have an impact on Tom's experience of health and well-being?

2. Environmental factors that have an impact on Tom's experience of health and well-being?

Go further – can you analyse issues using theory?
Discuss the relevance of the nature versus nurture debate with particular reference to Tom's experience of health and well-being.

Go further – can you evaluate using a range of theory?
Using a range of concepts, can you make judgements on the factors influencing Tom's health that were under his control and those which he would not be able to change.

1.3 Promoting health and well-being

Defining 'health' is a difficult task as it means many different things to people, rather like 'stress' or 'happiness' does. These words are almost indefinable except in the most general terms. We must, however, have some idea of the meaning of 'health' as we use the word in titles such as 'health visitor', 'health education' and '**health promotion**'.

Understanding 'health'

If you asked friends or members of your family what they understand by 'health' or 'being healthy', you will collect varied responses.

Most people will respond in terms of 'not being ill' indicating a rather negative view that health is something that you don't think about until you have not got it. In other words, health is something that you have until your daily life is disturbed by illness and you are unable to carry out your normal programme. Other people might produce a more wholesome or '**holistic**' view of health as being in the peak of physical, mental and emotional fitness. Some people might provide you with a very personal notion of health, such as 'when my rheumatism isn't giving me trouble'. Personal views like this might

FIGURE 1.51 *'Health' means different things to people; some associate it with decent accommodation*

SCENARIO

A state of health

Simin is 22 years old and uses a wheelchair after a road accident left him paralysed 4 years ago. He has totally recovered from the accident and travels by car to his local leisure centre to play basketball with other wheelchair users. Simin hopes to take part in national events next year and international competitions in a year or two. When asked, Simin replies that he is in excellent health.

Mary and her four children have lived in bed and breakfast accommodation for 2 years. Before that, Mary was homeless and the children were in residential care. Last month, Mary and her family moved into a partly furnished council house. Mary obtained two nursery places for her pre-school children and managed to get a part-time job in the local supermarket. When Mary met her friend yesterday she told her that she felt 'on top of the world'.

Stan is a 68-year-old ex-miner who is a widower, living alone. He smokes 20 cigarettes a day and enjoys a few pints at the local with his friends when he can manage the walk. Stan has chronic bronchitis and moderately severe arthritis, a legacy from his working days. On the days when he can meet his friends and spend a few hours chatting about old times, Stan says that 'he is in great shape'; on other days he will say that he is 'soldiering on'.

Simin probably links the perception of his health to his basketball prowess and considers himself 'ill' if he cannot attend practice sessions due to physical ailments.

Mary associates health with decent accommodation and being with her family. She is unlikely to worry about minor problems of physical health, like colds.

Stan is likely to concentrate on meeting his friends. It is likely he will dismiss his bronchitis and arthritis as being natural because of his age and previous occupation. When he cannot manage to get out to see his friends then life is more of a burden.

depend on age, social background, culture, circumstances and experience, as seen in the mini-case studies on page 46.

The scenerios show how each person's view of 'health' is different and closely linked to feelings, moods and being able to cope with daily activities, jobs or events.

Other people, especially those with different cultural inheritances, may view health as a spiritual form of well-being; for example, consuming alcohol is seen as an unholy thing to do as it leads to loss of self-control.

Think it over...

At this stage, you might like to think about how *you* might define health, bearing in mind the difficulties with care terminology already referred to.

Defining 'health'

The World Health Organisation (WHO), part of the United Nations Organisation, was set up in 1948 and at that time defined 'health' as being 'a state of complete physical, mental and social well-being and not merely the absence of disease or infirmity.' Later on, criticisms about the idealistic nature of 'complete state of well-being' and the unreal, implied view that health is static throughout one's lifespan, led to an expansion of this definition by several groups and individuals in the mid-1980s.

Seedhouse (1986) proposed health *as a foundation for achieving a person's realistic potential'*, whereas WHO offered a revised concept of health as *'the extent to which an individual or group is able, on the one hand, to realise aspirations and satisfy needs, and on the other hand, to change or cope with the environment.'*

Key concept

Health: Health is now seen as a positive concept that focuses on personal and physical capacities, together with social resources, adaptability and responsibility.

It is worth considering now the meaning behind 'health education' and 'health promotion'.

Health education and health promotion

Health education is now seen as a very important part of a wider 'umbrella-type' concept of health promotion. It involves trying to influence or direct a change of attitude or behaviour in people as a result of giving information about health.

When a group of people is informed about the dangers of cigarette smoking through statistics on smoking-related deaths and the potentially lethal composition of cigarette smoke, they are being given health education.

FIGURE 1.52 *Health education*

Rather like the original WHO definition of 'health', it became evident that while health education involved vital information that needed to be distributed, a wider, less individual initiative involving more activities was required. The umbrella term was 'health promotion' is therefore used to describe a process involving a wide range of activities to improve the health of individuals.

Key concept

Health Promotion: The WHO explanation of 'health promotion' is the process of enabling people to increase control over, and to improve, their health.

Health promotion campaigns

Special interest groups, organisations or national government frequently mount health promotion campaigns to enhance this process. Campaigns can be short-lived and locally focused, such as endeavouring to keep a community-based special needs playgroup open in opposition to planned closure, or long-term and nationwide, such as a 'don't drink and drive' campaign.

Planning is an essential part of any campaign, which should have a *purpose* (intention), stated *aims* (general statements of achievement) and *objectives* (specific outcomes within a time period).

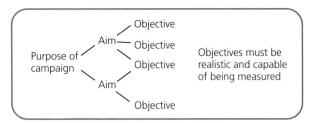

FIGURE 1.53 *Analysis of a campaign*

Think it over...

'Don't drink and drive' campaigns are familiar to most of us as they appear on TV, radio and hoardings. Individually or in a small group, try to work out the purpose, aims and objectives behind a recent campaign.

Aims of health promotion campaigns

What is any health promotion campaign trying to achieve?

* Is it trying to get people to be more knowledgeable about issues relating to healthy living? This is raising heath awareness.

* Is it trying to get people to generally improve their fitness?

* Is it trying to prevent people becoming ill?

The aims, as they exist in Figure 1.54, do not exist in isolation, for they are interconnected. Informing a group of school leavers about the reasons for continuing to take regular exercise in their leisure time means that you are raising their awareness about a health issue, thereby improving fitness levels and helping to prevent obesity, heart disease and respiratory problems in later life.

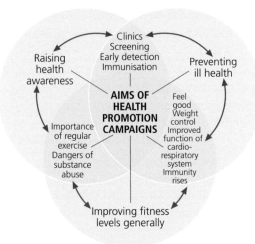

FIGURE 1.54 *The aims of health promotion campaigns and their links*

Different approaches to health promotion

Biomedical approach or model

This approach focuses on the prevention of disease or disability through intervention by medical (or other caring) professionals. It is important when using this model to have a group of clients who will act in accordance (be compliant) with medical advice and the use of preventive measures.

Examples of health promotion using a biomedical model include immunisation schedules,

SCENARIO

Biomedical approach

The West Piptree Group practice is located in an area favoured by retired people and those in later adulthood. Dr Wright, the senior partner in the practice, has sent letters to all his clients over the age of 65 years inviting them to the local community centre on a specific Friday in October to have 'anti-flu jabs'. The clerical assistants have telephoned all clients over 75 years of age as well, to reinforce the letter of invitation.

Influenza can have serious effects on older people and secondary bacterial infection is common, resulting in respiratory and circulatory problems that can be fatal.

FIGURE 1.55 *Service users receiving their 'flu jabs' (biomedical approach)*

cervical cytology, mammography, X-ray screening of the chest, family planning clinics, etc.

Giving 'flu jabs' is an example of health promotion using the biomedical approach. The biomedical approach can be seen to be 'expert-led', as in the scenario above, as far fewer people in later adulthood would have remembered to make appointments to protect themselves against influenza. This approach is also popular because it relies on medical science and, generally speaking, clients place great faith in such techniques. However, structures and resources need to be in place for this model to be successful.

Finally, the biomedical approach helps to avoid disease and prevents people becoming ill in the first place.

Educational / behavioural approach or model

This model emphasises information giving to promote better knowledge and understanding of health matters so that individuals, or groups, can adopt healthier lifestyles. The relevant, accurate information should be delivered at the right level to an audience capable of making informed decisions. Health promoters using this model will also believe in the rights of individuals to choose their own lifestyle.

Examples of the educational or behavioural approach include the distribution of leaflets explaining the dangers of all types of substance abuse, talks on the dangers of smoking, and advice on birth plans.

SCENARIO

Educational approach

Josh will soon be 16 years old and plans to leave school in the summer. He has no idea what he will do, as he doesn't expect to achieve any worthwhile qualifications. His best times have been spent in the local youth club, where he has made friends with Sam, one of the youth workers. Josh often smokes cannabis and sees no harm in it. Sam is aware of Josh's habit and they have talked about it several times. Sam has allowed Josh to continue attending the youth club, providing that he never encourages anyone else to use cannabis and never smokes in the club. Sam has invited a worker from the local drugs council to talk to the members about the dangers of substance abuse, particularly cannabis. Sam is sure that Josh is not aware of the mental health problems recently highlighted in the press and hopes that new information will encourage Josh to get 'clean' now that he is searching for work.

In this scenario Sam is using the educational/behavioural model of health promotion.

The behavioural aspect of this approach puts health firmly in the hands of the individual rather than the expert. The downside of this approach is that it places the blame for a poor lifestyle choice on the individual, especially if they are not yet ready to make 'healthy judgements' for other reasons such as peer pressure, life stage, environment and low income. The educational aspect of this approach assumes that the more an individual knows and understands about the health issue, the more likely he or she is to adopt a different way of thinking and consequently behave differently. This may take place with some clients and the resulting change in behaviour may not be the desired one; for example, information on the dangers associated with substance abuse may result not in the cessation of the habit but of a different substance being abused. Many smokers are fully aware of the dangers of tobacco consumption but continue to smoke cigarettes; some clients will change to cigars or pipe smoking, which are generally perceived to be less harmful.

Societal approach or model

This concentrates on changing society rather than the individual, so for the most part it encompasses either national or local political decisions to change physical, social or economic environments for the greater health of inhabitants. People using this model are not afraid to politicise health issues to improve the health of society.

Examples of the societal approach or model include imposing a ban on smoking in public places; making it illegal to purchase fireworks, tobacco and alcohol products under a certain age; banning the display of fireworks between 11.00 p.m. and 7.00 a.m. and permitting it only on certain dates.

In November 2004, the Secretary of State for Health unveiled a public health white paper, *Choosing health – making healthy choices easier.* It announced that all workplaces would be smoke-free by the end of 2008 except for private membership clubs and pubs, bars and clubs that do not prepare and serve food on the premises. These will have the freedom to allow smoking under licence, except at bar areas.

This partial ban on smoking in public places is an example of health promotion using the societal approach.

Which approach or model?

To differentiate between societal, biomedical and educational/behavioural approaches, decide whether the model affects society as a whole, individuals or groups of individuals. If it is the former and implementation has arisen through local or national political decisions then the approach is societal. When the improved health is likely to arise from medical intervention (using scientific methods) to large numbers of people to prevent ill health, disease or disability then the biomedical approach is being used. Lastly, when information has been dispatched to single individuals or groups and this is trying to persuade the recipients to change to healthier lifestyles, the educational/ behavioural approach is being followed.

Summary of Section 1.3

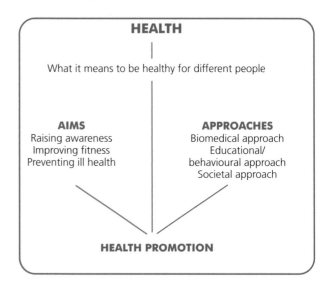

Tony wants to join the Army. In fact he really wants to become one of the elite SAS but knows that he will need experience in a regiment first. At the moment, Tony is still on holiday but he has his starting date for the Army. He enjoys leisure times with his friends in the snooker room of his 'local', playing snooker and billiards, smoking and having one or two pints of beer. In the evenings, he works behind the very busy bar serving drinks and collecting empty glasses. He likes the smoky, cosy atmosphere in the pub, but he also knows that it can only be for a limited time as he also likes the outdoor life. Tony has already had most of his immunisations brought up to date and picked up several leaflets on stopping smoking in the surgery, as he is beginning to think he needs to get fitter. The landlord has told him that he will be happy to have Tony back to work if the army life doesn't suit him and that the pub will not change, as he is applying for a smoking licence. Tony feels happy to know he has this safeguard.

Using concepts, can you identify?
1. When Tony becomes involved in the biomedical approach to health?
2. How the practice managers use the educational/behavioural approach to health promotion?

Go further – can you analyse issues using theory?
How might the practice managers know whether the educational/behavioural approach was being successful?

Go further – can you evaluate using a range of theory?
Feeling happy about the landlord's compliments, Tony begins to think around the issues of getting fitter and the landlord applying for a smoking licence. Imagine using a range of concepts to judge the values behind a partial smoking ban and to encourage the population to get fitter.

UNIT 1 ASSESSMENT

How you will be assessed

The external assessment is through a $1\frac{1}{2}$ hour written examination consisting of structured questions based on case studies. The material will include:

* aspects of growth and development throughout the different life stages

* environmental and genetic factors that can influence growth, development and health

* what it means to be healthy and how health can be promoted.

The examination will test your understanding and the ability to apply the knowledge you have gained from studying the units. You will be expected to analyse the issues and problems presented in the case studies as well as evaluate the evidence, make judgements and draw conclusions from the material. Remember to look carefully at the number of marks allocated to each question and try to make the same number of points in your answer.

Do not waste time or effort repeating the question or part of it, as this will gain zero marks. Read through each question in total before attempting to answer it. Candidates frequently answer a part of a question with an answer that belongs to another part that they haven't yet read. You will not be required to give the same answer twice; if you are tempted to do so, you are missing another point. Unless the question clearly needs a one- or two-word answer, write your answer in a properly constructed sentence or paragraph. The space allotted to each question is for guidance and you should not write either a great deal less or a great deal more.

Assessment preparation

FIGURE 1.56 *Sarah, her son and her daughter-in-law*

1 a) Sarah is 72 years old. She lives alone because her husband died six months ago, but her son John, 51 years old, and daughter-in-law Sue live only twenty miles away. Sue is 49 years old and is going through the menopause.

   (i)   Name Sarah's current life stage. (1)

   (ii) How many life stages has Sarah passed through *before* this current life stage? (1)

   (iii) Name the life stage that Sue is in now. (1)

   (iv) Identify and explain the likely effects of the menopause in Sue's life. (4)

   b) John was made redundant last year but they manage financially because Sue runs a corner shop in a deprived area on the edge of town. The shop is "a lock-up" and gets regularly vandalised. Sue visits her GP regularly with complaints related to stress.

   (i)   Identify and explain the likely effects of redundancy on John's social and emotional development. (4)

   (ii) Identify three possible reasons why Sue feels stressed. (3)

   (iii) Explain the possible effects of long-term stress on Sue's health. (5)

2. Sue often feels guilty about her ailments as she has many customers in the shop who suffer more stressful life events than she does. She also has support from her doctor who has encouraged her to join a gymnasium. There are no surgeries, medical or dental, on the estate so people buy a lot of over-the-counter drugs to treat their disorders. An hourly bus service runs through the estate in the daytime but drivers have refused to travel at night because of the number of aggressive youth gangs in the locality.

   a) (i)   Name three other life events that can lead to stress.   (3)

       (ii)   Discuss why large estates like this one frequently have no medical services.   (3)

       (iii)   Explain why Sue has been advised to do more physical exercise.   (4)

       (iv)   Discuss the advantages and disadvantages of purchasing over-the-counter drugs to treat your own health.   (6)

   b) (i)   How can living in a deprived area affect an individual's growth, development and health experience?   (6)

       (ii)   Why do some young people prefer to travel around in 'gangs'?   (2)

       (iii)   Minor gang members often have low self-esteem. Explain what is meant by self-esteem.   (2)

       (iv)   Give reasons why self-esteem is important.   (3)

3. Sue and John have a 17-year-old daughter, Melanie, who is a single mother with a 1-year-old son, Boris. She has left the parental home and is living with Sarah so that she can go to the college nearby. Sarah looks after Boris during the day and some evenings when Melanie wants to go out with her friends. Boris's father plays no part in supporting the child financially or in any other way.

   a) Name the life stages of:

       (i)   Melanie   (1)

       (ii)   Boris   (2)

       (iii)   Identify and explain the likely effects of these changes on Sarah.   (5)

       (iv)   Explain why it is important for Melanie to continue seeing her friends.   (3)

b) A few days after being born, Boris had a 'heel prick' test and this showed that he had a genetic condition known as Phenylketonuria or PKU. As a result, his health is carefully monitored and he has to take a special diet.

    (i)   What is a genetic condition? (2)

    (ii)   Explain how genetic factors can influence the health of an individual. (5)

    (iii) State three *other* factors that can influence the health of an individual. (3)

    (iv) Choose one of the named factors and give a precise account of the way it can affect the health of an individual. (5)

    (v)   Explain what is meant by the nature – nurture debate. (6)

4 a) Sue tried to sell fresh produce, especially fruit and vegetables, in her shop as she is enthusiastic about healthy eating, but she had too much wasted produce as people preferred cheaper frozen and tinned goods. Bread, cigarettes and sweets sell well and all types of meat products such as sausages, burgers and pies are popular.

    (i)   Explain why Sue can no longer sell fresh produce in the shop. (2)

    (ii)   What are the disadvantages of eating only processed food? (4)

    (iii) Discuss the harmful effects of smoking on the women and children of the estate. (6)

    (iv) Comment on the expected state of children's teeth on the estate. (4)

b) The health promotion unit in the nearby town has recently distributed information leaflets on 'Looking after your teeth' through people's letterboxes and in Sue's shop, hoping to see an improvement in dental hygiene in the area.

    (i)   Explain which approach is being used to promote a change in dental health. (2)

    (ii)   Which approach is being used if all the primary schools in the area are instructed (by the local authority) to provide at least one piece of fruit daily for each child? (2)

(Total marks = 100)

References and further reading

Acheson, D. (1998) *Independent enquiry into inequalities in health* (HMSO)

Argyle, M. (1987) *The Psychology of Happiness* (Methuen)

Bateson, ? (1995) (Independent Newspaper)

Blaxter, M. (1990) *Health and Lifestyles* (Routledge)

Bowlby, J. (1953) *Child care and the growth of love* (Penguin)

Dorling, D. et al. (1999) *The Widening gap: health inequalities and policy in Britain* (The Policy Press)

Erikson, E. (1963) *Childhood and Society* (Norton)

Ewles, L., Simnett, I. (2003) *Promoting Health – a practical guide* (Bailliere Tindall, London)

Havinghurst, R. J. (1970) *Developmental tasks and education* (David McKay)

HM Government (1997) *Saving Lives: Our Healthier Nation* (HMSO)

HM Government (2004) *Choosing Health – Making Healthier Choices Easier* (HMSO)

International Labour Organisation (2002) *Unemployment in the UK*

Naidoo, J., Wills, J. (2000) *Health Promotion – Foundations for Practice* (Bailliere Tindall, London)

Mead, G.H. (1934) *Mind, self and society* (ed. Morris, C.) (University of Chicago Press)

Moonie, N. (2000) *Advanced Health and Social Care* (Heinemann, Oxford)

Public Health News monthly magazine (Chadwick House Publishing)

Social Exclusion unit (1999) *Opportunity for all* (HMSO)

Unemployment unit (March 2000) *Working Brief*

Unemployment unit (May 1996) *Three Quarters of Job Growth is Part-Time*

Relevant websites

Please see www.heinemann.co.uk/hotlinks (express code 3718s) for links to the following websites which may provide a source of information:

✳ Joseph Rowntree Foundation findings online

UNIT 2

Communication and Values

This unit contains the following sections:

2.1 Communication

2.2 Care value base

2.3 Transmission of values

Introduction

This unit is designed to explore the importance of communication in all caring activities. When you have completed this unit you will understand a range of communication skills, the care value base and the transmission of values through communication. Your communication work might involve either people in health care settings, children in Early Years settings, older people in care settings, or people who have specific needs.

How you will be assessed

This unit is internally assessed. You must produce a written report.

2.1 Communication

Different types of communication

There are many different ways in which people communicate with each other. These can include language, body language, signs and symbols, written communication, art and music. Recorded information also enables communication to take place.

Many animals and insects communicate information between individuals, but no other species can communicate in the complex range of ways used by humans. Ways in which people communicate with each other are set out below.

Language

Spoken, signed, or written communication can communicate complex and subtle messages between individuals or groups of people. Language not only enables people to communicate information, but it also provides a basis for people to develop concepts. Concepts:

* influence the way individuals think

* enable us to group experiences together to help us understand events that we have experienced

* enable us to predict the future.

Human civilisation has developed because of our ability to classify experience using language.

Body language

Facial expressions, body posture and muscle tone all provide messages as to how we feel and perhaps what we are thinking. Mime and drama use body language to communicate complex ideas and emotions.

Signs and symbols

Gestures made with hands or arms, written symbols or diagrams such as traffic signs all communicate messages to people.

Signed languages

Language does not have to be based on sounds that are heard. Signing systems, such as British Sign Language, provide a full language system for people who do not use spoken language.

Visual, electronic and written communication

Humans can communicate across distance and time by using books, email, text messages, and so on. Recorded information such as books, magazines, newspapers, films, videos, tapes, CDs and other electronic mediums enable us to re-experience events or messages from the past. But recorded communication does not have to be visual.

Braille

Braille (a system of raised marks that can be felt with your fingers) provides a system of written communication based on the sense of touch for people who may have limited vision.

Arts and crafts

Paintings, photographs, sculptures, architecture, ornaments and other household objects can communicate messages and emotions to people. People often take photographs or buy souvenirs to remind them of happy experiences. Many individuals earn their living by designing and developing artwork.

Music

Music can provide an effective communication system for expressing emotion. Music is sometimes called the language of emotion.

Exchange of information

Some forms of communication involve simply sending a message within a fixed unambiguous system of meaning. An example might be an airline pilot trying to park an aircraft. But most communication between people is not simple and unambiguous. A lot of spoken and written communication is like music and artwork – rarely communicating straightforward information. It is normal for people to experience completely different messages from the same music or picture. Some communication is designed to stimulate thoughts and emotions in people.

Within care settings a great deal of communication is complex. It is important to understand that each person will have his or her own way of interpreting what they see and hear. Communication is not just about passing on information. Effective communication will depend on engaging in a 'communication cycle', which takes into account the way information is being received by the other person.

Listening skills and the communication cycle

When we communicate with people we become involved in a process of expressing our thoughts and interpreting the other person's understanding of what we are communicating. This process should usually involve the steps set out in Figure 2.1.

Communication needs to be a two-way process whereby each person tries to understand the viewpoint of the other. The **communication cycle** (see Figure 2.2) requires professionals (at least) to have advanced listening skills and the ability to check their understanding of the responses of others.

Listening is not the same as hearing the sounds people make when they talk. Listening involves hearing another person's words – then thinking about what they mean – then thinking what to say back. Some people call this process '**active listening**'. As well as thinking carefully and remembering what someone says, good listeners will also make sure their non-verbal communication demonstrates interest in the other person.

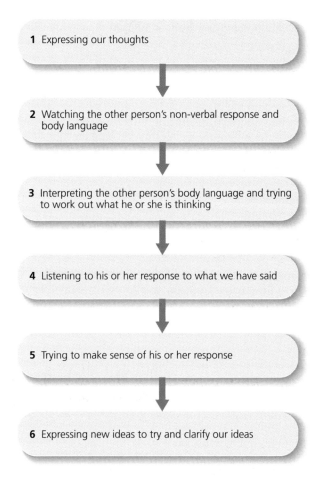

1 Expressing our thoughts

2 Watching the other person's non-verbal response and body language

3 Interpreting the other person's body language and trying to work out what he or she is thinking

4 Listening to his or her response to what we have said

5 Trying to make sense of his or her response

6 Expressing new ideas to try and clarify our ideas

FIGURE 2.1 *The process of expression and interpretation*

Key concept

Active listening: Active listening involves more than hearing – it also involves using the communication cycle and being able to demonstrate what you have understood when you listen to another person.

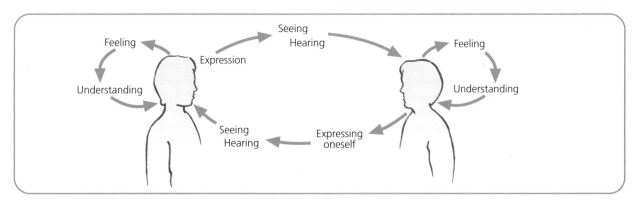

FIGURE 2.2 *The communication cycle*

So, skilled active listening involves:

* looking interested and ready to listen
* hearing what is said
* remembering what is said
* checking understanding with the other person.

It is usually easier to understand people who are similar to ourselves. We can learn about different people by checking our understanding of what we have heard.

Checking our understanding involves hearing what the other person says and asking them questions. Another way to check our understanding is to put what a person has just said into our own words and to say this back to them. This technique is called paraphrasing. Paraphrasing enables us to find out if we did understand what another person said.

When we listen to complicated details of other people's lives, we often begin to form mental pictures based on what they are telling us. Listening skills involve checking these mental pictures to make sure that we understand correctly. It can be very difficult to remember things accurately if we don't check how our ideas are developing.

Good listening involves thinking about what we hear while we are listening and checking our understanding as the conversation goes along. Sometimes this idea of checking is called 'reflection' because we reflect on the other person's ideas (see Figure 2.3).

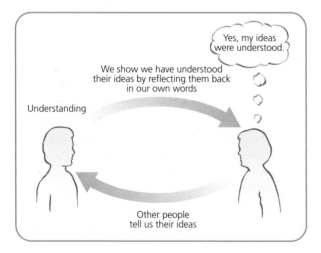

FIGURE 2.3 *Reflection*

The importance of cultural variation

Both words and non-verbal signs have to be understood in a particular context. For example, the word 'wicked' can have different meanings. If an older person used this phrase to describe his or her experience of World War II it would mean 'horrific' or 'terrible'. In a TV comedy made during the past 15 years the phrase would mean 'cool' – something very desirable. In a religious context 'wicked' might relate to the concept of sin.

Making sense of spoken language requires knowledge of the context and intentions of the speaker. Understanding non-verbal communication involves exactly the same need to understand 'where the person is coming from'; or, to put it more formally, the circumstances and cultural context of the other person.

> ### ✱ DID YOU KNOW?
>
> Both spoken and non-verbal communication is influenced by culture. For example, in the UK the hand gesture with palm up and facing forward means 'Stop, don't do that.' In Greece it can mean, 'You are dirt' and is a very rude gesture.

Why do the same physical movements have different meanings? One explanation for the hand signs is that the British version of the palm-and-fingers gesture means, 'I arrest you, you must not do it'; whereas the Greek interpretation goes back to medieval times when criminals had dirt rubbed in their faces to show how much people despised them.

Using care values means that carers must have respect for other people's culture. People learn different ways of communicating, and good carers will try to understand the different ways in which people use non-verbal messages. For instance, past research in the USA suggests that white and black Americans may have used different non-verbal signals when they listened. It suggests that some black Americans may tend not to look much at the speaker. This can be interpreted as a mark of respect – by looking away it demonstrates that you are really thinking hard about the message.

Unfortunately, not all white people understood this cultural difference in non-verbal communication. Some individuals misunderstood and assumed that this non-verbal behaviour meant exactly the same as it would mean if someone from their own cultural background had done it. That is, it would mean they were not listening.

Key concept

Cultural variation: Communication is always influenced by cultural systems of meaning. Different cultures interpret body language differently.

There is an almost infinite variety of meanings that can be given to any type of eye contact, facial expression, posture or gesture. Every culture develops its own special system of meanings. Carers have to understand and show respect and value for all of the different systems of sending messages. But how can you ever learn them all?

No one can learn every possible system of non-verbal message – but it is possible to learn about those the people you are with are using! It is possible to do this by first noticing and remembering what others around you do, i.e. what non-verbal messages they are sending. The next step is to make an intelligent guess as to what messages the person is trying to give you. Finally, check your understanding (your guesses) with the person.

Skilled interpersonal interaction involves:

* watching other people
* remembering what they do
* guessing what words and actions mean and then checking your guesses with the person
* never relying on your own guesses, because these might turn into assumptions
* understanding that assumptions can lead to discrimination.

Using care values involves getting to understand people – not acting on unchecked assumptions. So non-verbal messages should never be relied on; they should always be checked.

Think it over...

Imagine you are working with an older female person. Whenever you start to speak to her she always looks at the floor and never makes eye contact. Why is this?

Your first thought is that she might be depressed. Having made such an assumption, you might not want to talk to this person. But instead you could ask, 'How do you feel today? Would you like me to get you anything?' By checking out what she feels, you could test your own understanding. She might say she feels well and is quite happy, and then suggest something you could do for her. This would suggest that she cannot be depressed.

Why else would someone look at the floor rather than at you?

Age and gender

Perceptions of age-appropriate behaviour and gender-appropriate behaviour are strongly influenced by culture. People are socialised into the norms and values of a culture. Group norms and values – the 'rules' for behaviour – vary between different religious, ethnic, class, gender and age groups.

Group expectations of speech vary between social groups, but they also change with time within a particular group. People of different age groups have usually been socialised into different norms with respect to interpersonal behaviour.

Interpersonal interaction

Body language

When we meet and talk with people, we will usually use two language systems. We will use verbal or spoken language and non-verbal or body language. Effective communication in care work requires care workers to be able to analyse their own and other people's non-verbal behaviour. Our body sends messages to other people – often without us deliberately meaning to send these messages. Some of the most important body areas that send messages are outlined overleaf.

Florence Tucknell was born in 1922. When she was young there was a cultural norm that only close friends and family would call her by her first name. She was Miss Tucknell to everyone else. For a stranger to call her 'Florence' would be a sign of disrespect, a sign that they thought they were socially superior to her. When Florence went into care for a week she was upset that everyone used first names. She knows that this is common practice nowadays, but this was not how she was brought up to behave.

Miss Tucknell was very pleased to be greeted by her carer who introduced herself as, 'I'm Anthea Shakespeare, may I ask your name?' Miss Tucknell replied, 'I'm Miss Tucknell, please.'

Martin Howarth was born in the north of England in 1956. Some years ago he moved to the south-east of England and took a job as a care worker. Martin was surprised to find that many of his younger female colleagues were complaining about his behaviour. Martin had been socialised into the norm of calling women 'Flower' or even 'Petal.' When Martin used these terms he was expecting to communicate approval, comradeship and warmth. Martin believed that these were universal terms of endearment, i.e. 'You are likeable, we're all working together; we get on – don't we?'

His new colleagues in the south had never been referred to as 'Flower' before and saw it as sexist. Individually, Martin's colleagues' view of him was 'You are saying that I am weak, short-lived and that all that matters about my existence is my degree of sexual attractiveness!'

Can you think of other examples where age, gender and region influence how words are understood?

Key concept

Body language: The way we use our body can communicate messages to other people. People communicate using words and also by using body language.

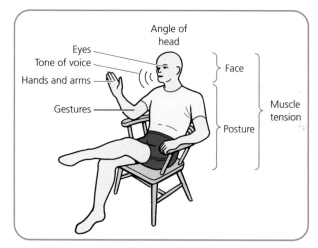

FIGURE 2.4 *Areas of the body that we use in communication*

We can guess the feelings and thoughts that another person has by looking at their eyes. One poet called the eye 'the window of the soul'. We can sometimes understand the thoughts and feelings of another person by eye-to-eye contact. Our eyes get wider when we are excited, attracted to, or interested in someone else. In European culture, a fixed stare may send the message that someone is angry and looking away is often interpreted as being bored or not interested.

The face

The face can send very complex messages and we can read them easily – even in diagram form (see Figure 2.5).

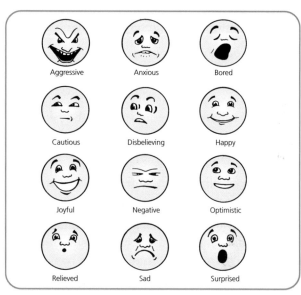

FIGURE 2.5 *The face expresses emotion*

Our face often indicates our emotional state. When a person is sad they may signal this emotion with eyes that look down, there may be tension in their face and their mouth will be closed. The muscles in the person's shoulders are likely to be relaxed but their face and neck may show tension. A happy person will have 'wide eyes' that make contact with you – their face will smile. When people are excited they may move their arms and hands to signal their excitement.

Voice tone

It's not just what we say, but the way that we say it. If we talk quickly in a loud voice with a fixed voice tone, people may see us as angry. A calm, slow voice with varying tone may send a message of being friendly.

Body movement

The way we walk, move our head, sit, cross our legs and so on, send messages about whether we are tired, happy, sad or bored.

Posture

The way we sit or stand can send messages. Sitting with crossed arms can mean 'I'm not taking any notice'. Leaning can send the message that you are relaxed or bored. Leaning forward can show interest. The body postures in Figure 2.6 below send messages.

Muscle tension

The tension in our feet, hands and fingers can tell others how relaxed or how tense we are. When people are very tense their shoulders might stiffen, their face muscles might tighten and they might sit or stand rigidly. A tense face might have a firmly closed mouth with lips and jaws clenched tight. A tense person might breathe quickly and become hot.

Gestures

Gestures are hand and arm movements that can help us to understand what a person is saying.

FIGURE 2.7 *Some gestures common in Britain*

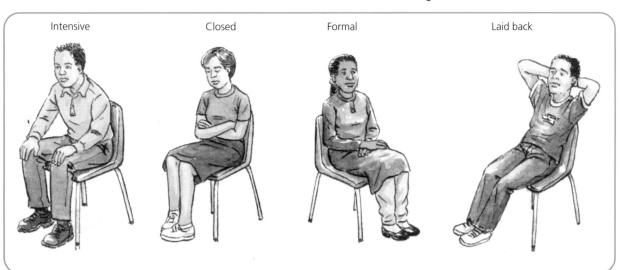

FIGURE 2.6 *Body postures that send messages*

Some gestures carry a meaning of their own. Some common gestures are shown in Figure 2.7.

Touch

Touching another person can send messages of care, affection, power over them, or sexual interest. The social setting and other body language usually help people to understand what touch might mean. Carers should not make assumptions about touch. Even holding someone's hand might be seen as trying to dominate them!

Proximity and personal space

The space between people can sometimes show how friendly or 'intimate' the conversation is. Different cultures have different assumptions about how close people should be (proximity) when they are talking.

In Britain there are expectations or 'norms' as to how close you should be when you talk to others. When talking to strangers you may stand an arm's-length apart. The ritual of shaking hands indicates that you have been introduced – you may come closer. When you are friendly with someone you may accept them being closer to you. Relatives and partners may not be restricted in how close they can come.

Personal space is a very important issue in care work. A care worker who assumes it is all right to enter a service user's personal space without asking or explaining, may be seen as being dominating or aggressive.

Face-to-face positions (orientation)

Standing or sitting eye-to-eye can send a message of being formal or being angry. A slight angle can create a more relaxed and friendly feeling. Examples of face-to-face interaction are shown in Figure 2.8.

Using appropriate language – degree of formality

Speaking is about much more than just communicating information between people. For a start, many people can speak with different degrees of formality or informality. The degree of formality or informality is called the language 'register'.

For example, suppose you went to a hospital reception area. You might expect the person on duty to greet you with a formal response, such as, 'Good morning, how can I help you'. An informal greeting of the kind used by white males in the south-east of England might be, 'Hello Mate, what's up then?' or 'How's it going?'

FIGURE 2.9 *Informality and informal humour may be perceived as disrespect*

It is possible that some people might prefer the informal greeting. An informal greeting could put you at ease; you might feel that the receptionist is like you. But in many situations the informal

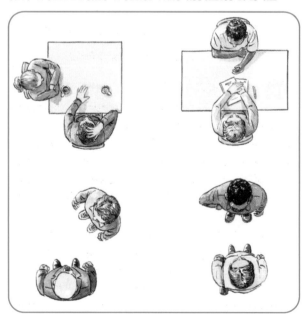

FIGURE 2.8 *Face-to-face interaction*

greeting might make people feel that they are not being respected.

The degree of formality or informality establishes a context. At a hospital reception you are unlikely to want to spend time making friends and chatting things over with the receptionist. You may be seeking urgent help. Your expectations of the situation might be that you want to be taken seriously and put in touch with professional services as soon as possible. You might see the situation as a very formal encounter. If you are treated informally, you may interpret this as not being treated seriously, or in other words 'not being respected'.

Speech communities

Another issue is that informal speech is very likely to identify a specific speech community. Different localities, different ethnic groups, different professions and work cultures all have their own special words, phrases and speech patterns. An elderly middle-class woman is very unlikely to start a conversation with the words 'Hello Mate'. Some service users may feel threatened or excluded by the kind of language they encounter. However, just using formal language will not solve this problem. The technical terminology used by social care workers may also create barriers for people who were not part of that 'speech community'.

Structuring a conversation

When we talk to people we have to start the conversation off. Usually we start with a greeting or ask how someone is. Conversations have a beginning, a middle and an end. We have to create the right kind of atmosphere for a conversation at the beginning. We might need to help someone relax by showing that we are friendly and relaxed. We then have the conversation. When we end the conversation we usually say something like 'See you soon'. When ending a conversation we have to leave the other person with the right feelings about what we have said. The conversation sandwich shown in Figure 2.10 illustrates this point.

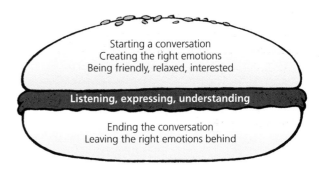

Starting a conversation
Creating the right emotions
Being friendly, relaxed, interested

Listening, expressing, understanding

Ending the conversation
Leaving the right emotions behind

FIGURE 2.10 *The conversation sandwich*

Asking questions

Some questions don't really encourage people to talk – these are called 'closed' questions. Questions like 'How old are you?' are closed. They are closed because there is only one, right, simple answer the person can give, for example, 'I'm 84', and so on. Closed questions don't lead on to discussion. 'Do you like butter?' is a closed question as the person can only say yes or no. 'Are you feeling well today?' is a closed question. Again, the person can only answer yes or no.

Open questions are 'open' for discussion. Instead of giving a yes or no answer, the person is encouraged to think and discuss their thoughts and feelings. A question like, 'How do you feel about the food here?' means that the other person has to think about the food and then discuss it.

In some formal conversations it can be important to ask direct closed questions; but the best way to ask closed questions is to ask open questions beforehand. There is an old saying that if you really want to find out what someone else thinks then 'Every closed question should start life as an open one'. Some examples of open and closed questions are given in Figure 2.11.

CLOSED QUESTION	OPEN QUESTION
Do you like your teacher?	What do you think about your teacher?
Is the food good in here?	What would you say the food is like here?
Do you like rock music?	What kind of music do you enjoy?
Do you sometimes feel lonely?	How do you feel about living on your own?
Do you enjoy drawing?	What are your favourite activities in school?

FIGURE 2.11 *Open and closed questions – some examples*

Silence

One definition of friends is 'people who can sit together and feel comfortable in silence'. Sometimes a pause in conversation can make people feel embarrassed. It may look as if you weren't listening or interested. Sometimes a silent pause can mean 'let's think' or 'I need time to think'. Silent pauses can be all right as long as non-verbal messages that show respect and interest are given. Silence doesn't always stop the conversation. Some carers use pauses in a conversation to show that they are listening and thinking about what a service user has said.

Probes and prompts

A probe is a very short question such as 'Can you tell me more?' This kind of short question usually follows on from an answer that the other person has given. Probes are used to 'dig deeper' into the person's answer; they probe or investigate what has just been said.

Prompts are short questions or words, which you offer to the other person in order to prompt them to answer. Questions such as 'So, was it enjoyable or not?' or, 'would you do it again?' might prompt a person to keep talking. Sometimes a prompt might just be a suggested answer. 'More than 50?' might be a prompt if you had just asked how many service users a carer worked with in a year and they seemed uncertain.

Here are some ideas for preventing unwanted silence:

✱ Use non-verbal behaviour like smiling and nodding your head to express interest.

✱ Use short periods of silence to prompt the other person to talk.

✱ Paraphrase or reflect back what the other person has said so that they will confirm that you have understood them.

✱ Ask direct questions.

✱ Use probes and prompts to follow-up your questions.

Assertive skills

Some people may seem shy and worried; they say little and avoid contact with people they don't know. Others may want people to be afraid of them; they may try to dominate and control others. Fear and aggression are two of the basic emotions that we experience. It is easy to give into our basic emotions and become either submissive or aggressive when we feel stressed. Assertion is an advanced skill that involves controlling the basic emotions involved in running away or fighting. Assertion involves a mental attitude of trying to negotiate, trying to solve problems rather than giving in to emotional impulses.

Key concept

Assertion: Assertion is different from both submission and aggression. Assertion involves being able to negotiate a solution to a problem.

Winning and losing

During an argument an aggressive person might demand that they are right and other people are wrong. They will want to win while others lose. The opposite of aggression is to be weak or submissive. A submissive person accepts that they will lose, get told off, or be put down. Assertive behaviour is different from both these responses. In an argument an assertive person will try to reach an answer where no one has to lose or be 'put down'. Assertion is a skill where 'win-win' situations can happen because no one has to be the loser. For example, suppose a service user is angry because his or her carer is late. Look at Figure 2.12 to compare the possible responses of a carer.

Assertive skills enable carers to cope with difficult and challenging situations. To be assertive a person usually has to:

* understand the situation that they are in – including the facts, details and other people's perceptions
* be able to control personal emotions and stay calm
* be able to act assertively using the right non-verbal behaviour
* be able to act assertively using the right words and statements.

Some verbal and non-verbal behaviours involved in assertion are summarised in Figure 2.13.

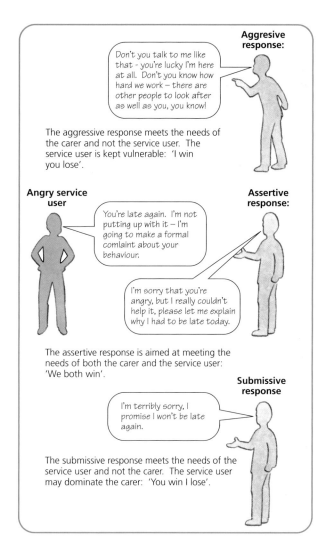

FIGURE 2.12 *How assertion enables both people to win*

Professional relationships

People who are good at communication and assertive skills are likely to be good at building social relationships. Professional relationships may be regarded as different from ordinary social relationships and friendships because:

* professionals must work within a framework of values (see Section 2.2)
* professional work always involves a duty of care for the welfare of service users (see Section 2.3)
* professional relationships involve establishing appropriate boundaries.

AGGRESSIVE BEHAVIOUR	ASSERTIVE BEHAVIOUR	SUBMISSIVE BEHAVIOUR
Main emotion: anger	*Main emotion*: staying in control of actions	*Main emotion*: fear
Wanting your own way Making demands Not listening to others Putting other people down Trying to win Shouting or talking very loudly	Negotiating with others Trying to solve problems Aiming that no one has to lose Showing respect for others Keeping a clear, calm voice	Letting others win Agreeing with others Not putting your views across Looking afraid Speaking quietly or not speaking at all
Threatening non-verbal behaviour including: fixed eye contact, tense muscles, waving or folding hands and arms, looking angry	**Normal non-verbal behaviour** including: varied eye contact, relaxed face muscles, looking 'in control', keeping hands and arms at your side	**Submissive non-verbal behaviour** including: looking down, not looking at others, looking frightened, tense muscles

FIGURE 2.13 *Some verbal and non-verbal behaviours involved in assertion*

A boundary is a line that must not be crossed. In care work the metaphor of a boundary means that there are limits to the degree of emotional involvement and commitment within a relationship. Although professionals care about what happens to service users, professionals do not form an emotional bond in the way that parents and children do.

Please see Section 2.2 for theory on confidentiality and Section 2.3 for theory on empathy.

Barriers to effective communication

Communication can become blocked if individual differences are not understood. There are three main ways that communication becomes blocked, and these are shown in Figure 2.14.

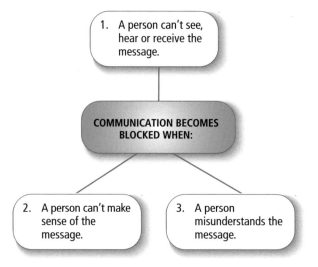

FIGURE 2.14 *Three main ways in which communication becomes blocked*

> ### Key concept
>
> *Barriers:* Effective communication depends on identifying barriers that may block understanding. Barriers can exist at a physical and sensory level, at the level of making sense of a message, and at a cultural and social context level, whereby the meaning of a message may be misunderstood.

Examples of the first kind of block, where people don't receive the communication, include visual disabilities, hearing disabilities, environmental problems such as poor lighting and noisy environments, and speaking from too far away.

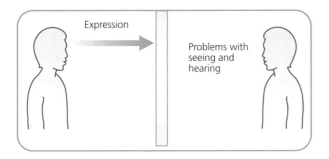

FIGURE 2.15 *Environmental problems like noise and poor light can create communication barriers*

Examples where people may not be able to make sense of the message include:

* the use of different languages, including signed languages

* the use of different terms in language, such as jargon (technical language), slang (different people using different terms), or dialect (different people making different sounds)

* physical and intellectual disabilities, such as dysphasia (difficulties with language expression or understanding) aphasia (an absence of language ability), being ill, or suffering memory loss or learning difficulty.

Reasons for misunderstanding a message include:

* cultural influences – different cultures interpret non-verbal and verbal messages, and humour, in different ways

* assumptions about people, e.g. about race, gender, disability and other groupings

* labelling or stereotyping of others (please see Section 2.2 for details of these concepts)

* social context – statements and behaviour that are understood by friends and family may not be understood by strangers

* emotional barriers – a worker's own emotional needs may stop them from wanting to know about others

* time pressures can mean that staff withdraw from wanting to know about others

* emotional differences – these can sometimes be interpreted as personality clashes or differences. Very angry, or very happy, or very shy people may misinterpret communication from others.

The psychologist Maslow (1970) explained human needs in terms of the five levels set out below. More detail of this theory can be found in Section 2.3 (page 96). Barriers to communication might block human need as shown in Figure 2.16.

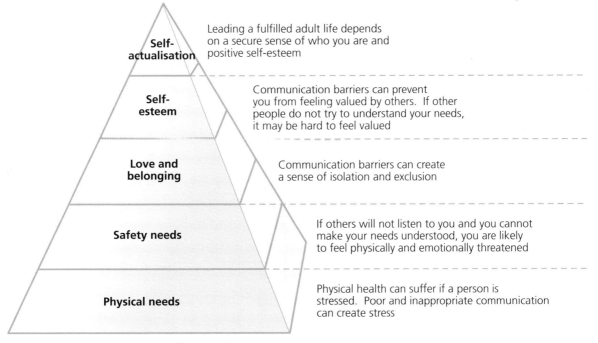

FIGURE 2.16 *Communication barriers can damage a person's quality of life*

Ways of overcoming difficulties in communication

It is always important to learn as much as possible about other people. People may have 'preferred forms of interaction'. This may include a reliance on non-verbal messages, sign language, lip-reading, use of description, slang phrases, choice of room or location for a conversation, and so on. Everyone has communication needs of some kind.

Some ideas of how you may overcome barriers to communication are given in Figure 2.17.

OVERCOMING BARRIERS TO COMMUNICATION	
BARRIERS	**TIPS**
Visual disability	Use language to describe things Assist people to touch things (e.g. touch your face to recognise you) Explain details that sighted people might take for granted Check what people can see (many registered blind people can see shapes, or tell light from dark) Explore technological aids such as information technology that can expand visual images Check glasses, other aids and equipment
Hearing disability	Don't shout, keep to normal clear speech and make sure your face is visible for people who can lip-read Show pictures, or write messages Learn to sign (for people who use signed languages) Ask for help from, or employ, a communicator or interpreter for signed languages Check that technological aids such as hearing aids are working
Environmental constraints	Check and improve lighting Reduce noise Move to a quieter or better-lit room Move to smaller groups to see and hear more easily Check seating arrangements
Language differences	Communicate using pictures, diagrams and non-verbal signs Use translators or interpreters Be careful not to make assumptions or stereotype (see Section 2.2 on stereotyping) Increase your knowledge of jargon, slang and dialects Re-word your messages – find different ways of saying things appropriate to the service user's 'speech community' Check your level of formality; speak in short, clear sentences if appropriate
Intellectual disabilities	Increase your knowledge of disabilities Use pictures and signs as well as clear, simple speech Be calm and patient Set up group meetings where people can share interests, experiences or reminiscences Check that people do not become isolated Use advocates – independent people who can spend time building an understanding of the needs of specific individuals to assist with communication work
Cultural differences	Try to increase your knowledge of different cultures and speech communities Watch out for different cultural interpretations Avoid making assumptions about, or discriminating against, people who are different Use active listening techniques to check that your understanding is correct Stay calm and try to create a calm atmosphere Be sensitive to different social settings and the form of communication that would be most appropriate in different contexts Check your work with advocates who will try to represent the best interests of the people that you are working with

FIGURE 2.17 *Some ways of overcoming barriers to communication*

Emotional barriers to communication

Service users often have serious emotional needs; they may be afraid or depressed because of the stresses they are experiencing. Sometimes service users may lack self-awareness or appear to be shy or aggressive. Listening involves learning about frightening and depressing situations. Carers sometimes avoid listening to avoid unpleasant emotional feelings.

Emotion can create barriers because care workers:

* are tired – listening takes mental energy

* believe that they do not have sufficient time to communicate properly

* are emotionally stressed by the needs of service users

* react with negative emotions towards the culture of others

* make assumptions about, or label or stereotype others.

Interpreters and translators

Translating and interpreting involve the communication of meaning between different languages. This is not just a technical act of changing the words from one system to another. Many languages do not have simple equivalence between words or signs. Interpreters and translators have to grasp the meaning of a message and find a way of expressing this meaning in a different language system. This is rarely a simple task even for professional translators.

Interpreters can be professional people, but they may also be friends or family members. For example, a mother might learn sign language in order to communicate information to a deaf child. It is possible for family members to interpret for each other.

Interpretation and translation are vital in any setting where communication is blocked due to different languages or communication systems. For example, many people may not use English as their first language. When these people need to access health care or social services, or legal support, the services of translators and interpreters are likely to be needed.

Issues surrounding interpretation

Interpretation raises a number of important issues. These are outlined below.

Interpretation can disrupt the communication cycle

It will often be important that the interpreter can confirm that he or she has understood things correctly before attempting to pass that understanding on to another person. Much interpretation in care and social work settings is consecutive interpretation. Consecutive interpretation is when the first person pauses to allow the interpreter to make sense of what they have communicated. When the interpreter is clear about the message, he or she then communicates it to the second person.

Another kind of interpretation is called simultaneous interpretation; this occurs when an interpreter explains what the first person is saying while they talk. Because of the need to clarify subject matter and emotions, this kind of interpretation is likely to be more difficult to use in care settings. Interpretation makes the communication cycle more complicated.

Knowledge of the subject matter

An interpreter is likely to be more effective when he or she understands the issues involved. Professional interpreters may be able to explain details of legislation or procedures for claiming benefit because they understand the issues. If relatives or friends act as interpreters they will have to make sense of the technical details before they can communicate clearly. Knowledge of languages alone is not always sufficient to enable clear and effective communication.

Trust

It is important that people have confidence in somebody who is acting as an interpreter. People from specific communities may find it hard to trust a member from a different community. Many women may not feel safe and confident discussing personal issues using a male interpreter. The issue may not be about the interpreter's language competence, but about the interpreter's ability to empathise with or understand and correctly convey what a person wants to say.

Social and cultural values

Many people may wish to use a professional interpreter or a specified member of their community or gender group because of social norms. Many people may feel that it is inappropriate to discuss personal details using an interpreter of the opposite sex. Some deaf people do not feel confident using interpreters who have not experienced deafness themselves. Choice of an interpreter must support the self-esteem needs of people who need to access interpretation services.

Confidentiality

Confidentiality is a right enshrined in the 1998 Data Protection Act as well as an ethical duty on professional staff. Professional interpreters are likely to offer guarantees of confidentiality. Using a relative or volunteer may not necessarily provide people with the same guarantee of confidentiality.

Non-judgemental support

A professional interpreter who has trained in social work is likely to offer advanced interpersonal skills which include the ability to remain non-judgemental when undertaking interpretation work. Volunteers, relatives and friends may have language competence, but they may not necessarily be able to interpret meaning without biasing their interpretation.

Advocates

Sometimes, when people have a very serious learning disability or an illness (such as **dementia**) it is not possible to communicate with them. In such situations, care services will often employ an advocate. An advocate is someone who speaks for someone else. A lawyer speaking for a client in a courtroom is working as an advocate for that client. In care work, a volunteer might try to get to know someone who has dementia or a learning disability. The volunteer tries to communicate the service user's needs and wants – as the volunteer understands them. Advocates should be independent of the staff team so they can argue for a service user's rights without being constrained by what the staff think is easiest or cheapest to do.

Advocacy is not straightforward, as volunteers may not always understand the feelings and needs of the people that they are advocating for. Some people argue it would be better if service users could be supported to argue their own case. Helping people to argue their own case is called self-advocacy. Self-advocacy may work very well for some people, but others may need very considerable help before they can do this.

Another kind of advocacy is called group advocacy. This is where people with similar needs come together and receive support to argue for their needs as a group. Different people may need different kinds of advocacy support.

Communication in groups

In everyday language 'group' can mean a collection or set of things, so any collection of people could be counted as a group. For example, a group of people might be waiting to cross the road. They are a group in the everyday sense of the word, but not in the special sense of 'group' that is often used in care work.

The stages groups may go through

Working with a group is usually taken to imply that the individuals identify themselves as belonging to a group. Groups have a sense of belonging that gives the members a 'group feeling'. This could be described as a group identity. Social scientists sometimes use the term 'primary group' and 'secondary group.'

Primary groups usually share the following features:

* people know each other
* there is a 'feeling of belonging' shared by people in the group
* people have a common purpose or reason for coming together
* people share a set of beliefs or norms.

The term 'secondary group' is used when people simply have something in common with each other.

Many theorists have studied the way people start to work together in a group. Before a sense of belonging can develop, people need to learn about each other. Most groups seem to go through some sort of struggle before people finally unite and work effectively together.

One of the best known theorists to explain group formation stages is Tuckman (1965). Tuckman suggests that most groups go through a process involving four stages before they can become effective (see Figure 2.18).

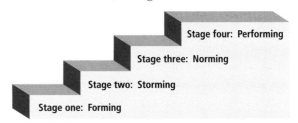

FIGURE 2.18 *Tuckman's four stages of group formation*

An outline explanation of Tuckman's four stages of group formation is shown in Figure 2.19.

PROCESS OF GROUP FORMATION	
STAGE	**BEHAVIOUR**
Stage one: Forming	When people first get together there is likely to be an introductory stage. People may be unsure why they are attending a meeting. The purpose of the group may not be clear. People may have little commitment to the group and there may be no clear value system. Stereotyping and prejudice may be expressed.
Stage two: Storming	There may be 'power struggles' within the group. Different individuals may contest each other for leadership of the group. There may be arguments about how the group should work, who should do tasks and so on. Groups can fail at this stage and individuals can decide to drop out because they do not feel comfortable with other people in the group. Staff teams sometimes split into sub-groups who refuse to communicate with each other if they become stuck in the storming stage.
Stage three: Norming	At this stage group members develop a set of common beliefs and values. People are likely to begin to trust each other and develop clear roles. Norms are shared expectations which group members have of each other. Norms enable people to work together as a group.
Stage four: Performing	Because people share the same values and norms the group is able to perform effectively. People may feel that they are comfortable and belong in the group. There may be a sense of high morale.

FIGURE 2.19 *An explanation of Tuckman's four stages of group formation*

Group values: For a group to perform effectively, group members will need to share a common system of beliefs or values relevant to the purpose of the group. It may be very important to identify the extent to which a group does share a value system when planning to run an activity.

Turn-taking

Working in a group can be more difficult than holding an individual conversation. If a group is worth belonging to, people must take turns in listening and speaking. Once everyone is speaking, no one is listening! Turn-taking between two individuals is easy, but turn-taking in groups is not so easy.

Turn-taking involves complicated non-verbal behaviour. When a speaker is finishing, he or she usually signals this by lowering and slowing the voice and looking around. Who speaks next depends on eye-contact around the group – not just with the speaker. Group members have to watch the faces and eyes of everyone else in order that just one person takes over and speaks in turn. If people get excited or tense, then they usually add gestures to their other non-verbal messages to signal forcefully that they want to speak next. Sometimes people will put their hand out or nod their head to say (non-verbally): 'Look, it's my turn next!'

Eventually turn-taking goes wrong, and two or more people start talking at once. This is called a failure to 'mesh'. Meshing means that conversation flows easily between people around the group. People link together in conversation, like the linking in 'wire mesh'. When two people talk at the same time, one person has to give way. A group leader can act as a 'conductor' to check that turns are taken.

Managing group activity

Most care groups have a purpose or task to work on. Children get together to play games, adults may get together in recreational groups. Groups often need a focus – a game to play, an activity to join in or a topic to discuss. Consider the observations on group behaviour shown overleaf in Figure 2.20.

As well as performing their tasks, groups have to be 'maintained'. Group maintenance consists of encouraging a sense of belonging and keeping the whole meeting enjoyable. The following list includes ideas of some behaviours that might be useful for maintaining group discussion:

* A bit of laughter can help to relieve tension and create a warm, friendly feeling that everyone can join in.

* Show interest in the people in the group – be prepared to negotiate and discuss different views.

* Be 'warm' and show respect and value when listening to people who are different from yourself or who have had different life experiences. This behaviour makes it safe to be in the group.

* Express feelings honestly and with sincerity. This will help others to understand your identity. Help others to understand you as well as trying to understand others.

* Take responsibility for ensuring that everyone has a chance to speak and contribute. Some people may need to be encouraged or invited to speak and some people may need organising, so that turn-taking works!

* If necessary, get people to explain what they have said, and to talk through – or negotiate – disagreements. Group members need to feel that their shared values will make it possible to arrive at solutions when people disagree.

A group leader must keep thinking about what is happening in the group. Do I need to guide the group back to the task? Is this the right time for a funny story? Should I make it clear that I am listening and that I value what is being said by this person? Every other group member who really wants the group to work will also monitor how the group is getting on with its task.

| If individuals are going to join in a supportive group meeting, then someone will need to introduce the activity – start the conversation. From time to time when the conversation wanders, someone will need to steer it back to the right topic. | Occasionally, group members will need to clarify, or make sense of, what is being said. |

GROUP BEHAVIOUR

| Throughout the group meeting, people will need to exchange ideas on the activity or topic being discussed. | Towards the end of a meeting, group members will need to agree on what has happened or what the group has decided. The group will come to some kind of conclusion. |

FIGURE 2.20 *Some observations on group behaviour*

Communication in a group might work best when groups:

* keep working on a task or discussion activity

* create a feeling of shared identity or belonging

* make sure each individual is supported and valued.

The dynamics of a care group are illustrated in Figure 2.21.

Group values

In care work the 'value base' should provide a basis around which groups can develop their 'ground rules' or norms. In practice, sharing the care value base is likely to mean that group members will encourage one another to speak, since everyone has an equal right to speak and be included in the group. Group members will try to understand and value differences between people. People will show respect and value for one another.

If people do not share caring values then it is quite likely that some people may try to dominate the group. Sometimes people 'pair' with others who think the same way, to fight for control of a group. Sometimes people can block the progress of a discussion with irrelevant or other deliberate distractions aimed at disrupting the discussion. Sometimes people may become withdrawn and

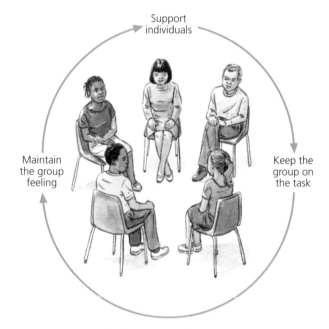

Support individuals

Maintain the group feeling

Keep the group on the task

FIGURE 2.21 *The dynamics of a care group*

ignore the group if they don't feel they belong. Groups have to develop shared beliefs and a feeling of 'belonging' if they are to work effectively.

Group discussion can sometimes be difficult. Some reasons for finding discussion difficult are listed below:

* not knowing the beliefs and values of others in the group

* not understanding the purpose of a meeting

* feeling different from others in the group

* not feeling confident of communication skills

* feeling threatened by other members (perhaps they may stereotype or label)

* feeling powerless and believing that others control the group.

Where individuals are not clear about the purpose of the group, or do not feel they belong, they may engage in disruptive behaviours such as:

* irrelevant talking

* trying to dominate other people

* changing the subject

* other kinds of behaviour that block the group from working such as splitting into pairs and excluding others.

Observing and evaluating group behaviour

The idea of classifying the behaviour of people in groups was put forward by Bales (1970). He suggested that observers could understand and analyse what was happening in a group by using an interaction analysis of individual member's behaviours. An interaction analysis involves classifying the way people behave using defined categories. Bales' categories are outlined in Figure 2.22.

Using categories can be a useful way of getting insight into how an individual is influencing the work and the emotional maintenance or feeling involved in group communication. It is possible to design a grid that can be used minute by minute to try to categorise the task and maintenance behaviours occurring in groups. An example relevant to the standards in this unit is offered in Figure 2.23.

A process of planning, doing and reviewing may enable individuals to understand how their own skills influence others (see Figure 2.24 on page 78). The ability to imagine and understand how an individual's behaviour will influence outcomes lies at the heart of getting a group activity to work.

CATEGORY	ANALYSIS
Group task	Gives suggestion (including taking the lead) Gives opinion (including feelings and wishes) Gives information (including clarifying and confirming) Asks for information Asks for opinion Asks for suggestion
Group maintenance (called 'Social-emotional Area' by Bales)	Seems friendly Dramatises Agrees Disagrees Shows tension Seems unfriendly

FIGURE 2.22 *Bales' categories of how people behave in groups*

Concluding group activity

When a group of people have worked together for a long period of time, there can be a feeling of loss when the group finishes. An example might be that a class of students who have worked together for a year might feel sad when the course comes to an end.

Benson (2001) offers a range of advice on a practical, emotional and intellectual level. This advice includes the need to feel that tasks have been completed. A group of students would need to feel that their course was over. Group members need to prepare to say goodbye and work through the emotions involved in parting. Most importantly, Benson stresses the need to encourage 'ritual and celebration'. Student groups might organise a farewell party – and this would be an example of celebrating the conclusion of belonging to a group.

In care settings the conclusion of a group activity might involve a period of time at the end of the session. When working with young children this might be a quiet time following practical work – perhaps listening to a story. When working with adults, group members

	Behaviour seen in each individual									
	1	2	3	4	5	6	7	8	9	10
Group task:										
Starting discussion										
Giving information										
Asking for information										
Clarifying discussion										
Summarising discussion										
Group maintenance:										
Humour										
Expressing group feelings										
Including other people in discussion										
Being supportive (using supportive skils)										
Behaviour which blocks communicaton:										
Excluding others										
Withdrawing										
Aggression										
Distracting or blocking disscusion										
Attention seeking and dominating discussion										

FIGURE 2.23 *A profile to monitor group behaviour*

SCENARIO:

Planning, managing and concluding a group activity

Alesha wants to involve a small group of adults who have learning disabilities in a cookery class. Alesha's idea is not to train the group to make cakes, but to provide an enjoyable social experience that the group can join in with to maintain their social skills. Before she can start, Alesha needs to plan. She needs to plan what ingredients to buy, and her own preparation of the ingredients, before the session begins. She also needs to organise the use of an oven for baking cakes, and so on.

As well as this, Alesha needs to plan how to support the group. Who does or doesn't get on with others? Who might be able to help with tasks? How could she interest and motivate the individuals? How will she keep the atmosphere enjoyable? All this planning depends on Alesha's ability to use her imagination, perhaps to picture the group and to work out how to organise the session.

Alesha will need to ensure that the tasks are enjoyable and appropriate to each individual.

Before moving on to the activity, she could also get advice on the plans from a senior member of staff – just to check that the activities are appropriate.

Doing the session would not necessarily be straightforward. Alesha will need to monitor how the session is going. Do the verbal and non verbal messages from her group suggest that they are enjoying themselves? Alesha will need feedback, so she could ask the group members what they thought. Another member of staff might help her by joining in and providing feedback. Whilst leading the cookery session Alesha will also be observing or taking in what is happening.

After the session is over Alesha will need to evaluate what has happened. Evaluation will depend on imagination. The evaluation will enable Alesha to make recommendations to improve her work in the future by thinking her work over before, during and after the cookery session. Alesha will thus be able to develop her own self-awareness and sense of skill.

THE PLANNING PHASE

- Choose a practical activity

- Plan this activity

- Get feedback on your ideas

- Finalise your plans

THE ACTION PHASE

- Observe and record what happened

- Make notes on own self-monitoring

- Note feedback from co-workers, clients, supervisors or teachers

THE REVIEW PHASE

- Evaluate what happened – use concepts and theory

- Identify own strengths and weaknesses – evaluate own skills

- Evaluate how theory and practice link in your work

- Check report against evidence indicators

FIGURE 2.24 *Three phases in getting an activity to work*

might be invited to talk through their feelings about the day's activity, or to talk through their feelings at the end of the day. Leaving a group for good might require more in-depth emotional work.

Summary of Section 2.1

The following key areas of theory have been covered in this section:

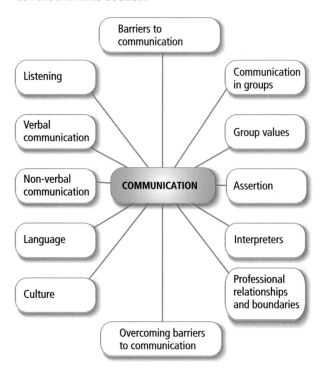

Chloe works at a day nursery. Parents sometimes make an appointment to see the nursery and to talk to the staff in order to decide whether the nursery would be appropriate for their children. Chloe expects to meet some parents in order to show them around the nursery and talk about the work they do. These parents do not live locally; they are from different ethnic and age groups to Chloe and have well-paid professional jobs.

Using concepts, can you identify?

1. What communication skills Chloe is likely to need in order to provide an appropriate welcome and to clearly explain the work of the nursery?

2. What barriers to communication Chloe should be prepared for as she takes the parents around the nursery?

Go further – can you analyse issues using theory?

How could Chloe know whether she was communicating clearly and effectively with the parents? How could Chloe know if she was successful at providing a warm and friendly welcome?

Go further – can you evaluate using a range of theory?

Chloe feels confident that she was highly skilled at holding the conversation with the parents. As she remembers how the conversation went, she can check what she did using the range of theory in this section. Can you imagine how you could use a range of concepts in order to judge the value of a conversation you have had?

2.2 Care value base

Principles that underlie care practice

The first standards for National Vocational Qualifications (NVQs) in care, published in 1992, included a unit of study that was called the 'value base'. Skilled caring is not simply about knowing the right techniques; a carer also needs to 'value' the service users that he or she works with. The 1992 value base stressed the importance of anti-discriminatory practice, confidentiality, rights, choice, effective communication and the importance of service users' personal beliefs and identity. Later standards in 1998 simplified these principles and emphasised equality and diversity, together with confidentiality and other rights and responsibilities. Proposed 2005 standards no longer specify a unit of study as a value base but do require that workers demonstrate an embedded framework of values. These values include the promotion of equality and diversity, the ability to challenge discrimination and an understanding of the rights and responsibilities of people involved in care settings.

Key concept

Care values/value base: Occupational standards and the GSCC code of practice identify a framework of values and moral rights of service users that can be referred to as care values or a value base for care.

In 2002 the **General Social Care Council (GSCC)** published a **code of practice** for both employees and employers. A summary of the code of practice for employees is set out in Figure 2.25.

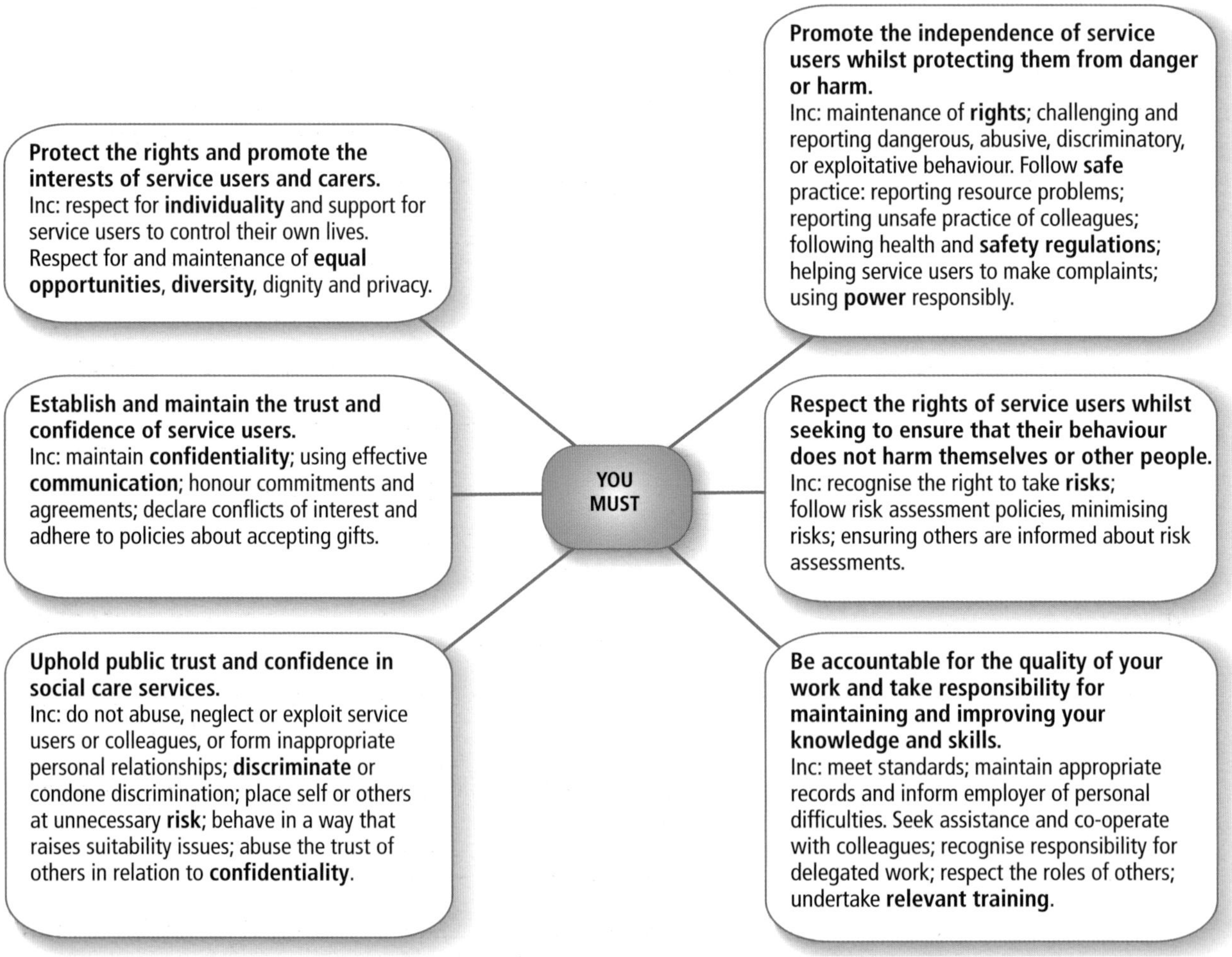

Protect the rights and promote the interests of service users and carers.
Inc: respect for **individuality** and support for service users to control their own lives. Respect for and maintenance of **equal opportunities**, **diversity**, dignity and privacy.

Promote the independence of service users whilst protecting them from danger or harm.
Inc: maintenance of **rights**; challenging and reporting dangerous, abusive, discriminatory, or exploitative behaviour. Follow **safe** practice: reporting resource problems; reporting unsafe practice of colleagues; following health and **safety regulations**; helping service users to make complaints; using **power** responsibly.

Establish and maintain the trust and confidence of service users.
Inc: maintain **confidentiality**; using effective **communication**; honour commitments and agreements; declare conflicts of interest and adhere to policies about accepting gifts.

YOU MUST

Respect the rights of service users whilst seeking to ensure that their behaviour does not harm themselves or other people.
Inc: recognise the right to take **risks**; follow risk assessment policies, minimising risks; ensuring others are informed about risk assessments.

Uphold public trust and confidence in social care services.
Inc: do not abuse, neglect or exploit service users or colleagues, or form inappropriate personal relationships; **discriminate** or condone discrimination; place self or others at unnecessary **risk**; behave in a way that raises suitability issues; abuse the trust of others in relation to **confidentiality**.

Be accountable for the quality of your work and take responsibility for maintaining and improving your knowledge and skills.
Inc: meet standards; maintain appropriate records and inform employer of personal difficulties. Seek assistance and co-operate with colleagues; recognise responsibility for delegated work; respect the roles of others; undertake **relevant training**.

FIGURE 2.25 *The GSCC code of practice for social care workers: an outline summary*

Value base principles and moral rights

Figure 2.26 lists key value base principles that might also be considered to be service users' moral rights, together with other rights that are specified within the GSCC code of practice.

Legislation standards and policies

It is important to know about legislation, such as the Care Standards Act 2000, because laws create a framework for the development of good practice. Laws can create commissions that develop standards and check that standards are being met. Each Care Service will develop its own written policies and procedures in order to monitor that service users' rights are respected. Figure 2.27 illustrates how law, standards and policies influence practice.

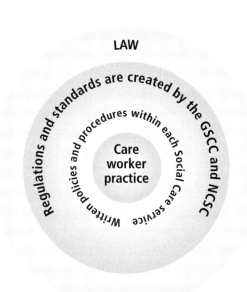

LAW

Regulations and standards are created by the GSCC and NCSC

Written policies and procedures within each Social Care service

Care worker practice

FIGURE 2.27 *How law, standards and policies influence practice*

MORAL RIGHTS OF SERVICE USERS	GSCC STANDARDS	
Diversity and respect for differences	1.1	treat each person as an individual
	1.2	respecting and promoting individual views
	1.6	respecting diversity and different cultures and values
Equality in care practice	1.5	promoting equal opportunities
Anti-discriminatory practice	5.5	care workers must not discriminate
	5.6	care workers must not condone discrimination
Confidentiality	2.3	respecting confidential information
The right to take control over one's own life – the right to choice and independence	1.3	supporting service users' rights to control their lives and make informed choices
	3.1	promoting the independence of service users
	3.7	helping service users and carers to make complaints
	3.8	recognising and using power responsibly
Dignity and privacy	1.4	respecting and maintaining the dignity and privacy of service users
The right to effective communication	2.2	communicating in an appropriate, open, accurate and straightforward way
The right to safety and security	Principle 3: promote independence while protecting service users, including health and safety policies, appropriate practice and procedures.	
	4.2 / 4.3	follow risk assessment policies, take steps to minimise risk
	5.2	must not exploit service users
	5.7	must not put self or others at risk
The right to take risks	4.1	service users have the right to take risks – help them to identify and manage risks

FIGURE 2.26 *A summary of the GSCC code of practice for employees*

Laws provide the background to policy making, and policy and standards guide managers when they design procedures.

Equal opportunities legislation

The main Acts of Parliament covering discrimination are shown in Figure 2.28.

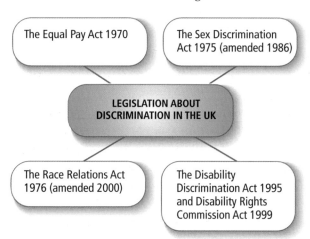

FIGURE 2.28 *Main Acts of Parliament covering discrimination in the UK*

The Equal Pay Act 1970

This Act made it unlawful for employers to discriminate between men and women in terms of their pay and conditions of work. Before this law was passed it was possible for an employer to pay men more than women – even though doing the same job!

Equal pay legislation was updated in 1975 and 1983 to make it possible to claim equal pay for work that was considered to be of 'equal value'.

The Sex Discrimination Act 1975

This Act made it unlawful to discriminate between men and women in respect of employment, goods and facilities. The Act also made it illegal to discriminate on the grounds of marital status. The Act identified two forms of discrimination: direct discrimination and indirect discrimination.

The Act tries to provide an equal opportunity for both men and women to get jobs and promotion. In order to make sure that people's rights were protected the government set up the **Equal Opportunities Commission** to monitor,

advise and provide information on men and women's rights under the law. People can ask the Equal Opportunities Commission for help and advice if they believe they have been discriminated against because of their gender. The law was updated in 1986 so that it also applied to small businesses.

The Race Relations Act 1976 (amended 2000)

This Act makes it unlawful to discriminate on 'racial grounds' in employment, housing or services. 'Racial grounds' means according to colour, race, nationality, ethnicity or national origins. The Act makes it an offence to incite or encourage racial hatred. As in the law against sex discrimination, both direct and indirect discrimination are made unlawful.

The Commission for Racial Equality was set up in 1976 to make sure that the law against racial discrimination works. The Commission can investigate cases of discrimination and give advice to people who wish to take legal action because of discrimination. The Race Relations Law was strengthened and widened by an amendment in 2000 in order to prevent discrimination in any public situation.

The Disability Discrimination Act 1995

This Act is designed to prevent discrimination against people with disabilities, covering employment, access to education and transport, housing and obtaining goods and services. Employers and landlords must not treat a disabled person less favourably than a non-disabled person. New transport must meet the needs of disabled people and colleges; shops and other services must ensure that disabled people can use their services.

The Disability Rights Commission was set up by the **Disability Rights Commission Act** of 1999. This commission has the power to conduct formal investigations and to serve non-discrimination notices, make agreements, and take other actions to prevent discrimination against people with a disability. The commission can give advice to people who believe they have experienced discrimination.

Confidentiality is an important right for all service users. Confidentiality is important because:

* service users may not trust a carer if the carer does not keep information to him or herself

* service users may not feel valued or able to keep their self-esteem if their private details are shared with others

* service users' safety may be put at risk if details of their property and habits are shared publicly

* a professional service which maintains respect for individuals must keep private information confidential

* there are legal requirements to keep personal records confidential.

The Data Protection Act 1998

The Data Protection Acts of 1984 and 1998, Access to Personal Files Act 1987, and Access to Health Records Act 1990 made it a legal requirement to keep service user information confidential. The 1998 Data Protection Act establishes rights to confidentiality covering both paper and electronic records. This Act provides people with a range of rights including:

* the right to know what information is held on you and to see and correct information held on you

* the right for you to refuse to provide information

* the right that data held on you should be accurate and up to date

* the right that data held on you should not be kept for longer than necessary

* the right to confidentiality – that information about you should not be accessible to unauthorised people.

See Unit 3 for more detail on confidentiality, and the recording and storage of records.

Other important laws relevant to care

The Children Act 1989 outlined 'parental responsibility' and established children's right to be protected from 'significant harm'. The NHS and Community Care Act 1990 established that all people who are in need of community care have the right to have their needs assessed and to have services if their needs meet criteria. The Care Standards Act 2000 created a new framework for defining and controlling quality within care work. (See Unit 3.)

Codes of practice charters and policies

Healthcare workers such as nurses follow a code of professional conduct published by the Nursing and Midwifery Council (NMC). The code has similar principles to the GSCC code for social care. Full details of the code can be found at the NMC website through www.heinemann.co.uk/ hotlinks (express code 37185). A summary of the key principles are listed below.

In caring for patients and clients, you must:

* respect each service user as an individual

* obtain consent before you give any treatment or care

* protect confidential information

* cooperate with others in the team

* maintain your professional knowledge and competence

* be trustworthy

* act to identify and minimise risk to patients and clients.

The majority of Early Years services are inspected by Ofsted and do not involve the Commission for Social Care Inspection (CSCI) or the GSCC code of practice. Instead, Early Years National Vocational Qualifications have a set of Underlying Principles; in outline these specify:

* that the welfare of the child is the most important issue
* that children must be kept safe
* workers must work in partnership with parents and families
* children's learning and development are centrally important
* that the principle of equality of opportunity is critically important
* that anti-discriminatory practice is vital
* that care practice must 'celebrate diversity'
* the principle of confidentiality must be followed
* workers must work with other professionals in the best interests of children and families
* early years workers must learn to reflect on their practice and principles.

After 2005 it is proposed that these principles should be revised and embedded within NVQ awards rather than being found as a separate set of principles.

Charters

Charters are another source of policies that define the values and principles of caring. Many health services – such as doctor's surgeries – may have a 'Charter' that specifies the quality of service that a patient may expect. Originally the idea for these charters may have come from the Patient's Charter, launched by the government in 1992. The Patient's Charter set out some general rights and quality standards that the public could expect from the National Health Service. This charter was replaced in 2001 by a lengthy publication called 'Your Guide to the NHS: Getting the Most from your National Health Service'.

National Minimum Standards of Care

The Care Standards Act 2000 established the National Care Standards Commission (NCSC). The NCSC produces a set of regulations and National Minimum Standards that care services must achieve. There are different sets of standards for different care services. The Standards provide very detailed guidance on how services must be delivered. Care services are now inspected by 'The Commission for Social Care Inspection'(CSCI) to make sure that they are providing high quality care. Further detail of National Minimum standards can be found in Unit 3.

Equality and respect for difference

Historically in the UK there have been major tensions between different social groups, such as religious groups. One idea for reducing conflict is the concept of 'tolerance'. This word was widely used two centuries ago to argue that different religious groups could co-exist without needing to fight each other. Tolerance and respect are values that could be argued to lay a foundation for anti-discriminatory practice. Celebrating diversity and anti-discriminatory practice involves much more than tolerance, however. Celebrating diversity involves being interested in and willing to learn about other cultures and belief systems. Anti-discrimination involves providing the same quality of service for everyone. If everybody is treated the same – if everyone were given the same dinner, for instance – then some people would be discriminated against. Vegetarians might not get the food they need, for example. Equality is about everybody getting the same *quality* of service – not the same service!

Anti-discriminatory practice

Some groups of people that are at risk of being discriminated against are listed in Figure 2.29. Discrimination may take the forms identified in Figure 2.30.

Key concept

Discrimination: In care work, discrimination means to treat some types of people less well than others. People are often discriminated against because of their race, beliefs, gender, religion, sexuality or age.

Direct and indirect discrimination

Direct discrimination is where the discrimination is open and obvious. In the 1950s and 1960s, properties for rent in London would sometimes have signs which read 'no blacks, no dogs, no Irish'. Such offensive and obvious discrimination is 'direct'; the

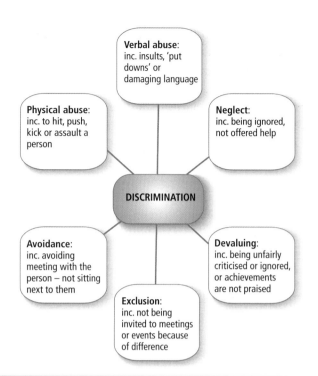

FIGURE 2.30 *Examples of some forms of discrimination*

FOCUS OF DISCRIMINATION	EXAMPLES OF RISK OF DISCRIMINATION DIFFERENCE IS SEEN AS A PROBLEM RATHER THAN AS SOMETHING POSITIVE
Race	People might not be included in activities, chosen as friends, or selected for a job because they are seen as 'not like us' and 'not to be trusted'
Religious belief	Assumptions are made that everybody follows the same cultural traditions. For example, Christmas is celebrated, but the festivals of other religions are not
Gender	Assumptions are made that male workers are the most reliable 'because they don't have to look after children'
Disability	People with a disability are thought of as being defective or damaged people who deserve pity because they are not 'normal'
Culture	A person from a different ethnic or even a different social class might be seen as inferior, 'having bad habits' and so on
Health status	HIV positive people are seen as 'untouchable' and a risk to others because of fears of **contagion**
Cognitive ability	People with learning difficulty being assumed to be 'children' who need everything decided for them
Mental health background	Assumptions that all people with a history of mental health problems are a risk to others
Place of origin	Assumptions that only people 'like us' can be trusted – even people from different geographical areas may be 'outsiders'
Marital status	Assumptions that only married adults are 'normal'. Alternatively, assumptions that married women will want to leave a job in order to have children
Sexuality	People might be avoided or made 'fun of' because they are seen as 'not normal'

FIGURE 2.29 *Groups of people that are at risk of being discriminated against*

advertisements were openly committing racial discrimination.

Indirect discrimination may do equal harm but it is less clear. On one occasion an employer produced an advert stating that applicants for a job must live in certain local areas. At first this sounds all right, but it became obvious that the areas had been carefully chosen to avoid the black and Asian communities. The advert was indirectly discriminating by identifying areas where only white people lived. Indirect discrimination involves unequal treatment that may not be obvious at first.

Receiving a worse service than others because of your age, gender, race, sexuality, or ability, could strike at the heart of a service user's sense of self, self-esteem and feelings of self-worth. Discrimination can damage a person's ability to develop and maintain a sense of identity.

Thompson's PCS Model for understanding discrimination

Thompson (1997) identifies three levels where discrimination and anti-discrimination practice can take place. These three levels are analysed as being P, C and S levels.

> **P** – personal and psychological
> **C** – cultural and conformity to norms
> **S** – structural and social forces

Discrimination can work on any of the three levels (see Figure 2.31). On a structural level, historical beliefs about gender role and about the superiority of ethnic groups influence the assumptions that surround us. Some organisations may still value male employees more highly than women. Men may find it easier to gain promotion because organisations have built-in or 'structural' systems that make it easier for men to succeed. Structural economic systems may result in some black communities living in more deprived housing conditions. Stressful housing conditions may represent one factor that can reduce life chances and opportunities.

On the cultural level, we mix with groups of people who share values and ways of behaving. A

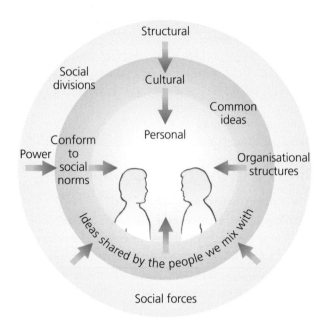

FIGURE 2.31 *Different levels of discrimination (P, C and S)*

great deal of discrimination happens because people conform to the expectations of others. People might, for instance, join in with jokes about a particular minority, not because they hold personal prejudices but because they want to fit in with others. On a personal level our own beliefs are often translated into our verbal and non-verbal behaviour. Our personal practice has a direct and immediate effect on others.

On an individual level, Thompson (1997) makes the point that carers can make a major difference to the quality of a service user's life by checking their own assumptions and their own behaviour. On a personal level, discrimination may result from emotional reactions as well as resulting from prejudice. Building an understanding of each service user's life and respecting service users' rights might enable a carer to avoid negative reactions to service users. Every carer has the power to develop his or her own skills and to employ appropriate skills when interacting with others. Lack of time may limit personal effectiveness, but there is nearly always something that could be achieved within person-to-person communication.

On a wider cultural level, individuals can 'make a difference'. Individuals can analyse what is happening and can challenge others to try to change group norms and values. Organisations must introduce management and quality systems, which aim to ensure that workplace norms and expectations conform to national standards and codes of practice for care.

On the very widest structural level, individuals may feel that they have little influence. Setting up quality standards and systems is a government function and the standards and the resources which services have to operate within are strongly influenced by

political views and values. Individuals may need to join pressure groups, or become involved in political debate in order to influence the structural level of discrimination.

Some obvious types of discriminatory practice are listed in Figure 2.32. It should be possible to monitor one's own and other's behaviour in order to minimise such risk.

Stereotyping and labelling

Sometimes people try to save mental energy and just make the assumption that groups of people are 'all the same'. Perhaps a younger person meets an 80 year old who has a problem with his or her memory. Perhaps they have seen someone with a poor memory on TV – it's easy then to think that 'all old people are forgetful'. This would be a stereotype.

A stereotype is a fixed way of thinking. People may make assumptions based on stereotyped thinking. For example, a carer working with older people might say 'I'll just go in and wash and dress this next one. I won't ask what she would like me to do because she's old – old people don't remember – so it doesn't matter what I do'. Stereotyped thinking may cause us to discriminate against people.

When people say 'All women are ...,' or 'all black people are ...,' or 'all gay people are ...,' they will probably go on to describe a stereotype or label for these groups.

Another way in which thinking can lead to discrimination is labelling. Labelling is similar to stereotyping but labels are simple. Instead of having a set of fixed thoughts about a group, a person gets summed up in just one word or term.

FIGURE 2.32 *Some types of discriminatory practice*

Diagram contents:
- Poor physical care, ignoring the needs of people who are different
- Conversations which do not value people because they are different
- Criticising or verbally abusing people who are different
- Making assumptions about people. Labelling or stereotyping people
- **DISCRIMINATORY PRACTICE**
- Avoiding people because they are different
- Excluding people from activities because they are different
- Treating everybody the same and ignoring their individual needs
- Negative body language towards people who are different

Many years ago there was a care setting for children with learning difficulties. Some children were not very skilled with holding plates, and so on. They were labelled 'clumsies.'

What effect do you think describing these children as 'clumsies' would have on their development of self-esteem?

Labels may be words such as 'aggressive', 'emotional', or 'naughty.' They can also be words that create a category of assumptions. Historically, a word like 'paranoid' was a medical term, but today it can be used as a label that neatly categorises and ignores another person's worries.

Labels are often used in order to categorise and discriminate against ethnic groups, women or old people. Labels may say that people are only one thing, such as aggressive, emotional or worthless. When individuals are labelled, it's almost as if they stop being people; they are just mentally ill, for example. That's all they are, no other details matter. Labels can reduce people's self-esteem, dignity and individuality.

Language differences often result in labelling or stereotyping. For example, people who have difficulty hearing or seeing are sometimes assumed to be 'awkward' or mentally ill. Older people are sometimes seen as 'demented' or 'confused' if they do not answer questions appropriately.

People can also be labelled or stereotyped when they use different language systems. Sometimes people shout at others who speak a different language, as if increasing the volume would help. People who sign to communicate are sometimes thought to be odd or to have learning difficulties, because they don't respond to written or spoken English.

The effects of discrimination

Discrimination that results in abuse can have permanent and extremely damaging effects on people. All forms of discrimination will harm people.

Discrimination may result in the outcomes shown in Figure 2.33.

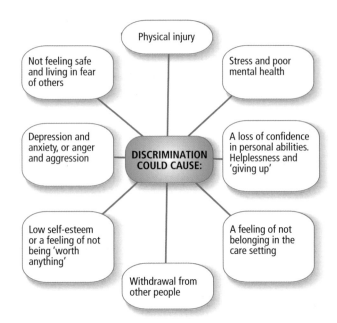

FIGURE 2.33 *Some effects of discrimination on people in care settings*

Empowerment

When a conversation takes place between a professional worker and a service user, who is the most powerful? Half-a-century ago, expert professionals held the power and made the decisions about what kind of treatment or care people would receive. For example, a person with learning difficulty might be sent to a specialist hospital that provided residential care. Within this institution, staff would decide the daily routine that each 'inmate' would follow. People with learning difficulty might not be consulted about their lifestyle – everything was decided for them. In this situation, the staff hold all the power; the service users have no power to choose how they would like to live or what they would like to do.

Half-a-century ago a visit to the doctor would involve the patient explaining his or her problem and accepting the advice received in return. The term 'doctor's orders' was sometimes used to describe a treatment plan that a patient had to follow. Patients often thought of doctors as being senior officers who were entitled to give them orders, rather like officers in the army.

The theory of empowerment is that health and care staff should not make decisions and take control of service users' lives. Care staff should communicate their knowledge to service users and enable service users to make their own decisions and choices about care plans or medical treatment. Empowering communication is communication that aims to give service users choice and control of the service that they receive.

An example of empowerment

In 2001, the government launched the 'Expert Patient Initiative'. The idea of an 'expert patient' is that a person with a long-term, or chronic, illness such as arthritis can learn to take control of the management of his or her condition. Expert medical staff can provide advice and guidance, but the patient is the expert on his or her own body. The patient works in partnership with medical staff in order to build his or her own treatment plan.

The 'expert patient' is empowered to take control of his or her own medical condition. The expert patient does not simply have to comply with the treatment prescribed.

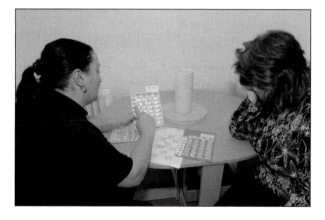

FIGURE 2.34 *A service user taking on the management of her health*

Bringing about empowerment

The idea that health and care workers should work in partnership with service users is closely associated with the value base of care work. But there are pressures that may limit the degree to which service users are empowered, as shown in Figure 2.35.

Descombes (2004: 94) provides evidence that within medical practice 'It is still the doctor who controls the whole patient–practitioner encounter. It is the doctor who decides just what information will be given and how much use can be made of it'. Establishing an empowering approach will require much more than simply giving clear information to service users.

Balancing the rights of individuals with the rights of others

Rights of individuality, freedom from discrimination, confidentiality, choice, dignity, independence, effective communication, and safety, all protect individual well-being and encourage self-esteem. Rights usually carry responsibilities with them. An individual can expect respect, but he or she has the responsibility not to interfere with or damage other people's rights. You have a right to be free from discrimination but a responsibility not to discriminate against others.

Think it over...

Nasil argues that he has a right to smoke – it's his life and he has a right to choose how he lives and dies. Nasil attends a day centre that has a no smoking policy inside the building. Nasil will often go outside to have a cigarette, but he complains that the cold damp air is unpleasant and bad for his health. 'Us smokers are discriminated against', he says. 'Why should we have to put up with being cold just because other people have got different habits?'

What are Nasil's rights and what are his responsibilities in relation to smoking?

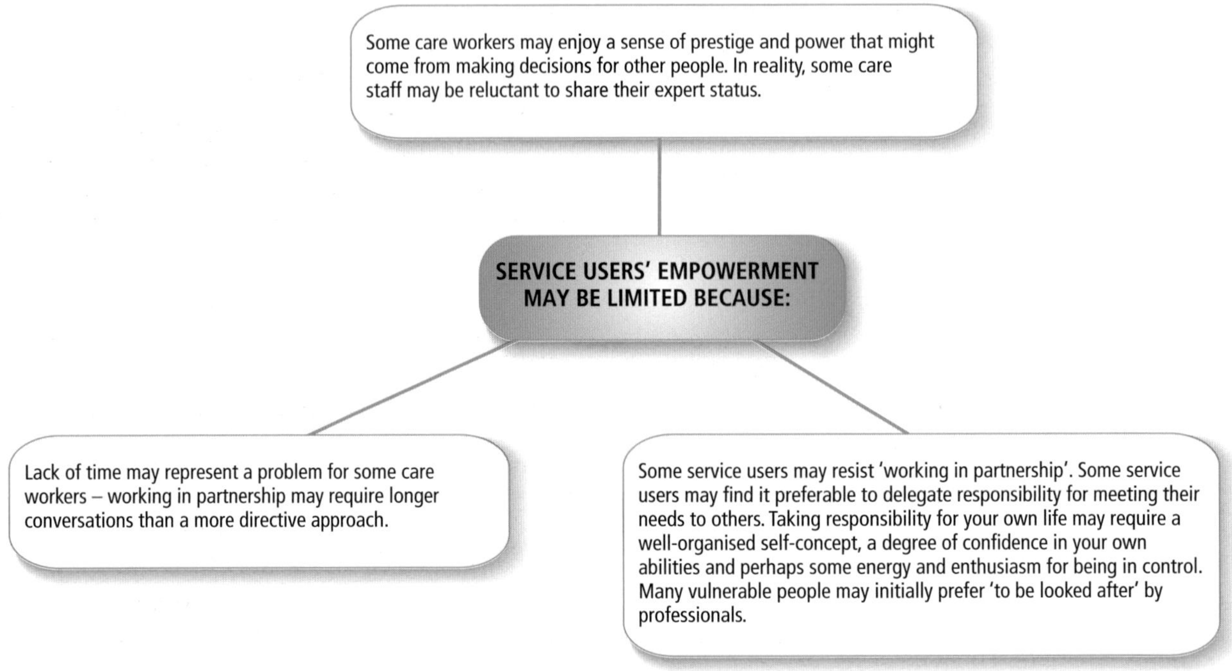
Some care workers may enjoy a sense of prestige and power that might come from making decisions for other people. In reality, some care staff may be reluctant to share their expert status.
SERVICE USERS' EMPOWERMENT MAY BE LIMITED BECAUSE:
Lack of time may represent a problem for some care workers – working in partnership may require longer conversations than a more directive approach.
Some service users may resist 'working in partnership'. Some service users may find it preferable to delegate responsibility for meeting their needs to others. Taking responsibility for your own life may require a well-organised self-concept, a degree of confidence in your own abilities and perhaps some energy and enthusiasm for being in control. Many vulnerable people may initially prefer 'to be looked after' by professionals.

FIGURE 2.35 *Limitations of service users' empowerment*

Adults have a right to choose to smoke even though smoking usually damages health and might shorten a person's life. Smokers have a responsibility not to put other people's health at risk because people have a right to health. Other people, including care staff, should not have to breathe in tobacco smoke. This means that in most places today, smoking is only allowed in specially designated areas.

In the past, service users' responsibilities may not have been a major focus because service users generally have less power than staff. Service users are generally vulnerable, whilst care workers generally have a degree of control over their own lives. But just because a person is vulnerable, it doesn't mean that he or she has a right to interfere with other people, or for instance, threaten people with racist or sexist behaviour.

Some ways of understanding rights and responsibilities are set out in Figure 2.37.

'It's my right to smoke'
'And it's my right not to have to breathe in your smoke'

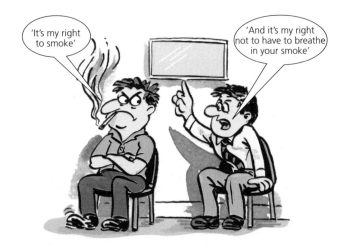

FIGURE 2.36 *Rights do not work without responsibilities*

Key concept

Rights and responsibilities: All moral rights also involve responsibilities towards others. Rights are part of a social system involving a two-way process of rights and responsibilities within UK society.

SOME MORAL RIGHTS OF SERVICE USERS	RESPONSIBILITIES OF SERVICE USERS
Diversity and the right to be different Including an individual's right to express his or her own identity / self-narrative and interpretation of life from the standpoint of different social group memberships	**To respect diversity in others** Including an acceptance that other people have a moral right to interpret life differently. A moral responsibility not to discriminate against others on the basis that own identity / social group membership is morally superior to that of others
Equality and freedom from discrimination Including freedom from discrimination on the basis of race, sex, ability, sexuality, religion	**Respect for the equality of others** Including respect for and not discriminating against members of other social groups
Control over own life, choice and independence Including the freedom to choose own lifestyle, self-presentation, diet and routine	**Respect for the independence, choice and lifestyle of others** Including arriving at a balance between the impact of own choices and the needs of other people who may be affected by the service user's choices – including care staff
Dignity and privacy Including the right to be responded to in terms of own interpretation of dignity and respect	**To share or disclose own assumptions about dignity and negotiate boundaries with others** Including boundaries associated with the health and safety or the identity needs of other users or carers
Confidentiality Including rights as established in law and local codes of practice	**Respect for the confidentiality of others** Including others' legal rights, and rights established in local codes of practice
Effective communication Including appropriately clear and supportive communication that minimises vulnerability	**Communication that does not threaten others** Including appropriate respect
Safety and security Including physical safety, living in an environment that promotes health and emotional safety. Security of property, and freedom from physical, social, emotional or economic threat	**Contributing to the safety and security of others** Including to behave in a way that does not compromise or threaten the physical or emotional safety and security of others
The right to take risks Including taking risks as a matter of choice, in order to maintain own identity or perceived well-being	**Not to expose self or others to unacceptable risks** Including a willingness to negotiate with respect to the impact of risk on others

FIGURE 2.37 *Rights and responsibilities of service users*

Inequalities within society

People have very different opportunities in their lives. The general income level a person has is likely to influence his or her expectations and assumptions about life.

> ✱ **DID YOU KNOW?**
>
> Just over one-sixth of Britain's population (17 per cent) were estimated by the Institute for Fiscal Studies to be living in relative poverty (low income) in the period 2001/2002 (Social Trends 2004). People who get less than 60 per cent of the level of income that an average person expects may be considered to be at risk of poverty and 'social exclusion'.

Key groups of people who have to live on very little money include: one-parent families, people who are unemployed, elderly people, people who are sick or disabled, a single earner, unskilled couples (where only one person works in an unskilled job).

People on low income may have enough money for food, for some clothes and for heating, but poverty means that there is little money for the interesting purchases that buy into exciting lifestyles. People who depend on benefits have limited life choices.

The government's 'Opportunity for all' (1999) publication states that:

* the number of people living in households with low incomes had more than doubled since the late 1970s

* one in three children lived in households with below half average income

* nearly one in five working-age households had no one in work

* the poorest communities had much more unemployment, poor housing, vandalism and crime than richer areas.

The problems which prevent people from making the most of their lives are characterised in the publication as:

* **Lack of opportunities to work** – work is the most important route out of low income but the consequences of being unemployed go wider than lack of money. It can contribute to ill health and can deny future employment opportunities.

* **Lack of opportunities to acquire education and skills** – adults without basic skills are much more likely to spend long periods out of work.

* **Childhood deprivation** – with its linked problems of low income, poor health, poor housing and unsafe environments.

* **Disrupted families** – the evidence shows that children in lone-parent families are particularly likely to suffer the effects of persistently low household incomes. Stresses within families can lead to exclusion; in extreme cases to homelessness.

* **Barriers to older people living active, fulfilling and healthy lives** – too many older people have low incomes, lack of independence and poor health. Lack of access to good-quality services are key barriers to social inclusion.

* **Inequalities in health** – health can be affected by low income and a range of socio-economic factors, such as access to good-quality health services and shops selling good-quality food at affordable prices.

* **Poor housing** – this directly diminishes people's quality of life and leads to a range of physical and mental health problems, and can cause difficulties for children trying to do homework.

* **Poor neighbourhoods** – the most deprived areas suffer from a combination of poor housing, high rates of crime, unemployment, poor health and family disruption.

* **Fear of crime** – crime and fear of crime can effectively exclude people within their own communities, especially older people.

* **Disadvantaged groups** – some people experience disadvantage or discrimination, for example, on the grounds of age, ethnicity, gender or disability. This makes them particularly vulnerable to **social exclusion**.

The cycle of disadvantage

When children are born into an environment in which they experience discrimination, poverty, poor housing and lack of opportunity they are less likely to develop the social and academic skills of more advantaged children. They are, therefore, unlikely to get the best jobs. Very often children who are born 'poor' are likely to stay 'poor'. This situation is called a 'cycle of disadvantage', because the disadvantage is recycled to each new generation.

Identifying own beliefs and prejudices

We all learn to simplify our world in order to make it easier to cope with. It is easy to make assumptions that people who are different are perhaps bad, frightening or 'best avoided'. Skilled care work might depend on identifying ways of coping with our own emotions. Some brief examples of prejudiced beliefs and reactions are set out in Figure 2.38, together with some ideas for avoiding discriminatory reactions.

Celebrating diversity

Equality between different groups in society cannot happen if some groups are seen as being superior to others. Differences between people such as race, gender, class, sexuality and age, must be valued. Learning about differences and trying to understand individual beliefs and needs is an essential skill for promoting equality.

One advantage of celebrating diversity is that it will help to create a fairer and more just society. But valuing diversity might also make your own life more interesting and exciting. If you are open to understanding other people's life experience and differences you may be able to achieve the benefits shown in Figure 2.39 for yourself.

Employers are likely to want to employ people who value diversity because:

* effective anti-discriminatory care depends on staff valuing diversity

* GSCC codes of practice require workers to respect diversity and employers to provide training to assist workers to develop skills

* people who value diversity are likely to be flexible and creative

* people who value diversity may make good relationships with one another and with service users

* diverse teams often work very effectively. If everyone has the same skills and interests then team members may compete.

SITUATION	RISK OF PREJUDICE	ALTERNATIVE
A service user comes from a different culture	Not understanding the service user's needs Avoidance, stereotyping and labelling	Using skilled conversation and listening in order to build an understanding of the other person
A service user has a learning difficulty	Thinking that the service user is a damaged or 'sad' individual	Using appropriate values and communication skills to learn about the unique individual nature of this person
A service user has different beliefs from you	Labelling difference as 'mad' or 'bad'	Thinking of difference as an interesting experience rather than a threat to one's own beliefs

FIGURE 2.38 *Some examples of prejudiced beliefs and reactions*

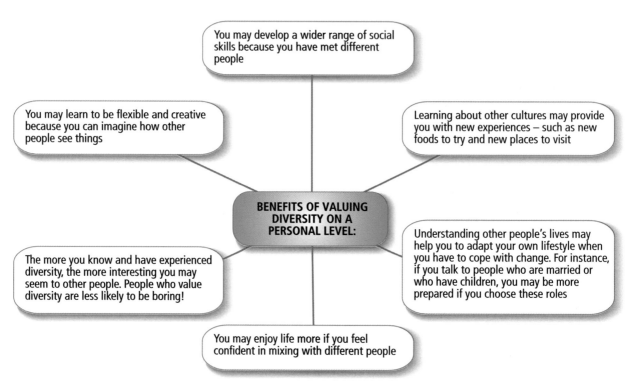

FIGURE 2.39 *Benefits gained through understanding other people's life experiences and differences*

Summary of Section 2.2

The following key areas of theory have been covered in this section:

Palvinder grew up in a low-income family on a housing estate. Palvinder was often ill and missed a great deal of school when he was young. Palvinder has bad memories of the school that he attended; he says that he was bullied and called names. Palvinder now lives in a housing complex with people who have a learning difficulty. He is happy there and says that the people who work in the housing complex are 'nice'.

Using concepts, can you identify?
1. Examples of the kind of discrimination that Palvinder may have experienced.

2. Examples of care worker values that might contribute to Palvinder feeling happy at the housing centre.

Go further – can you analyse issues using theory?
Staff in the housing complex say that they work in an anti-discriminatory way and that they try to empower service users. What might this mean for Palvinder?

Go further – can you evaluate using a range of theory?
Palvinder experienced a range of disadvantage and discrimination when he was young. In what way can care values expressed in codes of practice, and legislation that provide rights contribute to a better quality of life for service users?

2.3 Transmission of values

Awareness of needs

Care workers often work with people who have experienced abuse, are afraid, or who do not understand what might happen next. They are often vulnerable people who feel threatened by what they are experiencing. Care staff must use effective communication skills if they are to meet the needs of the people they work with.

Human needs are complex. In the past it was sometimes assumed that physical needs should always take priority over other social and cultural needs. Today physical needs are often seen as the foundation for working with people, but not always the most important issue to address. One way of understanding human needs is through the work of Abraham Maslow (1908–1970). Maslow's theory was that the purpose of human life was personal growth. That is, the quality of a human life can be understood in terms of an individual's development of his or her own ability and potential. Before a person can fully develop his or her potential, there are levels of need (called deficiency needs) which first have to be met. **Maslow's hierarchy** of needs is often set out as a pyramid, as shown below on the left-hand side of Figure 2.40. The role of communication in meeting human needs is described on the right-hand side of the diagram.

Effective communication needs to operate at every level of the triangle. It is important to give and receive clear information about physical needs in order to respond to those needs. A lack of clear communication may result in a person's physical needs being unmet.

Listening skills are vital in order to create the basis for psychological safety and to reduce the threat that members of the public may feel. If people do not feel that they have been listened to they may feel disrespected. A lack of respect may create a feeling of low self-esteem and emotional vulnerability. As well as this, individuals may feel that they are physically at risk because their needs have not been understood. Effective body

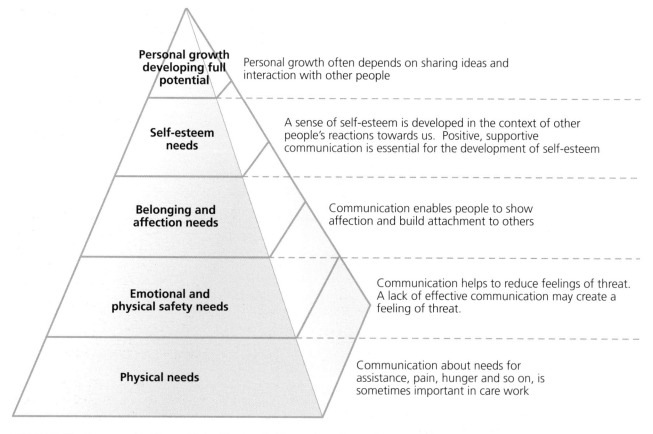

FIGURE 2.40 *Communication within Maslow's hierarchy of needs*

language is vital to establish professional relationships and create a sense of safety and belonging with people in care.

Establishing and maintaining relationships

Being good at establishing relationships may require supportive behaviour.

Supportive body language

Muscle tone, facial expression, eye contact and posture can send messages of being friendly. When meeting a person it is usually appropriate to smile, to express interest through eye contact and to maintain a relaxed posture – free of muscle tension. This indicates a readiness to talk and listen. It is difficult to define a simple set of rules for supportive body language because each individual will have his or her own expectations about what is appropriate and normal. The settings in which conversation takes place can influence how people should behave. The most important thing about supportive body language is to learn to monitor the effects that our behaviour is having on another person. Being supportive involves being aware of your own non-verbal behaviour and monitoring how your

non-verbal behaviour is affecting others. Section 2.1 explores the components of non-verbal communication in more depth.

As well as the communication skills outlined in Section 2.1, it is important that service users feel emotionally safe and able to share experiences. The skills for creating a sense of emotional safety were first identified by Carl Rogers (1902–1987). Originally these skills were seen as a basis for counselling relationships, but they have since become adopted as a basis for any befriending or **supportive relationship**. There are three conditions for a supportive conversation and these are that the carer must show (or convey) a sense of warmth, understanding and sincerity to the other person. These conditions sometimes have other names:

* warmth (sometimes called acceptance)
* understanding (originally called empathy)
* sincerity (originally called genuineness).

Showing warmth

The ideal is to get to know the service user in a sensitive manner and share experiences.

Warmth means being seen as a warm, accepting person. In order to influence another person to view you this way, you will need to demonstrate that you do not stereotype and label others. You will need to demonstrate that you do not judge other people as good or bad, right or

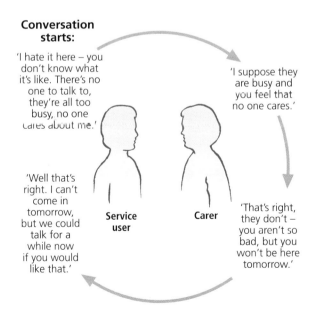

Conversation starts:

'I hate it here – you don't know what it's like. There's no one to talk to, they're all too busy, no one cares about me.'

'I suppose they are busy and you feel that no one cares.'

Service user

Carer

'Well that's right. I can't come in tomorrow, but we could talk for a while now if you would like that.'

'That's right, they don't – you aren't so bad, but you won't be here tomorrow.'

FIGURE 2.41 *Developing a supportive sense of warmth involves being non-judgemental*

> ### Think it over...
>
> Imagine that you feel sad about something and that you explain your problems to a friend. How would you feel if your friend did not look at you and instead seemed interested in what was happening outside the window? How would you feel if your friend just 'parroted' things you said back to you? How would you react if he or she just said things like 'I know', or 'Yes' all the time – without sounding sincere or interested?
>
> Being a good friend involves supportive behaviour. How good are you at showing others that you understand their feelings?

wrong. This is sometimes referred to as a non-judgemental attitude.

Conveying warmth means being willing to listen to others. It means being able to prove that you are listening to a person because you can remember what he or she has said to you. Warmth involves using **active listening**. That is, you give your attention to the person when talking, and remember what he or she said. You can then reflect the words back again.

In Figure 2.41, the carer is able to show the service user that she is listening by repeating some of the things that the service user has said. The repetition is not 'parrot fashion'; the carer has used her own way of speaking. The carer also avoids being judgmental. When the service user says that no one cares, the carer does not argue. The carer might have felt like saying, 'How can you say that – don't you know how hard we work for you? You want to think yourself lucky – there's plenty of people who would be pleased to be here; other people don't complain'. This advice to think yourself lucky and comparison with other people is judgmental. The statement does not value the other person, and it is not warm. If the carer had said these things it would have blocked the conversation. Warmth makes it safe for the service user to express his feelings. Warmth means that the carer can disagree with what the service user has said, since the service user feels safe that he will not be put down.

In developing the skill of showing warmth, it is important not to judge. Carers should accept that people have the right to be the way they are, and to make their own choices. While you may disapprove of a person's behaviour, you must show that you do not dislike him or her as an individual. This is particularly important when working with people with difficult behaviour. It is essential that individuals know it is the behaviour which is disliked, not them as a person.

Conveying understanding

Understanding means learning about the individual identity and beliefs that a person has. Carl Rogers saw the idea of understanding or empathy as the ability to experience another person's world as if it was your own world. The key part being the 'as if'. We always understand our own world and we know that other people have different experiences from our own. It is important to try to really understand others' thoughts and feelings.

Active listening provides a useful tool to enable carers to learn about people. If a person is listened to, he or she may experience a feeling of being understood. If the carer is warm and non-judgemental, it becomes safe for a service user to talk about his or her life. If the carer checks that he or she understands the service user, that person may feel valued. As the person feels that they are valued, so he or she may talk more. The more the person talks, the more the carer has a chance to learn about the service user.

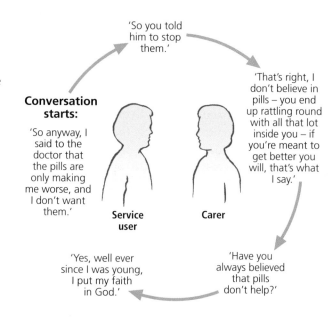

FIGURE 2.42 *Developing a supportive sense of understanding involves active listening*

In Figure 2.42, listening and conveying warmth the carer is being given the privilege of learning about the service user's religious views. Understanding can grow from a conversation that conveys value for the other person. A sense of trust may develop out of a sense of understanding. If you feel you are understood then you may feel it is safe to share your thoughts and worries.

Conveying sincerity

Being sincere means being open about what you say and the way that you speak. It means not acting – not using set phrases or professional styles that do not reflect your true self. In some ways being sincere means being yourself – being honest and real. Being real has to involve being non-judgemental though – trying to understand people rather than trying to give people advice. If being honest means giving other people your advice – don't do it! However, when you listen and learn about other people, do use your own normal language. Think about ways you might describe yourself and occasionally share details of your own life with the people you are helping. Sometimes it is necessary to share your thoughts to keep a conversation going. Sharing information from your own life might help to convey sincerity or genuineness in some situations.

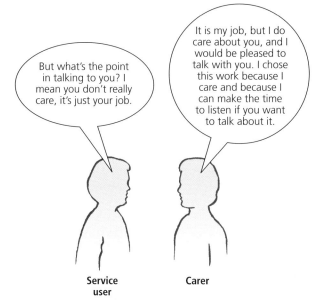

FIGURE 2.43 *Sharing information about your own life may help to convey sincerity*

Understanding, warmth and sincerity have to be combined in order to provide a safe, supportive setting.

Learning to create a supportive relationship with people will involve practice and a great deal of self-monitoring and reflection. If you practise conveying warmth, understanding and sincerity,

it will be important to get feedback from colleagues, supervisors and most importantly service users.

You may be able to tell if your communication is effective because the other person may reflect your behaviour. That is, if you are warm and understanding the other person may come to trust you; then you may find that this person is warm and friendly toward you. If you are honest and sincere, people may be honest and sincere with you. The quality of a supportive relationship should become a two-way process.

Establishing and maintaining relationships

The importance of identity and the worth of others

In order to enjoy life, it is very important that adults develop a sense of personal identity. If you feel confident that you understand your own abilities and your relationships with others then you may feel in control of your life.

Self-esteem and feeling that life is worthwhile depend on the development of a secure **identity**. Children develop a sense of self through the quality of their relationships with other people. If you work with children you may influence their development of identity in terms of the relationships that they experience.

If you work with adults or older adults it is very important that communication work shows respect for identity. One of the main ways to 'promote a person's identity' is to listen and build an understanding of his or her life. Listening and understanding skills are explained in Section 2.1. Listening and showing that you understand usually creates a feeling that you have been respectful.

Respect for difference

It is very important that people are not 'treated all the same'. Each person in care will be different from other people in terms of his or her ethnicity, gender, age group, religion, social class and chosen lifestyle. Together with these differences each person will have a unique set of personal characteristics, attitudes and emotions. If you get to know each person as an individual and you make it clear that you can remember some personal details, then you can show that you are working with or 'transmitting' care values.

Sometimes, listening involves switching into a store of knowledge and understanding. For some people, this is a conscious 'switching on' process. We switch on by remembering details of another person; perhaps we can recall when we last talked to this individual and what he or she said. Transmitting respect for individual differences may depend on being able to remember these important details; for example, greeting another person using a word of welcome in his or her own first language, remembering a recent event such as a visit of grandchildren, or discussing an interest that you know that person has, such as music.

Some key ideas for transmitting care values are set out in Figure 2.44.

Consider this

Sarah works as a home care worker with older people in their own homes. Sarah takes time to learn and remember the personal likes and dislikes of each person that she works with. Many service users feel safe to talk about their life histories and their current interests and worries with Sarah. Although service user plans specify the work that Sarah is supposed to do, Sarah always asks how service users would like tasks such as cleaning to be done. Service users are full of praise for Sarah, saying things like 'Oh you couldn't want for a better person – she is so kind and thoughtful.'

Using concepts, can you identify?
1. Evidence that suggests that Sarah is good at building supportive relationships with service users.

2. Examples of respect for service users' rights.

Go further – can you analyse issues using theory?
Service users say that Sarah is kind and thoughtful. Sarah might achieve this response because she is good at transmitting care values. What care values might guide Sarah's work?

Go further – can you evaluate using a range of theory?
Sarah is using a range of skilled communication, values and supportive skills in order to build successful caring relationships. Can you imagine how the theory in this unit can be used to explain successful caring relationships?

COMMUNICATING CARE VALUES THROUGH:	KEY IDEAS
Awareness of needs	It is very important to understand the self-development, self-esteem and belonging needs of service users and not be limited to understanding only the basic physical and safety needs of people
Relationships	Use the supportive skills of 'understanding', 'warmth' and 'sincerity' in order to build appropriate caring relationships
Understanding a service user	Learning about others is a key way to show that you value them. Formal techniques for understanding a service user's life history include: life story work with children and adults; life review and reminiscence work with older people
Respect for differences	Never 'treat everybody the same' – this is not equal opportunity. Alter your verbal and non-verbal behaviour to show respect for each different service user
Maintaining personal dignity	Giving physical care such as washing, dressing, feeding and cleaning should focus on making the service user feel that he or she is respected. Feeding someone should not be just about putting food in his or her mouth, it should also meet emotional and social needs
Providing choice	Always offer choices – when service users cannot do things for themselves they can still be offered a choice of how they would like you to do things for them. How would a service user like to be fed? When would he or she like to eat?
Encouraging independence	A sense of self grows out of the choices and decisions that we make. Learning to travel, learning independent living skills, learning to operate a computer helps to create a sense of self-esteem. Care workers often focus on helping people to be independent rather than being dependent on others
Confidentiality	Each work setting will have policies and procedures to follow in order to ensure confidentiality. Check out the procedures that you need to follow in relationship to a given care setting
Praise	Praise can be very effective in influencing children, but adults will interpret praise as patronising if it does not seem genuine. It is important to establish an understanding of another person's identity in order to be supportive and sincere when offering praise
Promoting identity	One theory of identity (Glynis Breakwell, 1986) suggests that identity involves self-esteem, a feeling of being special and a sense of own history or life journey. If you listen to service users and communicate the care values set out in this table, you will contribute to the development and maintenance of a service user's identity

FIGURE 2.44 *Some ideas for transmitting care values*

How you will be assessed

In order to achieve this unit you must produce a report of an interaction with at least one other person in a care setting. The person you are interacting with should be either a child, an older person, someone who is ill, or someone with specific needs such as learning or hearing difficulties.

If you want to work towards a higher grade your report will need to cover more than one interaction and might include communication with groups of people.

You will be given instructions regarding the structure of the report, but your report will need to include evidence for each of the following:

ASSESSMENT OBJECTIVE		DETAILS
A01	Types of Communication Used and Care Values	You must explain the types and range of communication skills you have used. Your discussion of communication must show that you are aware ofthe 'care value base'.
A02	Transmission of Care Values	You must explain how you have used and transmitted care values in the way you have communicated with other people.
A03	Barriers to Communication	You must explain possible barriers to communication that might have existed and explain how you overcame any barriers that you identified.
A04	Evaluation of your report	You must evaluate your interactions, explaining how well the interactions proceeded, and draw conclusions from the evidence of the interactions that you have collected.
		You must also discuss the features of a group, or individual situation that you would need to take into consideration when evaluating the success of your interaction(s).

Assessment preparation

A01 Communication skills

You need to produce a report that explains the types and range of communication skills that you have used in interactions with others. The Rating Scale below may help you to identify and then to evaluate some of the skills that you have used.

The rating scale

How good were different aspects of non-verbal communication?

How to rate behaviour

Place a circle around the number that fits your observation:

1 Very effective and appropriate use of a skill.
2 Some appropriate use of the skill.
3 The skill was not demonstrated or it does not seem appropriate to comment on the area.
4 Some slightly ineffective or inappropriate behaviour in relation to the area.
5 Very inappropriate or ineffective behaviour in relation to the area.

Eye contact	1	2	3	4	5
Facial expression	1	2	3	4	5
Angle of head	1	2	3	4	5
Tone of voice	1	2	3	4	5
Position of hands and arms	1	2	3	4	5
Gestures	1	2	3	4	5
Posture	1	2	3	4	5
Muscle tension	1	2	3	4	5
Touch	1	2	3	4	5
Proximity	1	2	3	4	5

How good were verbal communication and listening skills?

Appropriate language (speech community and register)	1	2	3	4	5
Encouraging others to talk	1	2	3	4	5
Reflecting back what others have said	1	2	3	4	5
Using appropriate questions	1	2	3	4	5
Use of prompts	1	2	3	4	5
Using silence as a listening skill	1	2	3	4	5
Clarity of conversation	1	2	3	4	5
Pace of conversation	1	2	3	4	5
Turn taking	1	2	3	4	5

(Use the same rating instructions as for non-verbal communication above.)

This grid may help you to analyse and provide examples of your communication skills. In order to achieve the highest marks your report will need to go beyond a description of skills and you will need to provide comparisons and contrasts between different interactions. You will also need to explain some of the theory that helps you to understand what is happening as you interact with others. Your analysis of interaction will also require an analysis of how effectively you transmitted care values (see below).

VALUE	WHAT EVIDENCE CAN YOU FIND THAT YOU TRANSMITTED THESE VALUES?
Respect for individual identity	
Valuing diversity and equality	
Preventing discrimination	
Maintaining confidentiality	
Respecting individual rights to make choices	
Empowering others rather than expecting them to be dependent	

A02 The transmission of care values

Thinking about your interactions, how far were you able to maintain care values? The grid above identifies some issues that you may wish to comment on in your report in order to evidence your awareness of the care value base.

In order to achieve the highest marks you should identify how your interaction has protected and maintained the self-esteem and identity of others. You will also need to discuss the importance of the care value base in relation to other care settings and not just in terms of your own analysis of interaction.

A03 Barriers

You must produce a report that explains possible barriers to communication within your interactions and how you overcame any barriers that you identified. The grid overleaf provides a starting point that might help you to identify barriers and analyse your interaction.

The barriers to communication grid

Rating scale:

1 Good – there are no barriers.
2 Quite good – few barriers.
3 Not possible to decide or not applicable.
4 Poor – barriers identified.
5 Very poor – major barriers to communication.

BARRIERS					
In the environment					
Lighting	1	2	3	4	5
Noise levels	1	2	3	4	5
Opportunity to communicate	1	2	3	4	5
Language differences					
Appropriate use of language:(terminology and level of formality)	1	2	3	4	5
Carer's skills with different languages	1	2	3	4	5
Carer's skills with non-verbal communication	1	2	3	4	5
Availability of translators or interpreters	1	2	3	4	5
Assumptions and/or stereotypes	1	2	3	4	5
Emotional barriers					
Stress levels and tiredness	1	2	3	4	5
Carer stressed by the emotional needs of others	1	2	3	4	5
Cultural barriers					
Inappropriate assumptions made about others	1	2	3	4	5
Labelling or stereotyping present	1	2	3	4	5
Interpersonal skills					
Degree of supportive non-verbal behaviour	1	2	3	4	5
Degree of supportive verbal behaviour	1	2	3	4	5
Appropriate use of listening skills	1	2	3	4	5
Appropriate use of assertive skills	1	2	3	4	5
Appropriate maintenance of confidentiality	1	2	3	4	5

Once you have identified potential barriers you need to research other people's perception of these issues. You might discuss your analysis of your interaction with a tutor or colleague. If possible it would be ideal to discuss your work with a member of staff in the care setting where your interactions took place.

The views of service users are vitally important when evaluating a service; and it might be possible for you to ask service users about language and environmental barriers. It will be important to plan any questioning work carefully and to check your plans with a tutor before undertaking any research.

In order to achieve the highest marks you will need to take the initiative in obtaining feedback from others. You should analyse why people have responded in the way that they have. You will need to gain information from different sources and to provide an analysis of the issues you have identified.

AO4 Evaluation of your report

You must provide an evaluation of how well your interactions went and draw conclusions from the evidence you were able to gather. To achieve the highest marks you will need to evidence independent thinking and initiative. You will need to be able to show that you have fully understood what took place during your interactions and what impact you had on others. You will need to be able to give reasons for any conclusions you make and these conclusions will need to be supported with evidence.

Unit test

1 Identify five examples of areas of the body that can send messages to other people as body language

2 Identify three verbal (including para-language) and three body language behaviours associated with assertive behaviour

3 If you talk to a four-year-old child, skilful verbal and non-verbal communication is likely to involve different skills compared with adult communication. Identify four verbal or non-verbal aspects of communication that you would adapt for creating a friendly conversation with young children.

4 If you plan to interview a care worker about values in care identify two issues that you would need to think about and plan before starting the interview.

5 List three ways in which you could help to 'promote a service user's identity.

6 Identify three communication skills that you believe would be important for a care worker to use in order to maintain a conversation about an older person's past life.

7 Explain how you could identify whether or not care values were being effectively transmitted within a conversation between an adult service user and a care worker.

8 Explain three different types of barriers to communication that you might identify within a day service for people with learning difficulty.

9 Why is it important to understand cultural differences in communication?

10a When service users receive a service they will have certain rights and responsibilities - where do these rights are responsibilities come from?

10b Why is it important that service users have rights?

The answers to these questions are provided on page 157 of this book.

References and further reading

Bales, R. (1970) *Personality and Interpersonal Behaviour* (New York: Holt, Rinehart & Winston)

Benson, J.F. (2001) *Working more creatively with Groups (2nd Ed.)* (London and New York: Routledge)

Breakwell, G. (1986) *Coping with Threatened Identities* (London and New York: Methuen)

Descombes, C. (2004) *The smoke and mirrors of empowerment: a critique of user-professional partnership* in *Communication, Relationships and Care*, Robb, M.,Barrett, S.,Komaromy, C., and Rogers, A. (eds) (i.e.) (London & New York OU & Routledge)

Maslow, A.H. (1970) *Motivation and Personality (2nd Edition)* (New York: Harper & Row)

Rogers, C.R. (1951) *Client Centred Therapy* (Boston: Houghton Mifflin)

Thompson, N. (1997) *Anti-discriminatory Practice* (Basingstoke and London: Macmillan)

Tuckman, B. (1965) *Development Sequence in Small Groups,* in Psychological Bulletin, Vol 63, No 6

Key resources

Johnson D. and Johnson F. (1997) *Joining together: group theory and group skills (6th Ed.)*(Allyn & Bacon)

Pease, A. (1997) *Body Language* (London: Sheldon Press)

Thompson N (1996) *People skills* (Basingstoke and London: Macmillan)

Thompson N. (2001) *Anti-Discriminatory Practice (2nd Ed.)* (Basingstoke and London: Macmillan)

At a more advanced level:

Hargie, O. (ed.) (1997) *The Handbook of Communication Skills (2nd Ed.)* (London and New York: Routledge)

Relevant websites

Please see www.heinemann.co.uk/hotlinks (express code 3718s) for links to the following websites, which may provide a source of updated information:

* Commission for Racial Equality
* Equal Opportunities Commission
* General Social Care Council
* The Nursing and Midwifery Council

UNIT 3

Positive Care Environments

This unit contains the following sections:

3.1   Values and individual rights

3.2   Barriers to access

3.3   Creating a positive environment

3.4   How society promotes service users' rights

Introduction

This unit addresses the main issues involved in achieving and maintaining a positive care environment. It begins by exploring the importance of values and beliefs in creating a positive care environment. An explanation of the different barriers to access is given, and the nature and dangers associated with discrimination are explored in detail. The third section considers the ways in which institutional policies, practices and culture can both hinder and promote service users' rights. Finally, the role of law in promoting service users' rights and the mechanisms that exist to enable service users to challenge unfair or discriminatory actions are examined. A discussion of current law and policy in relation to service user rights is also included.

How you will be assessed

This unit is internally assessed. You must produce a written report.

3.1 Values and individual rights

The nature of values and ethics

Positive care environments make an enormous difference to the quality of life of both the service users and the staff. It takes a lot of work to create and maintain a good care setting but the effort makes it a much more rewarding place to work. Consider the example below.

> ### SCENARIO
>
> **The Mansion**
>
> Staff spend the majority of time in face-to-face contact with the residents. Meal times are flexible and there is a choice of menus to ensure people's dietary and religious food needs are followed. The furniture is up to date and clean. Residents have activities arranged to suit their preferences and interests. The television is only put on when the residents request to watch it. There are often trips out to places of interest. A hairdresser and beautician visit every week. The manager speaks to the residents every day to check how they are feeling. Records are filled in three times per day with action points, which are ticked off when they have been completed. The staff get on well with each other and are keen to go on training courses to update their skills and knowledge. People enjoy their life in the Mansion.
>
> How should carers behave? Make a list of at least five values that might guide the staff in 'The Mansion'.

Today, a great deal of care is provided in people's own homes, but wherever care is provided it is important to understand that positive care environments do not just happen: they have to be created and require ongoing maintenance. This demands key skills of self-awareness and a commitment to the rights of others. Care environments reflect the **values** held by society in general, as well as the aims and goals of the organisation. The personal values of the manager and care workers also are very important in setting the atmosphere of the care environment.

Values involve a judgement that is made about the worth or importance of a particular action, attitude, behaviour, person or situation. These judgements are made on the basis of unconscious and conscious views that we hold. Some views may reflect our upbringing and the values we have learned from our parents. Other values may be shaped by public attitudes as expressed in the media. In health and social care environments, values relate to the judgements made about the moral worth and acceptable standards of behaviour in other people. Values have a fundamental effect on how a care environment is run. The values held by society and individuals change over time. In some cases the change is radical.

> ### ✱ DID YOU KNOW?
>
> One hundred years ago values and attitudes towards people with psychiatric illness were very negative. People with a mental illness were viewed as dangerous and therefore the care environments created were like massive hospitals, built in remote rural areas separated from the rest of society.

Even just 80 years ago a homeless, single mother could be deemed to be 'mentally defective' for having a child. This was because of a belief that all children should be born within marriage. Some single mothers were held in hospitals for the remainder of their lives.

So, although values may be held on an individual basis, general social values and attitudes also influence the type of care environments that are created.

> ### Key concept
>
> *Values:* Values are beliefs that identify 'something that is valued' or 'valuable' in a situation. Beliefs and values can influence what people do and the choices and decisions that they make.

Because health and social care workers take on a paid professional role they have a high level of responsibility towards service users. There must be

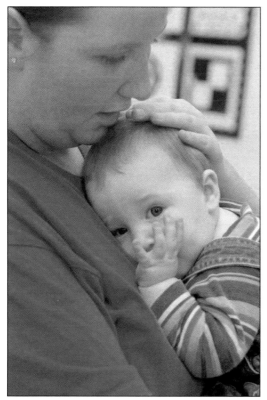

FIGURE 3.1 *Professional carers have a duty to act for the benefit of service users*

a bond of trust between a professional carer and a service user; this principle is stated in the GSCC code of practice (see Unit 2). Workers also have a duty to act for the benefit of service users. These responsibilities and duties are recognised in law and as a result the courts view abuse of a service user by a professional worker very seriously.

Within health and social care there are different approaches to the definition of values. Biestek (1961) compiled a list, which includes those shown in Figure 3.2.

Shardlow (1998) describes understanding values and ethics in social care as 'picking up a live, large and very wet fish out of a running stream. Even if you are lucky enough to grab a fish, the chances are, that just when you think you have caught it, the fish will vigorously slip out of your hands and jump back in the stream' (1998: 23). In this extract, he is referring to the different views and opinions in the areas of values and ethics. Often workers in this field might focus on practical tasks and not think more deeply about why they are working in a particular way.

Vulnerability

Values are very important because service users are vulnerable. Many service users are at high risk of experiencing harm. This may be from others in the form of abuse, or it may be that their health is more at risk because of the poor conditions they live in. People can also be vulnerable where they

DEFINITION OF VALUES	
Individualisation	This means that what is done with a service user and how is made to fit his or her individual needs and wishes. One size does not fit all situations and the need for an individual approach is essential
The purposeful expression of feelings	This means that for people to have a good quality of life they need to be able to express their thoughts and feelings and for these to be understood
Emotional acceptance	People need to feel that they belong and are accepted by others
A non-judgmental attitude	This refers to people's need to be understood and their views and feelings not being condemned
Self-determination	People need to feel they have choices and some control over their own lives
Confidentiality	When someone talks about private or sensitive information he or she needs to know that it is safe to do so

FIGURE 3.2 *Biestek's definition of values (1961)*

are ignored and have few services or people to support them. This is often referred to as being vulnerable. Many service users experience high levels of stress when care services are needed. They might be in pain or experiencing **marginalisation** because of their age, race, sexuality or gender; this will also affect their sense of well-being and ability to deal with the particular problems they may be facing.

The rights of an individual cannot be upheld where there is no commitment to a shared set of values. Values must not only be reflected in the policies and procedures of the organisation but also used by individuals on a daily and ongoing basis. To fully understand the fundamental importance of values you need self-awareness of your own beliefs and how you react to different

situations. If you are honest and open about your own beliefs and prejudices you can imagine the effect your values may have in a health and social care environment.

Having identified your values, think about how they compare with the values described below. In order to work effectively with vulnerable people it is centrally important that you value and work within the principles of:

* confidentiality
* effective communication
* anti-discriminatory practice
* **empowerment**
* respect for individual choice, identity, culture and beliefs

Together with the service user rights explained in Unit 2, these principles can be seen as forming a

Think it over...

How would you feel about carrying out the activities listed below?

1. Visiting someone who has admitted abusing a child.

2. Providing a care service for someone who has an alcohol addiction.

3. Telling a child they cannot return home.

4. Working with a teenager who tells you they don't want to know, as you will just let them down like everyone else.

5. Working with an asylum seeker who was actively involved in past war crimes.

6. Advising a pregnant teenager.

7. Working with a home owner who wishes to evict an older person because the local authority will not pay the home owner above a certain limit.

Give each activity a score ranging from 1–10 (where 1 equates to feeling confident to and 10 equates to feeling very uncomfortable).

Think about why you have given each score and list the main reason behind each of your answers.

Key concept

Care values/value base: Occupational standards and the GSCC code of practice identify a framework of values and moral rights of service users that can be referred to as care values or a value base for care.

value base for care work.

The role of values in positive care

Equality does not happen automatically. Indeed, the source of the many barriers that prevent equality being achieved can be traced back to the values that are held by individuals and **groups**, both consciously and unconsciously. These values are translated into attitudes systems and institutions that make it easier for some groups and individuals to access services, goods and opportunities than others.

The key to developing a positive care environment is to acknowledge how crucial values are (see Figure 3.3).

Values affect behaviour	In health and social care, workers have particular relationships of trust and responsibilities for ethical behaviour towards service users
Vulnerability of many services users and carers	Many service users and carers come from vulnerable groups whose needs have been ignored or pushed to the edges of society. The absence of status and power has a major impact on the life chances and well-being of such groups and individuals
The UK consists of many different cultures and groups. Difference is often seen as a threat	In biology, richness and diversity of plant and animal life is seen as a good thing and a sign of health. However, in terms of human society the same value is not always placed on diversity
Self-awareness	Recognising your own values and ways in which you judge the worth of a person or group is essential
Understanding of inequalities in society	You need to be aware of the ways (past and present) that society has failed to treat everyone fairly
Experience of discrimination	Discrimination will be a common experience for many people in need of health or social care services
Anti-discriminatory practices	Good practice in care work will recognise and challenge inequality through anti-discriminatory working
Policies and procedures	Policies and procedures are important in setting standards of behaviour and protecting service users rights, but in themselves they are not sufficient to guarantee that good quality care is maintained at all times
Actively promote equality in social and health care	Equality in social and health care is a meaningless term unless actively promoted at an individual and organisational level

FIGURE 3.3 *The importance of values in developing a positive care environment*

Think it over...

Consider the list below. Which are the most important qualities / values to you personally? Give a maximum of 5 points to the most important area and 1 to the least:

* honesty
* kindness
* efficiency
* support
* respect.
* fairness
* understanding
* being well organised
* authority

What are the most important qualities in a care environment? Are they any different to your own views and, if so, why?

Confidentiality

In situations of stress or need, personal information often needs to be shared. In order to feel comfortable about discussing private concerns, a person needs to feel that there is an emotional climate of safety in which to do so. Information is therefore given in trust to the care worker. A key principle in positive care environments requires that permission is needed from a service user before such information can be shared. It is essential that a service user is confident that the worker can be trusted. Information can also be seen as the property of a person. Breaking confidentiality can cause considerable damage to people whose rights have been infringed.

For example, an older female resident tells a care worker that she was not married when she gave birth to her children. The next day a woman in the next chair leans across and says: 'I hear you had your children when you weren't married'. The care worker has clearly broken the confidence without a good reason and the person whose confidence has been broken will be upset – at the very least – by this loss of trust.

Boundaries to confidentiality

The British Association of Social Workers (BASW) states that confidentiality is, in essence, concerned with faith and trust. The BASW acknowledges a direct relationship between the principle of confidentiality and respect for people. However, confidentiality cannot be seen as an absolute right and might at times conflict with the equally valid rights of others to protection.

SCENARIO

Within boundaries

Ross is a child, aged 6 years, and he tells his teacher that his stepfather has hit him with a belt. He then tells the teacher not to say anything to anyone else, but shows his teacher his bruises. There is a clear duty to protect Ross from further harm and the teacher must break Ross's wish for the information not to go any further. However, suppose that Ross is aged 74 years and tells his care worker that his son has hit him; but he also says that he does not want any action taken. The situation may not be as straightforward, as an adult does have rights to choose what he or she wishes to do.

So there are many difficult areas around the limits of confidentiality, and, at times, it is not easy to balance the right to confidentiality with the right of a vulnerable individual to be protected from harm.

Service users have a right to confidentiality but a responsibility in relation to the rights of others. Confidentiality often has to be kept within boundaries or broken where the rights of others have to balance with the service user's rights. Keeping confidentiality within boundaries occurs

when a carer tells his or her manager something that was learned in confidence. The information is not made public so it is still partly confidential. Examples of situations when information may need to be passed to managers are given in Figure 3.4.

A MANAGER NEEDS TO KNOW WHEN:	
SITUATION	**EXAMPLE**
There is a significant risk of harm to a service user	An older person in the community refuses to put her heating on in winter; she may be at risk of harm from the cold
When a service user might be abused	A person who explains that his son takes his money – he might be being financially abused
Where there is a significant risk of harm to others	A person who lives in a very dirty house with mice and rats may be creating a public health risk
Where there is a risk to the carer's health or well-being	A person is very aggressive, placing the carer at risk

FIGURE 3.4 *Examples of situations when information about service users may need to be passed by carers to their managers*

Confidentiality and the need to know

Good care practice involves asking service users if we can let other people know things. It would be wrong to pass on even the data of a person's birthday without asking him or her first. Some people might not want others to celebrate their birthday! Whatever we know about a service user should be kept private unless the person tells us that it is all right to share the information. The exception to this rule is that information can be passed on when others have a right and a need to know it.

Some examples of people who have a need to know about work with service users are:

✳ the manager – he or she may need to help make decisions, which affect the service user

* colleagues – these people may be working with the same person
* other professionals – these people may also be working with the service user and need to be kept up to date with information.

Giving information

When information is given to other professionals it should be passed on with the understanding that they will keep it confidential. It is important to check that other people are who they say they are. If you answer the phone and someone says they are a social worker or other professional, you should explain that you must phone them back before giving any information. By doing so you will be sure that you are talking to someone at a particular number or within a particular organisation. If you meet a person you don't know, you should ask for proof of identity before passing any information on.

Relatives will often say that they have a right to know about service users. Sometimes it is possible to ask relatives to discuss issues directly with the service user rather than giving information yourself.

Service users have a right to accurate recording of information about them.

FIGURE 3.5 *Sometimes it is possible to ask relatives to discuss issues directly*

The dangers of inaccurate information include:

* serious delays in meeting people's needs
* inability to follow up enquiries
* making mistakes with arrangements for people's care

SCENARIO

Confidentiality

Ethel is 88-years-old and receives home care. One day she says 'Keep this confidential, but I don't take my tablets (pain killers for arthritis and tablets for blood pressure) – I'm saving them so that I can take them all at once and finish my life if my pain gets worse.' Ethel manages to say this before you can tell her that some things can't be kept confidential.

Do you have to keep this information confidential? Ethel has a right to confidentiality, but she also has a responsibility not to involve other people in any harm she may do to herself. She doesn't have a right to involve you. The information about the tablets should be shared with managers and her GP, who can discuss the matter with Ethel.

Ethel's neighbour stops you as you are leaving one day. The neighbour asks 'How is Ethel, is she taking her tablets?'

Can you tell the neighbour of your worries? Before giving any information to anyone, carers have to ask the question 'Does this person have a need to know?' A need to know is different from wanting to know. Ethel's neighbour might just be nosy, and it would be wrong to break the confidentiality without an important reason. If Ethel's GP knows that Ethel doesn't take her tablets, he or she may be able to save Ethel's health or even her life. But the neighbour should not be told.

* missing meetings or important arrangements

* not providing a professional service to people

* failing to organise services for others properly

* other professional workers not having the right information.

Many organisations use printed forms to help staff to ask important questions and check that they have taken accurate information. Service users' personal records are likely to be written on forms that use headings.

The need for confidentiality is more than a moral right; it is a right that is made **law** by the **Data Protection Act 1998**.

The law set out in the Data Protection Act 1998 has been incorporated into the regulations set out by the NCSC and the GSCC. For example, Standard 10 of the **Commission for Social Care Inspection's National Minimum Standards** for Care Homes for Younger Adults is set out in Figure 3.6.

All services now need to have policies and procedures on the confidentiality of recorded information.

Effective communication

Principle 2.2 of the GSCC code of practice identifies that care workers must communicate in an appropriate, open, accurate and straightforward way. In many care situations this will involve the need for active listening skills (see Unit 2). Very often it is the little things that care workers do that will create a sense of trust and confidence when working with service users. Compare the two situations below:

TWO DIFFERENT SCENARIOS	
Scenario A	'Good morning. I'm afraid I haven't got long, just got to change this dressing like I've done before – won't take a minute – OK. All done – bye'.
Scenario B	'Good morning. How did your son get on with that job that you were telling me about yesterday? I'm afraid I can't stay long, I just called in to change the dressing, but I do enjoy our conversations. I often think about the things you tell me. So how does the dressing feel; is it OK? I do hope things work out for your son. I'll see you again in three days time.'

In both situations the technical work – changing a dressing – gets done. But the communication work in scenario A is very limited and might feel mechanical to the service user, who is being processed as though an object. The care worker only discusses the need to change the dressing –

	STANDARD 10
10.1	Staff respect information given by service users in confidence, and handle information about service users in accordance with their home's written policies and procedures and the Data Protection Act 1998, and in the best interests of the service user
10.2	Service users and their families have access to their home's policy and procedures on confidentiality and on dealing with breaches of confidentiality, and staff explain and / or ensure service users understand the policy
10.3	Service users' individual records are accurate, secure and confidential
10.4	Staff know when information given them in confidence must be shared with their manager or others
10.5	Information given in confidence is not shared with families / friends against the service user's wishes
10.6	The home gives a statement on confidentiality to partner agencies, setting out the principles governing the sharing of information

FIGURE 3.6 *Standard 10 of the Commission for Social Care Inspection's National Minimum Standards for Care Homes for Younger Adults*

quickly. In scenario B, the carer becomes involved with the service user, using a range of skills that will help to develop a bond of trust.

Think it over...

Using the theory in Unit 2 can you identify the communication skills that the carer is using in scenario B?

Anti-discriminatory practice

Anti-discriminatory practice means being able to recognise and identify the different levels of discrimination and disadvantage described in Unit 2.

A first step to developing anti-discriminatory practice is to be aware of the inner world that you believe is important and valuable. The beliefs of a person may affect how he or she understands the actions of other people. Generalised or **stereotyped** views about particular groups of people or types of behaviour will be reflected in your speech, language, decisions and actions. In health and social care, this explains why it is so important for workers to be self-aware of the views and attitudes they hold.

FIGURE 3.7 *Stereotyped thinking can result in discriminatory behaviour*

Anti-discriminatory practice firstly requires an understanding and recognition of what discrimination looks like. Secondly, it requires a willingness to change views and actions that disadvantage others. In practice, this means not only thinking about what happens on a day-to-day basis, but also thinking ahead. This will ensure that the rights of service users are being thought about in any future plans. An example of this might be a female Jewish service user. Is her diet in line with her faith? Does she have the opportunity to practise her faith on a daily and weekly basis? Might there be particular newspapers or television channels she might like? Do the staff understand about Jewish religious festivals that are important, and that the Jewish weekly day of worship is on a different day to that of Christians?

Key concept

Non-discrimination: Not discriminating – not damaging other people by providing some people with a better quality of service than others. Not stereotyping or labelling people (see Unit 2). Avoidance of assumptions associated with negative beliefs about disability, age, sexuality, gender, ethnicity, religion and other social groups.

Anti-discrimination: As for non-discrimination above, but with the added principle that you actively identify and challenge discriminatory behaviour – in yourself or in others – or systems that result in discrimination, within your work setting.

The main aim of anti-discriminatory practice is to value difference and to recognise that such differences do not mean that someone is of lesser worth or value. Honest self-awareness and understanding of social prejudice is the key to a lifelong approach to anti-discriminatory practice.

Empowerment

Global economic functioning involves assumptions about consumer choice. Worldwide, consumer behaviour often focuses on individuality and the assertion of individuality in the purchase of goods. European society operates within a framework of individual human rights. Within the United Kingdom there is an assumption that individuals have the right to choose their own lifestyle and make their own decisions as to how they wish to live.

The concept of '**empowerment**' identifies an individual's right to make choices and be independent. Historically, children and any adults who needed health or care services were seen as needing to be dependent on their carers. If a person was vulnerable then he or she needed to be 'looked after' by somebody, who would make choices and decisions for them. The idea of empowerment challenges this idea of dependency. Empowerment requires health and care services to support vulnerable people to make their own choices. A simple slogan for empowerment might be 'it's my life'. Principle 3 of the GSCC code of practice for social care workers requires workers to 'promote the independence of service users while protecting them as far as possible from danger or harm'. The

principle of empowerment might be developed with different service user groups as shown in Figure 3.8.

Respect for individual choice, identity, culture and beliefs

Anti-discrimination and empowerment are not possible without respect for diversity, respect for individual dignity and privacy, and respect for the individual rights of service users. The first principle of the GSCC code of practice emphasises the importance of respect for service users. Without receiving respect from other people it is difficult to feel that you belong, and perhaps impossible to develop positive self-esteem. If you are to maintain a sense of self-esteem you will need to feel that other people respect you.

Think it over...

Imagine you go into a shop and you are ignored whilst people behind you in the queue are served before you. You will probably feel that you are not being respected, and that perhaps you are being discriminated against. How will this affect you?

Imagine that you are in a residential situation and the care staff have favourite people that they look after – but you're not one of them! Care staff ignore you; they prioritise other people's needs and you often can't get attention or help. How will this affect you?

USER	CONCEPT
Young children	Empowerment will stress the educational needs of young people – the need to develop **self-confidence** and **self-esteem**
People with health care needs	Empowerment will stress the person's involvement in the management of an illness, together with the right to make choices about the type and nature of treatment
People with a learning difficulty	Empowerment will stress supporting people to understand possible choices, and enabling people to make important choices
People with a physical disability	Empowerment will stress the importance of the person – the right to be independent and the right to self-esteem. A person should not be seen as a problem!
Older people	Empowerment will again stress the individual's right to maintain personal decision-making, make choices about care and maintain **self-concept** and self-esteem

FIGURE 3.8 *Developing the concept of empowerment with different user groups*

Respecting and valuing others is not just the first principle in the GSCC code; it is perhaps the most central value in any social situation.

Both situations might make you feel angry; both situations might make you want to complain. But you are much more vulnerable in the care situation – it will be much more difficult to walk away from this. A lack of respect may damage your self-esteem whenever this happens, but in a care situation the effects are likely to be amplified.

Policies and procedures

All care organisations will have written policies and procedures that need to be followed with respect to service users' rights. **National Minimum Standards (NMS)** for the different care services will require every organisation to have a documented complaints procedure and a policy on confidentiality. Services are inspected by the **Commission for Social Care Inspection (CSCI)** and this organisation will refer to National Minimum Standards as a basis for its report. Care organisations may have a range of other policy documents including a policy on **advocacy**. Advocacy is explained in Unit 2. Service users may need to work with an advocate in order to understand the choices available to them. Sometimes an advocate might need to make a case for the service user, when the service user cannot express his or her own wishes. Sometimes an empowering approach may not be possible without the services of an advocate.

Redress

Things can and do go wrong in health and social care. However, it is only in the last 30 years that the rights of service users and carers to challenge processes, events and policies have been developed. Redress means making good, or righting a wrong. It also has the idea of compensation and making good the balance within it. All local authorities must have a complaints procedure. This was required by the Local Authorities and Social Services Act 1970.

Further directions and regulations have also been issued by the DOH (Department of Health). The Children Act 1989 requires a complaints procedure for actions involving children and families, as does the NHS and Community Care Act 1990.

Many care environments are privately owned or are in the voluntary sector. The requirements of the Care Standards Act 2000 have to be followed. Home Care agencies also now have to be registered. There are minimum standards for different areas as well as more detailed regulations. When the local authority buys a service from an agency the local authority is also responsible for that service as the agency is delivering services that in the past the local authority would have provided. Therefore, organisations like residential and nursing homes are required to have their own complaints procedures but have to follow additional regulations as well. For example, if a concern is raised about injury, ill treatment or neglect to a person in a care environment, the home must let the local Commission for Social Care Inspection know (under Regulation 37 of the Care Homes Regulations). The home must also advise the local authority social services under current Adult Protection Procedures.

Summary of Section 3.1

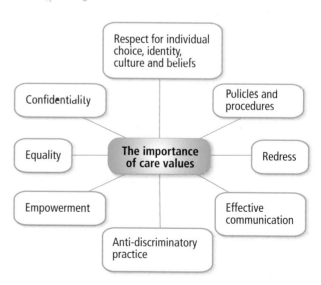

You are talking to an adult man who has a degenerative illness that will cause increasing difficulty in coping with daily life. The man says, 'One of the main problems is the way other people see me. People say things like, "Oh, I am so sorry for you". And you know they're trying to help – but it doesn't help. At the moment I can cope with them and make them see me for who I am. I talk about all my achievements, so they start to think about me, instead of seeing me as a diseased body. But I'm so afraid that as I get weaker I won't have the energy to challenge them. They will just see me as a problem and I will start to see myself as a problem. I could lose the will to live.'

Using concepts can you identify?

1 Examples of care values that are missing in the way that people treat this man.

2 What basic communication approaches might be needed in order to maintain this person's self-esteem.

Go further – can you analyse issues using theory?

What systems of support and redress should exist within a care service in order to help this person maintain personal choice and dignity and not see himself as a problem?

Go further – can you evaluate using a range of theory?

How might care workers use the value base of care in order to avoid assumptions and to communicate a feeling of being valued to this man?

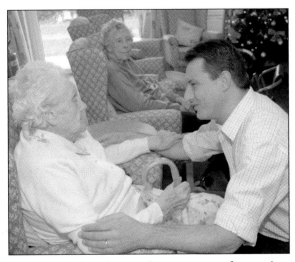

FIGURE 3.9 *Listening to the concerns of a service user*

3.2 Barriers to access

Some of the barriers that service users may encounter are identified below.

Language/communication barriers

People who do not speak English as a first language (or Welsh in Wales) may need the services of an interpreter or translator (see Unit 2) to be able to find out about, and be appropriately assessed for services. People who communicate using British Sign Language may also need an interpreter in order to access services. Having to access a different language system is an obvious barrier, but even within the same language, terminology can create a barrier to understanding. Words like 'assessment' may lead to misunderstandings about care services, causing people to ask 'Do I have to pass a test then?' The degree of formality in the communication (see Unit 2) may also have an impact on whether service users feel welcome and valued. The issues listed in Figure 3.11 provide a summary of communication barriers.

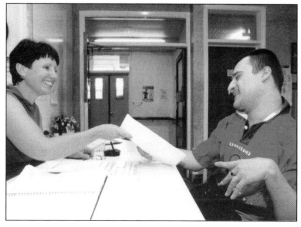

FIGURE 3.10 *Reception areas should be designed to assist communication*

Organisational barriers

Sometimes organisations have systems in place that unintentionally excludes certain people. Many organisations expect staff to work long hours and to put family commitments second to work commitments. Promotion to a senior post may depend on always being available to do overtime. But such an organisational culture

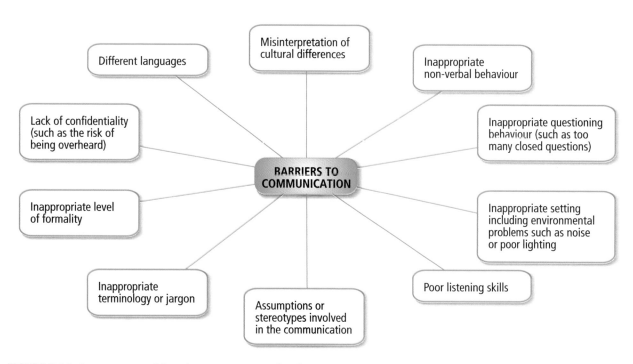

FIGURE 3.11 *A summary of barriers to communication*

might create a barrier for people (usually women) who have child-care responsibilities.

In many organisations 'invisible' organisational barriers exist. For example, less than 3 per cent of judges are black or Asian. Whilst there may well be bias in the selection process, there are underlying factors that place many black people at a disadvantage. For example, there is clear evidence of inequality in educational opportunities for minority communities. In addition, there are sustained high costs associated with entering the legal profession that some families may not be able to meet.

Many women complain of the 'glass ceiling' when it comes to career progression. They experience very real limits to their career, yet there are no obvious policies that are responsible for the lack of women in senior roles. In 2004 the Equal Opportunities Commission (EOC) published a paper entitled 'Sex and power: who runs Britain?' In a press release Julie Mellor, the chair of the Equal Opportunities Commission, stated: 'Almost 30 years since the Sex Discrimination Act was passed, women are still massively under-represented in positions of influence in Britain. No one can argue anymore that it's just a matter of time until more women make it to the top . . . Women are still often prevented from getting to the top because they take on more caring responsibilities than men. Until every organisation accepts that they can't capitalise on the talent available without taking account of people's caring roles, the profile of the people who run Britain will not change.'

Emotional barriers

Many people do not perceive themselves as carers or as in need of services. In practice, the level of services people request is relatively modest. One of the emotional barriers to accessing services is that people do not like to see themselves as needy or dependent.

The name of some benefits also sets up emotional barriers. For example, Attendance Allowance suggests that a claimant has to have someone attending to them. Likewise, until recently one benefit was called Invalid Care Allowance. Many people would not see themselves as an invalid – a term that can imply dependence and helplessness. Many older people do not feel they are 'elderly', associating that term with very frail people who have multiple impairments

Stereotypes exist around characteristics that particular **groups** are believed to show. These can impact and create barriers, sometimes with devastating consequences.

> ## ✴ DID YOU KNOW?
>
> The fastest growing numbers of people with HIV are heterosexual. This is, in part, a reflection of the emotional barrier created by the false belief that only gay people have HIV.

Geographical and physical barriers

Rural areas are often very poorly served with services. This is often made worse by the lack of reliable and affordable transport. Often facilities may be many miles away and there are often difficulties in recruiting home care staff for rural locations. Public transport – including bus services, for example – is often limited.

Physical and geographical barriers were deliberately created in the past. People with

FIGURE 3.12 *A workhouse/psychiatric hospital*

disabilities and people with mental or physical health problems were segregated from mainstream society. Many large hospitals were built in remote locations. People who had no income were treated harshly since being poor was seen as a sign of laziness. The workhouse existed from the mid-Victorian times and the last workhouses only ceased to function as late as the 1940s. Some older people have memories of the workhouse and still associate residential care with 'the workhouse'. This can create real barriers to accessing care services.

Physical barriers also create problems in terms of accessing facilities. It is only in recent years that architects have thought about disabled access. There are still many stations without lifts and only a small proportion of buses that are suitable for wheelchair users. The Disability Discrimination Act has new regulations that came into force in 2004, which require that reasonable adjustments are made to meet the needs (including physical access) of anyone with a disability. Many cinemas and theatres limit the number of people in wheelchairs who can attend at any one time. Many shops have steps to the interior and often changing-cubicles are not large enough to allow wheelchairs inside. The processes that a person with a disability has to go through in order to access everyday facilities are significantly different to the majority of the population. For many, it proves to be too stressful and reinforces disabled people's sense of difference and isolation.

Discrimination

Discrimination and prejudice result in many vulnerable groups and individuals experiencing barriers to accessing the services and support they need. These barriers can be traced back to the attitudes, values and beliefs that affect behaviour and the way society is organised. Good practice in health and social care is based on recognising discrimination and how it creates barriers to services.

Some beliefs are based on assumptions that one group is superior to another group. One example of this was the apartheid scheme in South Africa.

> ✳ **DID YOU KNOW?**
>
> South African society was based on the assumption that white people were superior. There where multiple barriers that prevented black people having equal chances, including physical and geographical barriers. Black people were not allowed on the same transport as white people and had to live in separate areas that had been designated by white people. Society was clearly separated to allow white people access to jobs, education, and housing, and to keep black people separate.

The direct discrimination experienced by people in South Africa has been outlawed in the UK by Acts of Parliament, such as the Race Relations Act 1976 (amended 2000). However, there are still major barriers for people who are in a minority. These barriers are often hidden and disguised as something else, making challenge very difficult. This type of indirect discrimination can be as intensely damaging as direct discrimination. This section looks at some of the barriers that are used on an everyday basis to reinforce prejudicial and discriminatory practices.

Types of discrimination

Anti-discriminatory law in the UK recognises different categories of discrimination:

✳ direct discrimination

✳ indirect discrimination

✳ victimisation

✳ harassment.

Some examples of discriminatory practices are shown in Figure 3.13.

Direct discrimination

This means treating one person or group less favourably than another on the grounds of race, disability, sexual orientation or gender.

Indirect discrimination

This refers to an organisation applying a general condition or requirement that is not justifiable in terms of the job requirements.

TYPE OF DISCRIMINATION	EXAMPLE
Direct discrimination	Phoning up for details of an advertised job. Any women who phone are told that the position has been filled, whereas an application form is sent out to any men who phone.
Indirect discrimination	A historical example of this was police recruitment policies that required a certain height for applicants. This had the effect of disadvantaging some ethnic groups. Being tall was not necessary for police work.
Victimisation	Not speaking to a colleague or sharing information with him or her because he or she had previously complained about discrimination.
Harassment	Anonymously sending rude or upsetting emails in order to make the victim feel threatened.

FIGURE 3.13 *Some examples of discriminatory practices*

Victimisation

This can occur where an individual has experienced difficulties and challenges the practices of an organisation, yet there is no protection for that employee. Employers may not make the working life of that employee more difficult and any such action is seen as unlawful discrimination. An employment tribunal can award damages if this takes place towards an employee involved in proceedings brought under anti-discriminatory legislation.

Harassment

This is defined as unwanted conduct that violates people's dignity or creates a hostile, degrading, humiliating or offensive environment. This has been introduced with recent changes brought in

under the Employment Equality (Sexual Orientation) Regulations and the Employment Equality (religion and belief) Regulations 2003. In October 2004 the outlawing of discrimination and harassment of people with a disability came into force and extended the requirements of the 1995 Disability Discrimination Act.

Areas of protection under anti-discriminatory legislation

There are four main areas that discrimination legislation covers, regarding access to and opportunities within:

* education
* housing
* employment
* goods and services.

How do you recognise discrimination?

Often people are not honest or open about admitting that they hold views that disadvantage and diminish particular groups or individuals in society. Some of the ways in which you can assess whether unfair values or attitudes are being put into practice are shown in Figure 3.14. Although some of these areas do overlap they do provide an insight and a way of beginning to assess whether discrimination exists.

Effects of discrimination

Negative and judgmental attitudes have significant effects on both the person and group that express it and the group or individual on the receiving end. For those who express their views and prejudices, it often gives a false sense of superiority and power. Ultimately, labels and judgmental views are about avoiding change and favouring one individual or group over another. One group might be favoured in terms of power or access to resources.

For the person or group on the receiving end of discrimination there are several possible

Subjective criteria used	This is when unfair decisions are made about the type of qualities or attributes needed for a particular job. One example would be not employing women as they are viewed as less reliable employees – in the event that they should have children
Ignorance	Ignorance is no defence in law and the fact that someone may argue that they did not realise an action or policy was discriminatory does not lessen the damage it may cause to the person at the receiving end
Pressure from others	Groups often develop shared 'cultures'. In other words, an agreed (although often unsaid) agreement about who is acceptable and who is not. An example might be arranging meetings at a time that undesirable group members will not be able to attend
Traditional criteria	A strongly held belief that has always been accepted and seems like good 'common-sense' may have its roots in a blinkered view of what roles and jobs people should do. For example, the idea that women make good carers and that men do not is based more on a world view than any objective evidence to support this
Unintentional discrimination	This refers to individuals and groups who are committed to equality, but have not evaluated their views or practices and realised that some practices have the effect of excluding certain groups. For example, arranging to meet in a pub, since setting that serves alcohol might be offensive to certain religious groups such as Muslims and Methodist Christians
Stereotyping	This refers to rigid and simplistic assumptions made about individuals or groups, the outcome of which is that they are viewed and treated less favourably than the group or individual making that judgement. An example of this is a generalised assumption that anyone with mental health concerns is a danger to others
Unsatisfactory procedures	For example, not making issues clear, assuming that everyone thinks the same way and knows the same information that you do
Personal prejudice	This means an opinion formed beforehand that is based on inadequate facts. Give-away phrases often used include 'those people' or 'people like that', which often indicate prejudice

FIGURE 3.14 *Recognising discrimination*

negative outcomes. This can be understood as a process that repeats itself as a circle or negative downward spiral.

A cycle of oppression

When a person experiences discrimination there will always be an effect, even if at a subconscious level. Over time, an individual or group may feel threatened or devalued. If this concern is not recognised or addressed by the organisation a negative spiral may result. The person on the receiving end will experience anger or **depression**. Either anger or depression can be interpreted as 'over-sensitivity' or 'proof that this person is aggressive or difficult' by the people responsible for the discrimination.

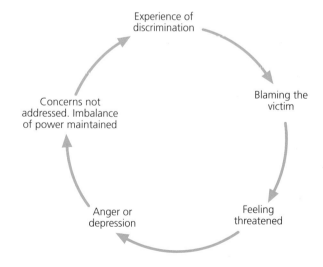

FIGURE 3.15 *The circular effects of discrimination*

For many people, the spiral of discrimination will be a daily experience. Individuals may feel that it is impossible to fight this process. This cycle also shows the injustice of expecting the victim of the discrimination to be the one to fight it (see Figure 3.15). It is the responsibility of everyone in social care to identify and challenge discrimination.

Approaches to equal opportunities

Three approaches to equal opportunities are shown in Figure 3.16.

Anti-discriminatory legislation

Some of the main Acts of Parliament covering discrimination are:

* The Race Relations Act 1976/2000

* Sex Discrimination Act 1975 and 1986

* Equal Pay Act 1970/1983

* Disability Discrimination Act 1995 and Employment Directive Regulations Article 13

* Employment Equality (Sexual Orientation) Regulations 2003

* Employment Equality (Culture and Belief) Regulations 2003.

However, there are many areas where there is no **law** about discrimination. For example, there are no laws about less favourable treatment on the grounds of size or class. Law on age discrimination is due in 2006

The law does provide a method of challenging discrimination, but, equally, some laws and practices are very discriminatory in themselves. For example, recent actions by the government regarding asylum seekers have been so harsh in proposing to leave people in total poverty, with no provision of money, that the courts have judged this to have broken the basic requirements of the Human Rights Act 1998.

Processes of discrimination – stereotyping and labelling

Stereotyping refers to generalised assumptions made about a particular group of people. The generalisations are usually negative and may identify a particular physical or social characteristic. These views are not usually flexible and are used as the basis for treating one group of people less favourably than another. Often these views are held very rigidly, even in the face of direct evidence that indicates their inaccuracy.

Stereotypes can lead to groups missing out on support and services that are really needed.

APPROACHES TO EQUAL OPPORTUNITIES	
Equal treatment	This is an inadequate approach that assumes that as long as there is no direct discrimination that will be enough. If there are barriers to access on the grounds of prejudice it is up to the disadvantaged group to 'assimilate' and adapt to the majority culture. This approach treats everyone as the same and does not recognise that there may be differences. This approach is not acceptable within the care value base.
Equal access	This approach focuses on removing barriers. All practices and procedures, therefore, need to be checked. Access to disadvantaged groups should be facilitated. One example is recruitment to the police force. The number of people applying from minority communities is very low. Previous poor experiences of policing may be one reason but the police are taking active steps to increase the number of minority police officers, to put right the imbalance and more fairly represent the community as a whole. This approach is the one that you are most likely to see in care organisations.
Equal share	This approach focuses on equality of outcome rather than any particular procedure for achieving this. It is the responsibility of the State to put right any unfairness and to redistribute resources more fairly. Some equal opportunities authors argue that this more radical approach would be best.

FIGURE 3.16 *Creating equal opportunities*

Key concept

Stereotyping: Stereotyping is a fixed way of thinking that involves generalisations and expectations about an issue or a group of people.

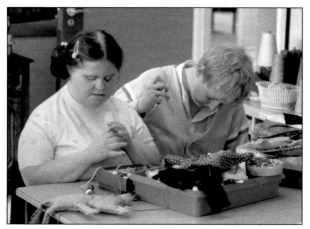

FIGURE 3.17 *Health Warning: Do not make assumptions about our lifestyles or needs. You will damage our health*

When labels are attached to people they carry with them strong meanings and views. This is nown as attaching a stigma.

The stigma of telling an employer or school that you are HIV positive is one example. Another example would be of letting it be known that you are gay or lesbian. Many people have experienced other people becoming more distant and being treated as though they do not belong. At worst there may be obvious unfair treatment. Attaching labels to people either as

Key concept

Discrimination: Katz (1978) defined discrimination as prejudice plus power.

sense of their worth or value and creates a false sense of 'them and us'.

Katz's definition firstly draws attention to the fundamental influence of personal values but indicates that where this is combined with personal, institutional or organisational power, discrimination moves beyond the realms of personal views. Thompson (1997) identifies how discrimination can work at the personal, community or structural levels (see Unit 2). Senior people in an organisation have the power to prevent prejudice resulting in discrimination.

Consequences of discrimination

Behaviour and attitudes that exclude and reduce the worth of others do have serious consequences, both for the person expressing the attitude and for those on the receiving end. On a personal level, being constantly seen as inferior can be internalised, creating depression and low **self-esteem**, and it can cause withdrawal from the people or institutions who treat individuals in this way. Anger is another response to rejection. Often when this anger is expressed it may be that other people see this as a sign that the victim is 'oversensitive'; this feeds into the cycle of oppression (see Figure 3.15). Both the person who is discriminating and the person on the receiving end may, therefore, show the effects of discrimination in the form of an emotional reaction.

Discrimination can result in a failure to provide services that are suitable to minority groups. Discrimination also results in failing to make any effort to reach out to minority groups with services, employment, education or housing.

Marginalisation and exclusion

Marginalisation describes the process whereby individuals or groups are pushed to the fringes or edges of mainstream activity. Where minority groups are excluded from the opportunities available to the majority of people in the UK the term 'social exclusion' is used. The effect of marginalisation is to disadvantage many people and to sideline any social, economic or moral concern for their well-being. The government in 2005 set up the Social Exclusion Unit to monitor progress on tackling poverty and disadvantage.

Disempowerment

Disempowerment refers to the loss of life chances and power. Many people are disempowered by the way society views them as a group and the absence of recognition or resources to enable them to improve their lives. Many parents of children with a disability describe their experience with social services as disempowering, or as 'being a fight'. Morally, it seems right that children or adults with a disability should have automatic entitlement to the services that they need. But in reality the experience is very different. The amount of help and services available are limited since local authorities have strict budgets that they have to work within. The reason for this is a political decision made by successive governments that the cost of health and social care must be limited and focused on those in most need.

Because people may be disempowered by the high cost of services they need, the government introduced a system called Fairer Charging in 2003. This means that the full details of each service user's financial situation is recorded. Adults who have savings over £20,000 are assessed as paying full cost for services. Many Social Services departments have a top limit to the contribution from the service user. Currently this may be around £125 per week.

The real cost of care may be around £400 per week in residential care and around £550 per week for nursing care, although prices do vary throughout the country. Many service users and their families feel financially disempowered by the cost of services. Scotland has made nursing and residential care services free, but in England the government felt that such a scheme would be too expensive.

Summary of Section 3.2

This section has looked at some of the different types of barriers that can prevent people from having the health and social care services and support they need; the key messages include:

Davinder is an older woman who came to the UK 30 years ago. Davinder is disorientated and cannot communicate easily in English. She also has mobility problems and diabetes. Her close family have recently emigrated, and she is living temporarily at her local temple. The temple guardians have approached Social Services for help, as they can only support Davinder on a temporary basis. The message that Davinder receives is that there are no services available to her.

Using concepts can you identify?

1 Reasons why Davinder may be vulnerable that are associated with the bases of discrimination.

2 Potential barriers to services that may exist for Davinder.

Go further – can you analyse issues using theory?

What might be the consequences for Davinder if she believes that she is marginalised and excluded from the quality of life most people expect?

Go further – can you evaluate using a range of theory?

What kind of support and help might Davinder need in order to feel safe, supported and of value to other people?

3.3 Creating a positive environment

There are two key elements to creating a positive **environment**. The first is the responsibility of individual care practitioners to challenge behaviour and practices that discriminate against service users; the second is to understand the role of the organisation. The size, structure and practices of an organisation will have a major effect on the quality of the care environment.

The individual practitioner

Why do people have discriminatory beliefs? One explanation is that they are socialised into thinking this way. **Socialisation** in its boldest sense means to become social.

> ### Key concept
>
> *Socialisation:* Giddens (1997) explains that 'socialisation is the process whereby the helpless infant gradually becomes a self-aware, knowledgeable person, skilled in the ways of the culture into which he or she is born' (1997:25). Socialisation involves learning the social norms of your culture.

Theories put forward by both Vygotsky (1869–1934) and Bandura (b.1925) argue that people learn by copying others. This happens from a young age. When a child learns effective ways of behaving this encourages **self-confidence**. However, many people do not have such positive experiences and learn to see themselves as ineffective at changing or controlling what happens to them. This will be carried forward into adult life and make a significant difference to how people approach the problems that they face.

A child's parents or carers will be the main people who influence early socialisation. They pass on what they see as right or good, as well as what is not valued. Prejudice and discriminatory attitudes are, therefore, communicated at a very early age. Ethnic minority parents, for example, may have to ensure their children develop a positive **self-image** by trying to protect them

from prejudiced views that other children have learned from their parents. Parents may have to act as a '**buffer**' to protect their children from discrimination and at the same time teach their children to be able to deal with prejudice.

The effect of experiencing constant negative responses has been described by Seligmann (1975) as 'learned helplessness'. When a child particularly experiences constant rejection or discrimination, he or she learns to withdraw and to give up trying. This can produce feelings of helplessness, which can further develop into anxiety and **depression**. These theories help to explain the devastating impact of prejudice on individuals and the lifelong consequences of prejudice.

> ### Key concept
>
> *Prejudice:* A prejudice is a 'pre' 'judgement' of an issue. The term is used to mean a negative judgmental attitude about an issue or about a **group** of people. Like **stereotypes**, prejudiced beliefs tend to be fixed rigid systems of thinking that are difficult to change.

Norms

A **norm** is a word describing the general standards of expected behaviour of a particular group or individual. Ideas about how people should behave vary over time. The generally held views of society are reflected in how institutions and systems are set up and run.

The importance of the care value base

When people work together they may develop a common group identity (explained in Unit 2) that involves shared values or norms. Tuckman (1965) argued that a group of people become a functioning group when they have been through the stage of 'norming'; this involves sharing beliefs and expectations about the purpose of the work of the group. Creating a positive care environment needs care workers to adopt the care value base (see Figure 3.18).

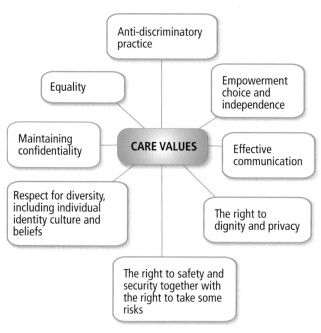

FIGURE 3.18 *Care values are important in creating a positive caring environment*

Consider the following statements made by two carers who work with different service users.

Early Years worker: 'I chose this job because I really enjoy working with young children. I know that I'm making a difference to their lives. I mean you can see the excitement in their faces when they are successful at an activity. And I think to myself that I'm helping them to develop as confident, successful people. Then that makes me feel that I'm valuable.'

Worker with older people: 'Yes, I know exactly what you mean. I get really interested in the life stories that some of the service users tell me. Just by listening to people, I think that I can make a difference to their quality of life and they value the work I do.'

Both workers look after different service user groups, but they work with similar values. Can you analyse how their experience relates to working within the value base? Can you see how the value base is associated with a general attitude towards people? Can you see how values are much more than just rules or procedures?

The terminology of the care value base provides a way of analysing the issues that care workers need to value. Most people develop their attitudes, **values** and beliefs by copying other people. To begin with we are socialised into beliefs. The main way in which care workers will begin to use the care value base will be by following the role models provided by senior care workers and managers. A truly positive care environment will be one in which care workers are treated with respect and valued by their employers. Care workers are likely to reflect this respect back to managers. The care value base then becomes a 'way of being', an attitude that affects every interchange between people whether they are managers, carers or service users. The GSCC combines the published code of practice for care workers with a code of practice for employers, and this emphasises that values are not just an issue for individual workers.

Aspects of care values – Empowerment

Many people's problems are rooted in the wider prejudices and disadvantages that exist in society. Historically, it was often assumed that individual people had problems as a result of their inability to cope. Radical social work argues that blaming service users for not coping was not only unfair but in fact 'blamed the victim' for his or her own misfortune.

Thompson (1991) explained the need to look at problems people face from a variety of different viewpoints. He argued that whilst it is important to look at the problems an individual is facing, it is also essential to understand the experience of different social groups. He argued that it is the interaction of individual and social factors that result in people's experiences of **marginalisation**, or being pushed to the edges of society. This theory opened the way to look at the bigger picture and to make it acceptable to point out where systems were causing injustice. Giving individuals and groups more power is referred to as **empowerment**, which includes harnessing awareness of unfairness to achieve social change. In recent years much more attention has been paid to disadvantaged groups such as ethnic minorities and older people.

Empowerment involves identifying areas of oppression and disadvantage then analysing biased policies and challenging these in order to achieve change. There is a need for any support and assistance given to individuals to be matched by a similar level of effort going into challenging institutions and society to change unfair views and practices.

✱ DID YOU KNOW?

Radical social work has its roots in a much older theory about society called Marxism. Marxism explained how the working people in society were made poor by the action of their employers (the ruling classes) in taking so much money for themselves. Radical (or empowering) social work has a much wider focus than money and looks at areas such as racism, sexism, sexual orientation, ageism and many others as areas of disadvantage that are created by the general actions of people in society as a whole.

However, although challenging unfairness and disadvantage may be seen as a noble and worthwhile cause, it is important to recognise that health and social care workers have control functions as well as having a responsibility to support people. For example, local authorities have clear legal duties to protect children from harm, following the requirements of the Children Act 1989. This may involve removing a child from home against a parent's wishes. Similarly, under the Mental Health Act 1983 a person with a mental disorder can be admitted by force to a psychiatric hospital if they are a danger to themselves or others. Balancing the need to control behaviour with the need to work in a supporting way can be very stressful for care workers. Law, policies, guidelines and procedures may be helpful in showing what good practice should be, but they do not provide all the answers for every situation.

Respect for individual choice

One of the main aims of the NHS and Community Care Act 1990 was to allow people to have choice over the services and care available to them. The purpose of this was to enable people to stay independent for as long as possible. The role of the social care worker was to provide clear and accurate information and to work together with people to identify their needs and the risks that threatened their independence. The law is also very clear in outlining the duties of local authorities to provide information.

There are three main acts that guide local authorities about providing information for adults. They are:

✱ The Chronically Sick and Disabled Persons Act 1970

✱ The Disabled Persons Act 1986

✱ The NHS and Community Care Act 1990.

The Children Act 1989 also makes requirements about providing information to children and families.

Choice and independence through Direct Payments

In recent years there has been a new way of encouraging choice and independence through the introduction of Direct Payments. Normally, once a social worker has assessed a person's needs the real cost of the care is worked out. Then the local authority might either provide the services themselves or buy in the services needed from a private or voluntary agency.

With Direct Payments, instead of the local authority buying the service, the money is given to the disabled person in order that he or she may purchase the services needed. Support is available for the disabled person to assist with the extra responsibilities of managing a direct payment. These include making tax and National Insurance payments. The Direct Payments scheme allows a person direct control over whom they employ and the hours they work. The current government strongly wants this scheme to be more widely used. The scheme started with the Direct Payments Act 1996 when only people between 18–65 years could apply. This was extended in 2000 to people over 65 years and also to parents with children under 16 years and carers. Since April 2003 all local authorities must have a Direct Payments scheme and must also assess anyone who asks to be part of the scheme.

The importance of identity

Identity means having sense of who you are. Feeling comfortable and happy with who you are is seen as a sign of good mental and physical health. For many years, how people felt about themselves was not seen as important in health and social care work, but in recent years the strong links between health and a secure sense of self have increasingly been recognised.

One example of this is that in the past many young black children were placed with white people who had no experience of any black communities. Many of these young people grew up to feel they did not belong in either white or black groups. Many people were found to have a very low opinion of themselves and often this reflected the views that black people were somehow less important than white people.

Thompson (2000) argues that identity is not a single and solid fact. A person's sense of self may change. Identity is not something that exists but is created by the way in which we interact with others. Thompson indicates that when these interactions with others feed back either negative or mixed messages this often results in people having a low opinion of their own worth and identity. Problems associated with identity can result in low **self-esteem** and this may be associated with poor relationships with other people. One crucial factor is the quality of the relationship of an individual with his or her parents or carers during the early years stage of life. Theorists such as Carl Rogers (1902–1987) argued that if a child did not receive love without conditions, his or her view of self could be severely affected. Mixed messages in childhood were seen to result in an inner uncertainty for the child about his or her own worth. These views would be carried through to adulthood. One

saying has it that there are three causes to mental ill health: low self-esteem, low self-esteem and low self-esteem.

A further factor affecting identity relates to what is seen as 'normal'. Society makes value judgements around difference. This is reflected in generally held views about worth and value. For example, older people are often seen as dependent burdens. Likewise, **stereotypes** around race, sexuality, religion, and gender all play a major part in establishing identity.

A key value in social work focuses around the worth of the individual. Anti-discriminatory practice is based around avoiding generalisations and treating people as if they were all the same. It is easy in towns and cities for individuals to lose their importance as individual human beings, and become lost in health and social care systems. Therefore, in health and social care it is vital to look at each person as an unique individual with his or her own beliefs, wishes and views. This is called working in a person-centred way and has the effect of supporting and strengthening a person's sense of self-worth and identity.

The importance of culture and beliefs

Culture refers to the traditions, beliefs, values and ideas that are inherited or passed on within a group of people, and the way in which these affect their roles, activities and actions. Culture is, therefore, a major factor in establishing the identity of an individual or group of people. Linked with the understanding of identity is also the idea of difference. For many people, difference automatically means that a culture or way of relating to the world is not as good as their own way. Difference can often be seen as threatening. Threatened groups may develop ideas of one group being superior to another.

Culture, therefore, has a major impact on how people experience and interpret what happens to them. Therefore, all health and social care workers need to be aware of and sensitive to culture and race. Anti-racist practice will need to acknowledge the reality of racism and the fundamental way this will affect groups and individuals.

Effective communication

Effective communication requires a number of attributes on the part of the social or health care worker. Key elements of effective communication are shown in Figure 3.19.

Effective communication depends on a mixture of actions, behaviour and attitudes. In turn, these are strongly connected to the underlying value base held by the individual.

Effective communication is also related to using straightforward language and avoiding jargon or complicated language that may not be understood. One example of this is when care workers talk about 'eligibility criteria'. This has little meaning to many but, in fact, relates to the conditions set down about who may receive a service. Given the diversity of the population in the UK, it is also essential to ensure that information is available in a variety of languages and formats. People with sight impairment may need a guide in Braille. People with learning difficulties also need to receive and understand information about the services that may affect their lives.

An essential skill in communication is the manner in which it is carried out. In highly emotional situations it is essential for care staff to understand that it may be difficult for the other person to fully take in what is being said.

Language is very powerful in conveying underlying attitudes. In the UK, discriminatory comments are often justified by stating 'it was only a joke', then blaming the victim as someone who 'can't take a joke'. Terminology can also act as a label; for example, describing a group of people as 'the elderly' reflects underlying stereotypical generalisations. Thompson (1993) argues such terms are depersonalising and ageist.

SCENARIO

Arriving in a care home

John was aged 80 years and had memory problems when he was brought into a care home. His wife had just been taken into hospital. He could not look after himself at home. John was bewildered and kept asking if he had hurt his wife and whether it was his fault that she was ill. He couldn't understand that she had a heart problem and that he could not stay at home. The staff needed kindness and patience and their warmth and kindly manner helped John to settle rather than anything that they said.

Can you identify the aspect of effective communication that care staff used here?

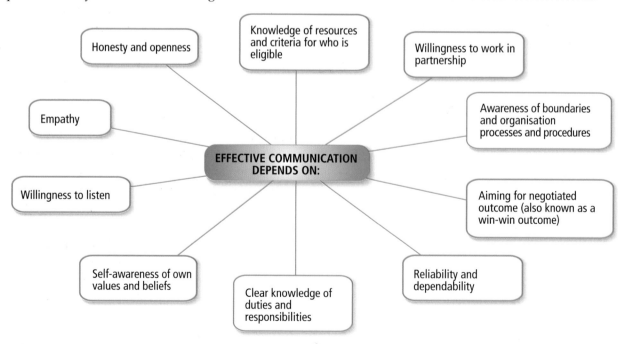

FIGURE 3.19 *Key elements of effective communication*

How to challenge discrimination or poor practice

The first step in challenging discrimination is to recognise its existence and the damaging effects it has on people. This also requires a degree of personal honesty and reflection about the views and prejudices that you may hold about particular situations or people. Training opportunities can really help to build your awareness of different types of discrimination and how it affects individuals, groups and organisations. Thompson (1993) argues that groups can have a much greater effect than individuals working alone, so change is much more likely to happen if staff develop group values and norms associated with the value base.

Challenging discrimination often involves challenging stereotypes or attitudes that fail to convey respect and value for service users. You may often need to challenge behaviour and assumptions that do not fit the value base for care. Some examples of discriminatory statements and possible challenges are set out in Figure 3.21.

Pressure groups can also play a major role in bringing issues to local and national awareness and are important factors in the process of change. Appreciating how crucial the role of **anti-discriminatory** practice is in social and health care will have a major impact on creating and sustaining a positive care environment. Awareness of discrimination is not an added extra or a separate area of learning, but is the bedrock of good practice and positive care environments.

The organisation

Some of the key organisational factors that impact on creating a positive environment are outlined below.

Policies and procedures

Policies reflect organisations' views about a particular area; this is usually combined with an expectation and procedures as to how staff working for that organisation will behave. Many

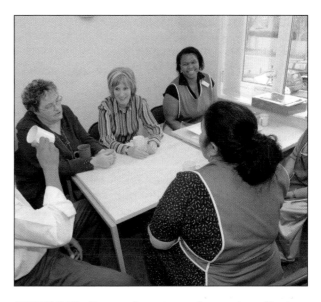

FIGURE 3.20 *Groups have a much greater effect than individuals in challenging discrimination*

organisations have policies on equal opportunities with a clear sequence of actions that staff must take if discriminatory language or behaviour occurs.

Policies and procedures play a vital part in establishing the 'culture' of an organisation. This refers to a set of commonly held beliefs, values, and behaviours. The culture of an organisation will affect how things get done and will also affect the staff's views and attitudes to learning.

In order to be effective, policies need to be made clear and regularly updated. Having a first aid policy is of little use if no one knows the policy and the approved first aider is on holiday when help is needed. The same applies to fire procedures.

Policies and procedures do provide a clear structure for how to work and what to do in particular situations. They are essential in promoting the rights of service users and also define the limits of a worker's role or responsibilities. However, policies alone are not enough. Staff need not only to have knowledge of them but above all a commitment to implementing and maintaining policies and procedures; unless they are believed in and adopted into everyday behaviour, high quality care practice cannot be achieved or maintained.

SETTING OR SERVICE USER GROUP	DISCRIMINATORY STATEMENT	POSSIBLE WAYS OF CHALLENGING THE STATEMENT
Early years setting	'Children from this ethnic group never mix with others, do they?'	A statement like this is a generalisation/stereotype. There could be a variety of reasons for a child not mixing with others; for example, due to shyness or feeling unsafe. It is important not to blame the child – the problem may be with the attitude of the staff.
People with a learning difficulty	'There is no point in asking these people what they want. They haven't got the ability to know!'	This discriminatory statement labels people as having 'no ability'. All living people have some abilities. Skilled care workers must work with people and not see 'the person as the problem'. If there are communication barriers then an advocacy approach can be used.
Healthcare setting	'It's the lifestyle that these people live. They bring the problems on themselves. Why should we have to work with them?'	A judgmental statement that assumes that some people deserve help and others do not. There is an assumption that people who are socially disadvantaged automatically do not deserve help. The attitude is almost as absurd as the argument that only healthy people should receive health care.
A service setting for older people	'Well, these people have had their lives haven't they.'	A discriminatory statement that regards service users as 'non-people' valued as 'already dead'. A positive, value-base approach might emphasise the richness of life experience and the life story of each service user together with the communication skills needed to maintain the service user's self-esteem.

FIGURE 3.21 *Examples of discriminatory statements and possible challenges*

SCENARIO

Organisational culture

Care Home A has a strict rule-bound way of working. The manager constantly criticises the staff and has threatened to sack someone who was late because she had to take her daughter to hospital as an emergency. Staff have no choice other than to work double shifts and the manager rarely talks to the residents. The staff are afraid and resentful of the manager and only do what they are told to do. The manager sees herself as the expert in all areas of knowledge and does not like the staff having any training, as she knows what to do. The staff only hear about policies and procedures when the manager tells them that they have done something wrong. They do not know any of the written policies

In Care Home B the staff are encouraged to use their own ideas and common sense to deal with

difficult situations, and receive support and back-up from their manager. They are often able to attend training courses and are encouraged to put new ideas into practice. The residents enjoy a laugh and a joke with the staff. The manager offers regular supervision to the staff and spends time with the residents every day. They have regular staff meetings and work together to solve problems. Policies and procedures are always looked at as part of the staff meetings.

The culture of Care Home B means that policies and procedures are seen as helpful tools to keep up good standards, whereas in Care Home A they are used negatively. Policies and procedures on their own are not enough to ensure that there is a positive care environment. The culture of each organisation will also play a major part.

Effect of organisational size, structure and culture

Many organisations providing social care are commercially run in order to make a profit. Many care homes have closed in the last 4 years, and in 2003 alone over 15,000 care home beds disappeared. Many smaller homes cannot survive financially and larger commercial groups are taking over ownership of many residential and nursing homes. The larger the home the more savings can be made (called economies of scale). There is a trend for homes to become larger, but this brings with it problems of keeping individual residents as the main focus.

Each home is required to meet **National Minimum Standards** as set down in the Care Standards Act 2000. There can sometimes be tensions as providing the best quality care would mean far higher costs in staff and supplies. Maintaining a balance between good standards of care and making a profit is not easy to get right.

Key organisational policies and procedures

Policies and procedures are vital elements in creating and maintaining a positive care environment (see Figure 3.22).

Equal opportunities policies

The Commission for Racial Equality recommends that equal opportunity policies should include a policy that covers recruitment, training and promotion. The policy should contain clear targets, following a thorough assessment of the organisation's current position on equal opportunities. Consideration should be given to pre-employment training that prepares job applicants for tests and interviews. In addition, applications from under-represented groups should be encouraged and effective links built with the community. The Commission also recommends that flexible working options should be considered and special equipment should be provided to meet the needs of people who are disabled.

Mission statement

This should be a clear short statement indicating the name and type of agency, its location, what it

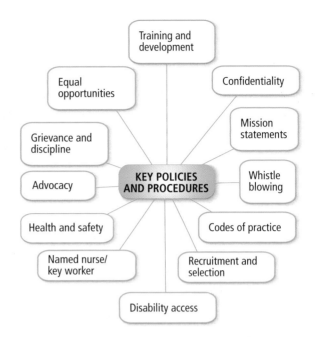

FIGURE 3.22 *Areas requiring clearly defined policies and procedures*

does, where and for whom. The vision and purpose of the agency also need to be included together with a statement of where the organisation wishes to go.

An example of a mission statement for a local authority social services department might be 'To provide accessible, quality services to the people of the borough'.

An example of a mission statement for an organisation working with people with learning difficulty might be 'To provide quality, **person-centred care** that values the individuality and potential of every service user'.

Codes of practice

These are statements of good practice and help to make clear what standards a service user can expect. They are useful for reviewing the quality of care. The Commissions that deal with areas of discrimination, such as the Disability Rights Commission, produce codes of practice to give guidance about good practice in the area of discrimination. They provide professionals with advice and guidelines and often can give detailed values relevant to a specific service. The codes of practice for nurses and the code of ethics for social workers can be found by accessing www.heinemann.co.uk/hotlinks (express code 37185) for the relevant websites.

FIGURE 3.23 *Codes of practice for care workers can be found on the Internet*

Recruitment and selection

Recruiting and selecting the right people is of the highest importance to a health or social care organisation and will affect its future success. The processes for recruiting and retaining staff must be free from bias and discrimination.

> ✱ DID YOU KNOW?
>
> The Race Relations Amendment Act 2000 places the responsibility on organisations to prove they are not discriminatory and to monitor their practices.

Whistle blowing

This is the process whereby employees can safely state their concerns if bad practice occurs. The Public Interest Disclosure Act 1998 protects staff from victimisation provided they make their concern known 'in good faith'. An example of this would be if someone was being abused in a care home. The normal first step would be to talk to the manager. Where an employee cannot safely talk to someone within their own organisation, the organisation should provide a list of other people that can be contacted.

Confidentiality

As a result of legislation and National Minimum Standards all care organisations must have a policy about confidentiality including the safety and security of recorded information. There will be procedures to follow when accessing information about service users or when records are updated.

Advocacy

Advocacy developed from radical social work and focuses on increasing the control and power of service users and carers over their own lives. On one level, it could be argued that social care workers empower service users by enabling them to access and receive the services they need. In more recent years, advocacy has developed to provide support and a voice for people who may have a mental health problem or learning difficulty, enabling them to fully participate in decision-making over their own lives. Such occasions might be an appeal against compulsory detention in a psychiatric hospital. It might also involve enabling someone with learning difficulties to plan short- and long-term goals for their lives in a person-centred planning meeting.

The task of an advocate is to enter into the life of a service user and to identify the service user's view of the world and to represent those views, where the person may find it hard to state these for himself or herself.

Advocacy recognises the powerlessness of particular groups. One area of empowerment has focused on black communities in the UK, who have traditionally experienced lower levels of employment, access to health services and mental health.

Person-centred planning

There are five key features to person-centred planning, as shown in Figure 3.24.

The White Paper 'Caring for People' (1991) indicates that the views and wishes of people with learning difficulties as to how they wish to live must be listened to; this is called person-centred planning. For example, a person with learning difficulties who lives in a shared house with care staff might wish to live in his or her own flat and get a part-time job. Such an individual might like to learn to horse ride and would like to go abroad once a year for a holiday. He or she might also want to buy different

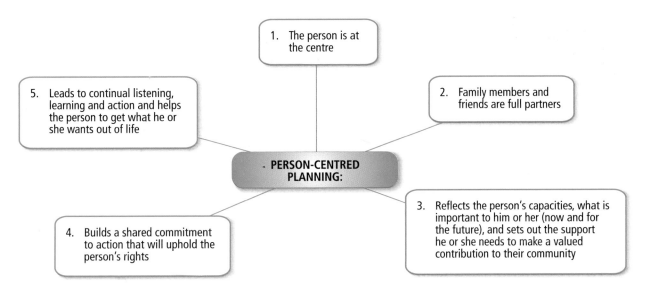

FIGURE 3.24 *Key features to person-centred planning*

Source: Planning With People: Guidance for Implementation Groups (Department of Health, 2002:13–14).

pictures for his or her room and change the wallpaper. So person-centred planning is about the little things as well as wider goals and ambitions. For people to have choices they need to know what is available, together with information about costs, as many services are chargeable. The provision of clear information is also essential.

Health and safety

Under The Health and Safety at Work Act (1974) both the employer and the employee are jointly responsible for safeguarding the health and safety of themselves and anyone using the premises. Each workplace must have a written statement of its health and safety policy with the name of the person responsible for implementing the policy. A list of hazards and risks should be put together and a clear procedure for recording accidents at work established. There should also be a clear statement about how the premises would be cleared in an emergency. All employers have to assess any risks under the Management of Health and Safety at Work Regulations 1992. Risk control measures must also be put in place.

Training and professional development

Under the Care Standards Act 2000 there are clear training requirements for social care workers. By 2005 at least 50 per cent of the workforce must have achieved NVQ qualifications at level 2/3. Eventually, all social care workers will be registered with the General Social Care Council. Training and professional development is an essential part of all health and social care work, in order to improve the standards and quality of care environments. In Early Years settings, 'Sure Start' estimates that the expansion of childcare services will require 175,000 to 185,000 new childcare workers, who will all need to be trained or retrained to meet current standards.

Named nurse and key worker

Effective care requires workers to know important information about service users. A named nurse or a key worker is a person who has a specific responsibility to get to know certain individual service users. A key worker will have a responsibility for coordinating the service user's plan of individual care. This may involve contact with relatives and friends in order to update and monitor the individual plan of care.

Grievance and discipline

The Labour Relations Commission has developed a code of practice to advise on how these procedures should be set up and operated. Grievance means a concern an employee has about the employer or another employee. Disciplinary procedures cover situations in which the employer has serious concerns about the professional behaviour of the worker. In the health and social care field, a list of those people considered unsuitable to be working with vulnerable adults was set up in June 2004 under the Care Standards Act 2000. If the result of the disciplinary procedure indicates concerns about a worker's suitability to work with vulnerable people, his or her name may be added to this list. However, there are very clear rules about the process of how this might happen.

Disability access

Part Three of the Disability Discrimination Act 1995 came into force in October 2004 and requires that reasonable adjustments are made to enable disabled people physical access to the buildings they need. Fines of up to £50,000 can be imposed on employers who do not make these adjustments. However, in practice the majority of stores are still not fully accessible for people in wheelchairs.

How organisations can promote positive practice

Promoting positive practice is the responsibility of every worker, but the organisation bears responsibility for ensuring that policies and procedures are in place to support and encourage good practice. Regular inspections by the Commission for Social Care Inspection do play a valuable role in monitoring the progress of an organisation. Care environments have to conform to clear standards. Inspection can monitor the quality of record keeping and other procedures. However, measuring the quality of care is not always so easy. Each organisation will develop its own culture and way of doing things.

It is important to become familiar with formal policy and legal requirements. Care environments operate where the personal and individual world of the individual overlaps with the legal and formal requirements of the law and guidance. Codes of practice and organisational policy documents give helpful guidelines about positive practice (see Figure 3.25).

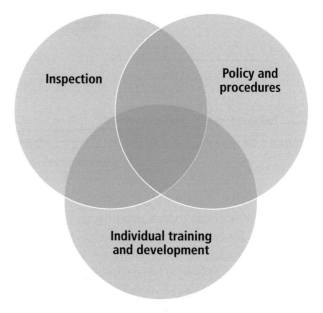

FIGURE 3.25 *The overlapping world of the individual and the legal and formal requirements in care environments*

It is also important to identify what changes are needed in order to improve the care environment. Whilst this can be done on an individual and personal basis, each organisation should have procedures whereby staff can become involved in changing and improving the practices of the organisation. Having clear goals and objectives is one of the most effective ways of achieving change.

Reviewing the position of the organisation and individuals on an ongoing basis is also a key to maintaining high standards. Training on a regular basis is also important in ensuring that consistently high standards are maintained. As part of the implementation of the Care Standards Act 2000 the goal is for at least 50 per cent of care workers to have achieved NVQ level 2/3 by 2005.

Summary of Section 3.3

Both the individual worker and the organisation must take an active part in creating and promoting a positive environment:

Individual worker's knowledge and understanding of the processes of discrimination, advocacy and empowerment

Organisations must ensure training is provided for health and social care workers

Organisations have responsibilities to ensure the law is followed with policies and procedures

CREATING A POSITIVE ENVIRONMENT

Individual workers need good communication skills

Organisations must ensure they are working in an anti-discriminatory way

Consider this

You visit a care setting. The staff are welcoming and friendly; they seem to have good communication skills and no difficulty remembering important details relevant to the lifestyle of service users. You hear that staff meetings focus on positive attitudes about working together; the staff seem to value and support each other. The care workers you talk to enjoy working with the service users and clearly value diversity and difference. The staff enjoy team development days, and each full-time member of staff has a personal development plan of training.

Using concepts can you identify?

1 Some of the organisational policies and procedures that might support the good practice you have seen.

2 Some of the care values that care workers must be using.

Go further – can you analyse using theory?
Can you analyse some of the influences that might have resulted in the staff team adopting care values as part of their norms for working as a group. What part might staff training have played?

Go further – can you evaluate using a range of theory?
Can you evaluate the extent to which organisational policy may have contributed to good practice and the extent to which personal commitment to care values may have contributed to this good practice?

3.4 How society promotes service user's rights

This section looks at the rights of service users and how they are defined and protected in **law**. In working in the field of health and social care there are specific and general areas of law that affect people's rights.

Acts of Parliament are divided into parts (like chapters in a book) and they have sections (like paragraphs). At the end are schedules, which contain important principles about how the law should operate.

Essential general law

These are laws that underpin any work within the health and social care field. These can be seen as bedrock or underpinning law, as all actions must follow these general laws. This means that they are in force and are as important as particular laws such as the Children Act 1989, which cover special areas. The important basic laws include:

✳ Human Rights Act 1998

✳ Discrimination legislation

✳ Data Protection and Freedom of Information.

Human Rights Act 1998 ✓

FIGURE 3.26 *Rights are defined and protected in law*

The Human Rights Act 1998 adopted the European Convention of Human Rights. The Act is based on a commitment to individual rights and freedom from the State acting against groups or individuals in an illegal way. The Act came into force in October 2000 and is now part of UK law. Previously people had to apply to the European Court of Human Rights in Strasburg, but this is no longer the case as any legal proceedings in the UK must take account the Human Rights Act. The Act contains 16 Rights and is very clear that discrimination is not allowed.

Absolute Rights

There are four Absolute Rights (see Figure 3.27). This means there is no compromise or change and they must not be broken.

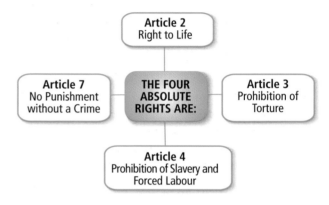

FIGURE 3.27 *The four Absolute Rights of the Human Rights Act 1998*

Limited Rights

Others rights, such as Article 8: Right to respect for Private and Family Life, are limited or qualified rights, so they need to be balanced with risks. This means that if a child were at risk of being hurt then the child could be removed, as his or her need for protection would override the family's right to respect for their privacy. This means that in certain situations these rights can be overridden.

The Human Rights Act applies to social care placements such as residential and nursing homes as well as voluntary organisations. This is because they provide services, which would otherwise be offered by the local authority. This means that social care establishments need to incorporate the principles of the Act into its policies and rules: how to make decisions, staffing and personnel procedures, how to run the establishment and also in the manner of relating to the public. Much of the Human Rights Act 1998 will apply in the social care field, as social care is very much involved with protecting and promoting people's mental and physical health.

Where it has been proved in court that any of a person's human rights has been broken, a range of legal **redress** is possible. These include damages, and the courts can also declare that the practice of an organisation is not legal.

Discrimination legislation

Sex Discrimination Act 1975 and 1986

Whilst pay was addressed in the Equal Pay Act (1970), other areas of discrimination against women were not covered. The Sex Discrimination laws cover discrimination and make direct and indirect discrimination illegal. The Equal Opportunities Commission plays the major role in helping individuals who experience discrimination, and they also have the power to issue a 'non-discrimination notice' to stop unfair practices. The notice can be enforced by injunction in the High Court. Compensation can be awarded by an employment tribunal and the employer may be ordered to change its practices. If there is discrimination in terms of provision of goods and services an individual can bring the matter before a county court, which have the power to award damages and issue injunctions (legal orders) to prevent further discrimination.

The Sex Discrimination Act also covers discrimination on the grounds of marital status as well as on the basis of **gender**. This means that the fact that someone is married or has children cannot be used as a reason to treat them unfairly. Under the Sex Discrimination Act interviewers must not ask about childcare or other caring responsibilities during employment interviews. Good practice would also ensure that there is a balance in terms of gender of those sitting on interviewing panels. The view that jobs such as dinner lady or nurse are 'women's jobs' has had to be radically re-thought in the light of the legislation.

The Sex Discrimination Act 1986 widened the areas covered by legislation. Employment by

small firms, employment in private households and collective agreements by employers were also included under the law as required by the European Community.

Employment Equality (Sexual Orientation) Regulations 2003

These regulations came into force in December 2003 and now cover direct and indirect discrimination, victimisation and harassment on the grounds of sexual orientation. Until these regulations came into force there had been a major gap in the legislation. Harassment is defined in the regulations as unwanted conduct that violates people's dignity or causes an intimidating, hostile, degrading, offensive or humiliating environment. These regulations cover heterosexual relationships as well as same-sex and bi-sexual relationships. If an individual is harassed or discriminated against on the grounds of who he or she associates with, this is also covered by these regulations. However, these regulations only cover areas relating to employment.

Race Relations Act 1976 and Amendment Act 2000

The Race Relations Act 1976 made discrimination unlawful on the grounds of colour, race, ethnic or national origin or nationality. The legislation applies as much to discrimination towards a white person on the above grounds as to any other nationality or race. In 2001, case law identified that Scottish, Irish, English and Welsh are recognised as national origins and are, therefore, covered by this area of legislation. In certain situations the Race Relations Act 1976 allows 'permitted discrimination'. This covers the issues outlined in Figure 3.28.

The Act also established the Commission for Racial Equality, which not only assists individuals but has a key role in publishing codes of practice to identify good practice. Of particular importance in the area of health and social care, section 71 of the Race Relations Act requires all public bodies to eliminate unlawful discrimination, and to promote equality of opportunity and good relationships between people of different racial groups. These duties have been extended to all public authorities

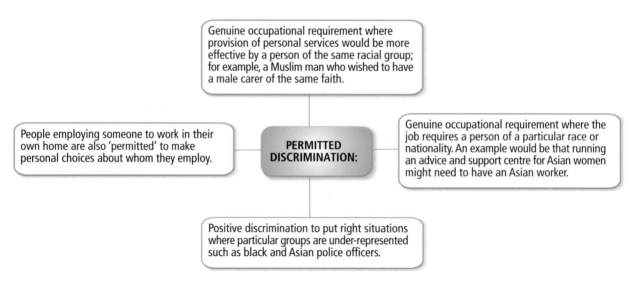

Genuine occupational requirement where provision of personal services would be more effective by a person of the same racial group; for example, a Muslim man who wished to have a male carer of the same faith.

People employing someone to work in their own home are also 'permitted' to make personal choices about whom they employ.

PERMITTED DISCRIMINATION:

Genuine occupational requirement where the job requires a person of a particular race or nationality. An example would be that running an advice and support centre for Asian women might need to have an Asian worker.

Positive discrimination to put right situations where particular groups are under-represented such as black and Asian police officers.

FIGURE 3.28 *Areas of permitted discrimination under the Race Relations Act 1976*

(including the police force) by the Race Relations Amendment Act 2000. All functions carried out by public authorities are now covered, whereas previously the areas covered only included employment, provision of facilities, goods and services, employment and housing.

These two Acts now make clear requirements on all public bodies to:

* review policies and functions every 3 years to ensure they are compliant
* monitor ethnic background of staff and in applications for employment
* ensure minority groups have access to information about the services provided
* identify and publish a race equality scheme
* identify arrangements to consult on the impact of new policies.

Employment does not just cover recruitment but also includes promotion, training opportunities and access to facilities

Employment Equality Religion and Belief Regulations 2003

These are similar to the regulations regarding sexual orientation; people are now protected from harassment, prejudice, victimisation and harassment on the grounds of religious belief. Both sexual orientation and religion/belief regulations bring the UK into line with European law and also protect people from discrimination on the grounds

of perceived, as well as actual, religion or belief (this means assuming correctly or incorrectly that someone has a belief or religion). The government aims to bring consistency to the field of **anti-discriminatory** practice. At tribunals the employer must show that any difference in treatment is justified rather than the claimant having to prove that he or she has been discriminated against.

Disability Discrimination Act 1995

This Act is different to the Race Relations Acts and the Sex Discrimination legislation in that there is not a clear category of indirect discrimination. The requirement on employers to 'make reasonable adjustment' is seen as the equivalent. Under this Act, discrimination in employment, buying or renting land and property, and the provision of goods and services is illegal. Transport services were not covered directly by the Act although 'right of access' provisions are included in Part III of the Act together with a separate code of practice, which came into force in October 2004. In terms of education, the Special Educational Needs and Disability Act amended the Disability Discrimination Act by making it unlawful for the bodies responsible for schools to discriminate against existing or prospective disabled pupils. A Special Educational Needs Tribunal has also been established to make judgments in this area of education. In 1999 the Disability Rights Commission was set up by an Act of Parliament.

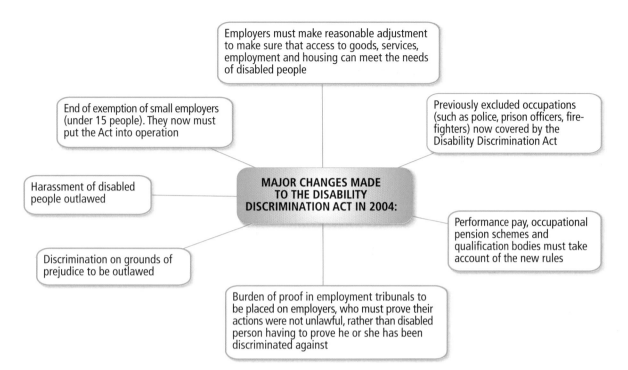

FIGURE 2.29 *Changes introduced by Part 111 of the Disability Discrimination Act in 2004*

Like other commissions it can issue a 'non-discrimination notice'. Individuals can seek redress through the county court in relation to goods and services.

The third part of the Disability Discrimination Act came into force in October 2004. The main points that have changed are shown in Figure 3.29.

✓Data Protection Act 1998 and Freedom of Information Act 2000

The Data Protection Acts of 1984 and 1998, Access to Personal Files Act 1987 and Access to Health Records Act 1990 made it a legal requirement to keep service user information confidential.

The 1998 Data Protection Act establishes rights to confidentiality covering both paper and electronic records. This Act provides people with a range of rights including those shown in Figure 3.30.

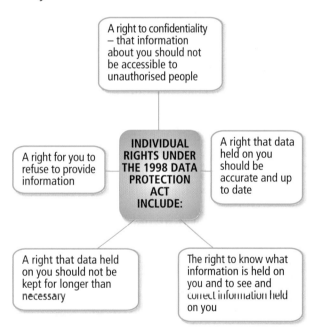

FIGURE 3.30 *Rights introduced by the 1998 Data Protection Act*

> **✱ DID YOU KNOW?**
>
> All services now have to have policies and procedures on the confidentiality of recorded information. The Data Protection Act 1998 has implications for confidentiality and the disclosure of records to friends and family; it also covers a person's right to see his or her own records.

The Data Protection Act was passed by Parliament to protect people's rights in relation to the way information could be stored about them. The Data Protection Act 1998 replaced an earlier law from 1984. All information about people now has to be kept in accordance with the following principles:

* information or data must be fairly and legally obtained. People must not be misled about the purposes for which information is gathered

* data must be gathered with the permission of the people involved and processed for limited purposes

* data gathered has to be adequate, relevant and not excessive

* data must be accurate and kept up to date

* data must not be kept for longer than is necessary for the purpose it was originally gathered for

* people have the right to find out or access personal data being kept about them and certain other rights about the way in which data can be used

* data must be kept secure. Organisations must make sure that data is not lost or made available to unauthorised persons. The security principle means that data must be kept confidential

* data must not be transferred to a country out side of the European Union unless there are guarantees of data protection.

The Freedom of Information Act 2001

This was implemented in three stages and came into force in January 2005. It is part of government policy to increase openness and to reduce unnecessary secrecy. The Data Protection Act 1998 covers access to information by individuals, whereas the Freedom of Information Act covers information about public bodies. The principle underlying this Act is that information should be readily released unless there is evidence that harm would be caused. The Act identified rights to access information and also set up an Information Commissioner and Information Tribunal hear cases of complaints. All public authorities need to have schemes for publication of information. The format for these schemes has to be approved by the Information Commissioner.

Specific laws in social care

Within health and social care there are important Acts of Parliament that cover particular areas of practice. Three of the main acts – the Children Act, the National Health Service and Community Care Act, and the Mental Health Act – are considered below. The White Paper 'Valuing People,' for people with learning difficulties, is also included.

The Children Act 1989

The Act defined the duties and responsibilities of local authorities and established clear principles to follow. The Act established **rights and responsibilities** of parents and tried to set a framework for balancing the rights of children and parents against the responsibilities of the local authority to protect children from harm. The Children Act applies to all statutory and voluntary organisations providing care to children.

Key principles for working with children were established. They include:

* that children are better brought up within their own families

* the welfare of the child is always the highest priority (known as the paramountcy principle)

* no court order should be made unless it is essential to do so (no order principle)

* the views of the child must be sought and taken into account if of a suitable age or mature enough to express his or her wishes

* the child's race and cultural needs must be taken into account in order to maintain his or her identity

* no delay in working with children

* a welfare checklist must be followed by the court in any decision involving children.

The Children Act 1989 also emphasised that local authorities *must* work in partnership with families. A new Children Bill is going through Parliament in 2004/5 and this will make partnership a duty in law that local authorities must carry out.

Gender Equality	
Equal Pay Act Northern Ireland (1970)	Broadly similar legislation to the equivalent Acts within other UK countries
Sex Discrimination, Northern Ireland Order (1976)	Broadly similar legislation to the equivalent Acts within other UK countries
Race Equality	
Race Relations Northern Ireland Order (1997)	Legislation that introduced similar provision to the 1976 Race Relations Act in other UK countries
Disability	
Disability Discrimination Act (1995)	Legislation that applies across the UK
Equality, Northern Ireland Order (2000)	Legislation that expanded the duties and powers of the Equality Commission for Northern Ireland in relation to disability matter
Sexuality	
Employment Equality (Sexual Orientation) Regulations Northern Ireland (2003)	Similar legislation to other UK provision to prevent discrimination on the basis of a person's sexuality
Religion and Political Beliefs	
Fair Employment and Treatment, Northern Ireland Order (1998)	Legislation that makes it unlawful to discriminate against someone on the grounds of religious belief or political opinion. All UK countries now have legislation to prevent discrimination within employment on the basis of religion. Citizens of Northern Ireland currently have some additional rights preventing discrimination on the basis of religion or politics, as compared with other UK countries

The Children Act also sets out the responsibilities of local authorities towards children in need. The Act defines a child in need as one whose health and welfare would suffer without support from social services. Any child with a disability is automatically considered to be a child in need. There are also clear duties under the Act for local authorities to provide support services such as nurseries and family centres.

Social services also have duties to protect children from harm. Significant harm was a term adopted by the Act and is defined as ill treatment, impairment of health or impairment of development. The Adoption and Children Act 2002 has added an extra category of children witnessing violence as another important area to be taken into account when deciding if a child is in danger of being harmed. Social services must take into account not only the harm a child may have already experienced, but also the future possibilities of significant harm.

Parental responsibility was established by the Children Act and sets down the idea that parents have fundamental responsibilities as well as rights towards their children. Parents cannot lose their rights (except trough adoption) but their responsibilities can sometimes be shared with the local authority. Even if a child is living away from his or her parents as a result of a Care Order, the parents still keep their responsibilities. Clear guidelines were set down by the Children Act defining who automatically has parental responsibility and how it can be acquired through the courts.

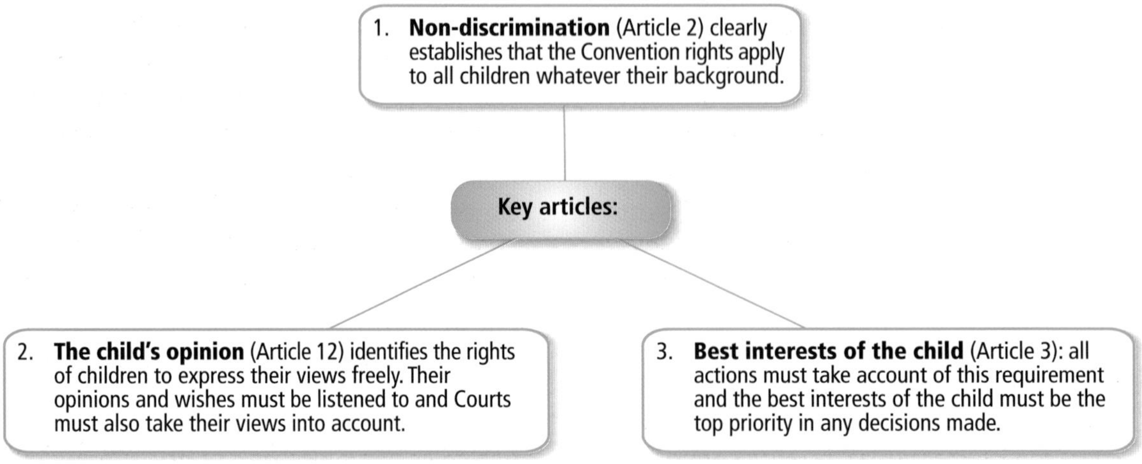

1. **Non-discrimination** (Article 2) clearly establishes that the Convention rights apply to all children whatever their background.

Key articles:

2. **The child's opinion** (Article 12) identifies the rights of children to express their views freely. Their opinions and wishes must be listened to and Courts must also take their views into account.

3. **Best interests of the child** (Article 3): all actions must take account of this requirement and the best interests of the child must be the top priority in any decisions made.

FIGURE 3.31 *Key articles of the United Nations Convention on the Rights of the Child*

In addition to the principles laid down in the Children Act, social services must also ensure that work with children follows the key requirements of the United Nations Convention on the Rights of the Child. These rights were agreed to in the UK in 1991 and set important standards and rights for children. The principles must be taken into account by English Courts. There are three key principles:

* participation in expression of views, protection of privacy

* protection from abuse and exploitation

* provision of education, and an adequate standard of living.

There are three Key articles that must also be followed. These are shown in Figure 3.31.

The United Nations Convention on the Rights of the Child, together with the Children Act 1989, sets out a clear framework that the welfare of all children must be taken very seriously. Social services must look at all aspects of a child's welfare as well as his or her physical safety. A child's need for identity, education and healthy development must always be taken into account.

Figure 3.32 shows how the different laws work together in the field of childcare.

As can be seen from the pyramid, the principles and important parts of the Act are underpinned by law which covers the rights of all people in terms of discrimination, information

and their Human Rights. These laws must be followed as well as the particular instructions that laws specific to children impose.

In addition to the law around the welfare of children there are clear duties and responsibilities towards children who commit offences. Like the Children Act 1989, there are clear principles that

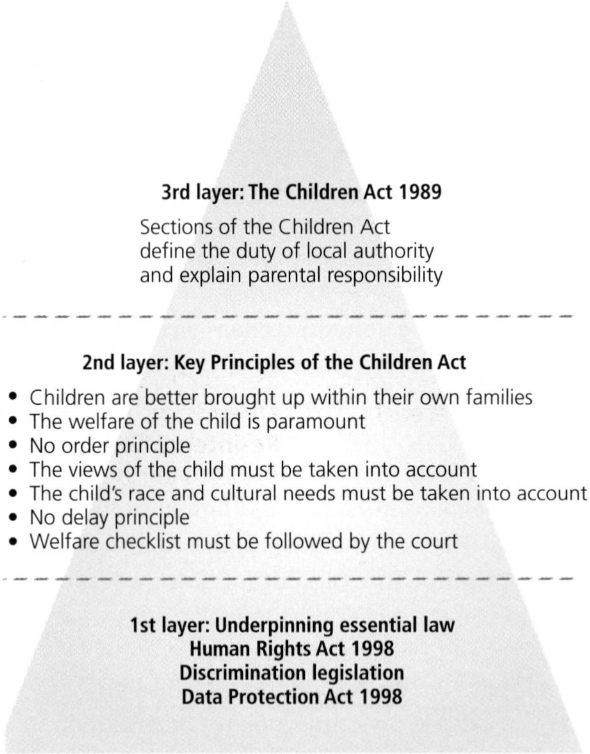

3rd layer: The Children Act 1989

Sections of the Children Act define the duty of local authority and explain parental responsibility

2nd layer: Key Principles of the Children Act

• Children are better brought up within their own families
• The welfare of the child is paramount
• No order principle
• The views of the child must be taken into account
• The child's race and cultural needs must be taken into account
• No delay principle
• Welfare checklist must be followed by the court

1st layer: Underpinning essential law
Human Rights Act 1998
Discrimination legislation
Data Protection Act 1998

FIGURE 3.32 *Different laws working together in childcare*

youth justice workers, the courts and the police have to follow. They are shown in Figure 3.33.

In addition, the local authority has responsibilities to reduce the need to bring criminal proceedings and must also encourage children not to commit offences. Current laws in the youth justice area provide a variety of measures to deal with juvenile crime. Under the Crime and Disorder Act 1998 local child care curfews can be used for children and young people under 16 years of age. These give the police powers to take children home if they are in a particular area or out after a particular time at night. Another order under the same Act is an Anti-Social Behaviour Order (ASBO) whereby young people who are causing a continued nuisance or damage can be banned by a youth court from being in one or a number of particular places. The conditions of the ASBO can be very detailed even to the extent of specifying what someone is allowed to wear. The strong connection between truanting and crime has led to the police having the power under the Crime and Disorder Act 1998 to pick up children who they believe are truanting from school.

NHS and Community Care Act 1990

The aim of the NHS and Community Care Act was to enable people to stay at home for as long as possible. Admission to residential or nursing care was seen as the last resort under the Act. Prior to this, people did not receive an assessment of need before going into long-term care. The Act also introduced business ideas into social care services. Eighty-five per cent of a local authority's budget has to be spent in buying care services from private, voluntary and independent providers of care.

Before this Act, the local authority was a major provider of services, whereas under the NHS and Community Care Act the key roles for local authorities are now:

* assessment of need – this means identifying what help a person needs
* commissioning/purchasing of services such as residential care and home care
* monitoring of services in terms of quality and value for money
* hospital discharges – key role in arranging quick hospital discharges Community Care (Delayed discharges) Act 2004
* protection of vulnerable adults from abuse.

Assessment of need of a disabled person

The NHS and Community Care Act gave people with a disability much clearer rights in terms of automatic entitlement to an assessment. The NHS and Community Care Act 1990 makes it clear that there are two situations when someone is eligible for an assessment. These are:

DUTIES AND RESPONSIBILITIES TOWARDS CHILDREN WHO COMMIT OFFENCES	
Restorative justice: (covers 3 areas)	**Restoration:** where the young offender acknowledges and makes amends for their crime, including apologising to the victim **Re-integration:** an offender moving away from offending behaviour **Responsibility:** offenders and parents taking responsibility for their actions and preventing further behaviour occurring
Welfare principle	The youth justice system must take into account the welfare of the child in terms of removing him or her from undesirable surroundings and ensuring a proper education
Prevention of re-offending	This is the primary responsibility of Youth Courts

FIGURE 3.33 *Principles that youth justice workers, the courts and the police have to follow in dealing with child offenders*

* when they need or appear to need community care services

* when someone is disabled they now have an automatic right to an assessment and should be informed of this.

The Act makes it clear that it should not be difficult for an assessment to be made. Sometimes this goes wrong, as is shown in the following situation.

SCENARIO

Individual needs

In one case, a woman whose husband was due to have an operation on his brain phoned social services, asking for help with her mother who had Alzheimer's disease (memory problems) and was living with her. Clearly, looking at the above Act the woman's mother and husband should have been offered an assessment. The woman herself should have been offered a Carer's Assessment, as she was looking after both of them. Instead, social services asked how much money her mother had saved, as the worker was muddled between the rules about offering an assessment and charging for services offered. No assessment was made and the only help the woman received was a booklet containing a list of private care homes. The situation came to a crisis point some months later after the woman had struggled alone to cope and had placed her mother in a residential home that was unsympathetic to her mother's needs and wanted her moved within 24 hours. An assessment was then made and a suitable place eventually found for her mother; but this example shows how important it is for a social care worker to understand what the law says.

The purposes of the NHS and Community Care Act have been set down as key objectives. These are shown in Figure 3.34.

The Mental Health Act 1983

The Mental Health Act defines who is regarded as mentally disordered and sets out rules detailing

KEY OBJECTIVES OF THE NHS AND COMMUNITY CARE ACT:	
Home	Keeping people within their own home wherever possible
Carers	Support and help for carers is a high priority
Assessment	This is the cornerstone of good quality care
Mixed economy of care	85 per cent of the local authorities' budgets are to be spent in the private, independent and voluntary sector to buy in the services people need
Responsibility	Clear statement of who is responsible for assessing need and arranging services
Better value for taxpayers money	The money given to local authorities must be spent wisely

FIGURE 3.34 *Purposes of the NHS and Community Care Act*

when someone can be admitted to a hospital against their wishes.

The principles covering the Mental Health Act 1983 are defined by the Mental Health Act Code of Practice 1983, revised in 1999. They include:

* recognition of human rights

* respect for individuals and anti-discriminatory practice

* needs to be assessed

* treatment must be the least controlling possible, taking into account risks to others

* care should promote self-determination and personal responsibility

* to discharge a person from compulsory sections as soon as possible and safely.

The Act is due to be changed within the next two years, as parts of it do not meet the requirements of the Human Rights Act.

Before someone can be compulsorily detained in hospital they have to be diagnosed as suffering from a mental disorder. This is defined under section 1 of the Mental Health Act 1983 as:

'Mental illness, arrested or incomplete development of mind, psychopathic disorder and any other disorder or disability of mind.'

White Paper 'Valuing People'

In 2001 the government published a White Paper for people with learning difficulties. A White Paper is a statement of the government's policy or plans. Although no Act of Parliament has followed this, 'Valuing People' is now the driving force directing service provision for people with learning difficulties in England.

There are four key principles in the White Paper:

✱ legal and civil rights

✱ choice

✱ inclusion

✱ independence.

Up to £50 million has been made available to change the services available for people with learning difficulties. People are to move out of long-stay hospitals; day services are to become more personal and meaningful; everyone will have a health plan and those with a learning difficulty will have a personal plan for their lives including housing, employment and leisure services. The process for this is called **person-centred planning**.

Redress for service users

Within current legislation there has been growing awareness that service users need mechanisms to make their voice heard. This can be linked to the consumer movement, which began in the 1970s to ensure that organisations were more accountable for their actions and to provide ways in which injustices could be addressed and put right. Within social care and discrimination law there are clearly defined procedures for service users. These operate at two levels:

✱ local complaints procedures

✱ formal and legal avenues of challenge.

Local complaints procedures

Complaints within social and health care organisations

Agencies must have their own complaints procedures as required by the Care Standards Act 2000, but they are also accountable to the complaints procedures in the local authority. As purchasers of the service, the local authority is also accountable for the standards and quality of care provided.

In a local authority, complaints follow a 3-stage procedure as shown in Figure 3.35. There are clearly defined time limits that each stage has to follow as required by government regulations.

There are also conditions about who can make a complaint. Technically, complaints must relate to a 'qualifying individual.' A qualifying individual is someone for whom the local authority has a **power** or a duty to provide social services; and the person is known to the social services. Financial compensation can be offered where complaints are upheld, but this is by no means commonplace. If policies and procedures are changed as a result of a complaint it is good practice for the person who has complained to be advised of this.

Formal and legal avenues of challenge

If the local complaints procedures have not resulted in the problem being resolved there are other legal options for the service user. These include:

✱ the Commissioner for local administration (Ombudsman)

3-STAGE PROCEDURE FOR LOCAL AUTHORITY COMPLAINTS:		
1	Informal	Attempts are made to resolve concerns at a local level with the social worker or team manager. The complaint does not have to be written; it may be made by a phone call
2	Formal	The complaint must be written and is dealt with by the local authority's designated complaints officer. Senior managers in social services may be involved
3	Review	An independent person leads and chairs a panel, which may require people involved in the complaint to attend a hearing. Their conclusions are made as a recommendation to the Director of Social Services. Although the Director is not legally bound to follow these recommendations, he/she has to show good cause why they are not followed if the matter is contested in court

FIGURE 3.35 *Procedure in local authorities for complaints*

* default powers
* judicial review
* civil action for damages/negligence
* whistle-blowing procedures.

Ombudsman

A person with a complaint can approach the Commissioner for Local Administration (also known as the Ombudsman). The Ombudsman looks at the actions of the local authority to see whether there has been maladministration. Maladministration is where the local authority has handled a situation dishonestly or inefficiently and this has caused an injustice to the service user. The Ombudsman can make recommendations about compensation but often it takes a long period for an investigation to be carried out. The process is free and the Ombudsman has powers to access information from local authorities (but is not able to look at general policies). The recommendations made by the Ombudsman are not legally binding on local authorities, although in practice most accept them as such.

Default powers

The Secretary of State has powers under the Local Authority Social Services Act to hold an inquiry where a local authority fails to carry out any of its statutory duties for adults. However, this power has never been used in practice, although the

Secretary of State can require a local authority to comply with the requirements of the law.

Judicial review

A decision can be challenged in court but the courts are limited in that they look at the process followed rather than the content of the decision. The courts identify if the process followed was legal, rational and reasonable. As from October 2000 the courts also have to check if the local authority has followed the requirements of the Human Rights Act.

Negligence and damages

A service user has to prove that he or she has suffered a 'wrong' as a result of the actions of a local authority. Proving negligence can be very difficult as three separate conditions have to be evidenced. Although the civil courts work in terms of 'balance of probabilities' rather than 'beyond reasonable doubt' (as for criminal cases) it is still by no means easy and straightforward for negligence to be proved in law.

Whistle blowing

The Public Interest Disclosure Act 1998 now gives protection to workers who 'blow the whistle' on bad practice, to protect them from being penalised or losing their job as a result. It is a sad fact that in many scandals in health and social care the person who is brave enough to speak out is victimised. Disclosures must be made 'in good faith' to prevent malicious allegations from being made. All local authorities have to have whistle-blowing procedures and social and health care providers would also be covered by these.

Implementing redress involving discrimination

Tribunals

Tribunals are special courts put in place to administer specific areas of civil law.

Currently there are over 2,000 different tribunals administering legislation such as that relating to appeals against compulsory detention in a psychiatric hospital (Mental Health Tribunal). Other examples are rent tribunals and employment tribunals, which hear cases where either a tenant or an employee feels they have been treated unfairly. People are encouraged to state their own case for themselves. There are appeal mechanisms for some but not all tribunals. There are advantages to this system as it does not take as long for a tribunal to hear a case as it would do for a court case to be heard. The proceedings are not as formal as in a court. However, it is not always clear why a tribunal has made a particular decision. Some tribunals have the power to award compensation and in the field

FIGURE 3.36 *Tribunals are not as formal as courts*

of employment some very big pay outs have been awarded.

Commissions

Commissions are government-appointed agencies that implement and monitor key areas of legislation. Examples include the Commission for Racial Equality. In April 2004 the **Commission for Social Care Inspection (CSCI)** was created, the role of which is to inspect social care services. The Commission also has responsibilities for inspecting the standards for some health services.

The work of each Commission will focus around specific legislation. Common tasks for Commissions involve investigating complaints or concerns such as standards of care in the case of CSCI. The Commissions also have a role in providing information and support about good quality practice. The codes of practice are valuable for measuring whether good standards are being achieved. The Equal Opportunities Commission and the Commission for Racial Equality both have published codes of practice to guide employers and workers on how to eliminate discrimination.

Codes of practice for social care workers have been published by the General Social Care Council (See Unit 2). These define the standards of professional behaviour that must be upheld.

Ofsted

The Care Standards Act 2000 modified the Children Act 1989. The modified Children Act now places the responsibility for quality inspection of childcare services with the Office for Standards in Education (Ofsted). Since 2001 Ofsted has been responsible for the registration and inspection of day-care and child minding. Ofsted is responsible for the:

* registration of all day-care providers

* inspection of all day-care provision

* investigation of complaints or concerns about day-care provision

* enforcement of quality standards

* provision of advice to central and local government on childcare issues.

Ofsted uses National Standards published by the Department for Education and Skills to guide its inspection work.

FIGURE 3.37 *National standards have to be met for all types of childcare*

There are national standards for each type of childcare provision including:

* full day-care

* sessional day-care

* crèches

* out-of-school care

* child minders.

The relationship between law and rights for service users

There are different ways that service user rights can be understood. These range from generalised human rights and protection from discrimination to the belief commonly held that individuals have an automatic right to services. Each approach has limitations and many of these approaches are the subject of misunderstanding by the general public. The ability to know the problems in the area of rights is essential in understanding how to promote a positive care environment.

Clear rights in law

One of the clearest lists of rights in law has been made by Brammer (2002).

The list includes the right:

* to an assessment for services under the NHSCCA 90

* of a carer to an assessment of their needs under Carer and Disabled Children Act 2000

* not to be discriminated against in specified circumstances, e.g. provision of goods and services on specified grounds, race, sex, disability, sexual orientation, religion or belief

* of a child (of sufficient understanding) to make an informed choice to refuse a medical and/or psychiatric examination under the CA 89 (Gillick Competence)

* of access to information held about you under the Data Protection Act 1998.

Right to protection from discrimination

Another major area of development in terms of service users' rights has been the development of anti-discriminatory legislation. The enforcement of these rights is through Commissions such as the Commission for Racial Equality, which can provide advice and support for individuals. However, the codes of practice published by the different Commissions do not have the same force of law as an Act of Parliament. Law on its own does not always change people's behaviour or attitudes.

Rights as an automatic entitlement to a service

This is the biggest area of misunderstanding in the area of service user rights. There is a widespread belief that people are automatically entitled to services and provisions from the local authority. In reality, this is not the case as successive governments since the 1970s have been concerned about local authorities' increasing expenditure. When the Welfare State was set up in the 1940s the key principle was that the State would provide for all its citizens' needs 'from cradle to grave'; this is the foundation of many people's belief that they are entitled to services. The reality is that people may be entitled to an assessment and it is only if, as a result of that assessment, it is agreed that the conditions set by the local authority have been met that services will be provided. However, charges are also made for those services.

Rights to information and consultation

FIGURE 3.38 *Local authorities are responsible for up-to-date information on services*

The law is very clear that local authorities must provide information about the services it provides. This dates back to the National Assistance Act 1948. Three other Acts also emphasise what local authorities must do. These include the 1970 Chronically Sick and Disabled Persons Act, and the Disabled Persons Act 1986. The NHS and Community Care Act 1990 requires each local authority to publish a plan of its current services. The Children Act 1989 also makes it very clear that an essential part of working in partnership is to provide accurate and up-to-date information to parents and children.

There are also clear duties for each local authority to consult with service users about service provision. Providing information about people's rights is crucial to good practice in health and social care. For example, many carers do not know they are legally entitled to an assessment of their needs. People with a disability also have an automatic right to an assessment.

However, many people still do not receive up-to-date information, as this is expensive for local authorities to produce and there are concerns about creating more demand when local authorities cannot cope with the present level of demand.

Summary of Section 3.4

A positive care environment must take account of legislation and also understand how service users can complain

A clear understanding of the rights of service users is essential together with the awareness that there are real limits to their rights

PROMOTING SERVICE USERS' RIGHTS

Health and social care workers must uphold people's rights through services and keep to the main principles of good practice in their professional practice

Law, policies and procedures are not enough in themselves to ensure good practice

Kai has a learning difficulty and has worked out a number of life goals that he would like to achieve through a process of person-centred planning with his key worker. Kai would like support to enable him to attend religious meetings now that he has become a Muslim. Kai would also like help to identify appropriate food, and to advise him of what he should not eat. Kai's key worker has since left and no progress has been made on meeting his needs. Kai has an advocate who intends to try and get social services to do something for him.

Using concepts can you identify?
1. What actions could an advocate consider in order to achieve an improvement of services?

2. What moral rights might Kai have in relationship to the value base of care?

Go further – can you analyse issues using theory?
What legal rights does Kai have in relation to his religious and ethnic group identity. As a person with a learning difficulty, what legal rights does Kai have for services to meet his needs?

Go further – can you evaluate using a range of theory?
Can you explain why many people believe they are entitled to services, and yet legislation does not provide a legal right to the services that they might expect?

UNIT 3 ASSESSMENT

How you will be assessed

In order to achieve this unit you must produce a report that explains how a service user group accesses services. Your report must focus on either people who are ill, young children, older people or individuals with special needs.

You will be given instructions regarding the structure of the report, but your report will need to include evidence for each of the following:

ASSESSMENT OBJECTIVE	DETAILS
AO1 Rights of service users	You must explain the rights of service users when accessing services.
AO2 Barriers to accessing services	You must explain the potential barriers experienced by that service user group when accessing services and the effect of these barriers.
AO3 Policies and practices	You must explain the policies and practices designed to create a positive care environment.
AO4 Legislation	You must evaluate how legislation safeguards and promotes the rights of service users, together with an evaluation of organisations' responsibilities under relevant legislation and an explanation of methods of redress open to service users.

Assessment preparation

The best way to write report might be to focus on a real local service, and to research the way that service works. Ideally, you may be able to listen to talks, and go and visit work settings where you can explore what senior staff say about the importance of: care values, how to overcome barriers to accessing services and how policies and legal requirements enable staff to promote positive care environments. Again, if the opportunities exist, it would be ideal if you could actually interview a care worker after you have collected some ideas about care values, potential barriers, and what it takes to create a positive environment. If you can interview someone you may be able to get detailed guidance on legal issues as well as examples of how barriers to access can be overcome. The material you get from talking to care workers can be used in conjunction with the theory in this chapter to help write a report.

In order to undertake a successful interview you will need to plan the questions you would like to ask and perhaps discuss your plans with a tutor. It will be important to discuss the issue of confidentiality before starting any interview.

AO1 Rights of service users

To achieve the highest marks you need to show that you have in-depth knowledge and understanding of service users' rights. You must be able to clearly explain the importance of a value base in relation to the support of these rights. Overall, you must demonstrate that you have excellent understanding of the issues by providing full and accurate explanations in you work.

AO2 Barriers to accessing services

To achieve the highest marks you need to show that you can thoroughly apply your knowledge and understanding of potential barriers to access. You must be able to Identify the different barriers, provide a full explanation and discussion of each and their effects. The application of your knowledge to the promotion of positive care environments must be appropriate and accurate.

AO3 Policies and practices

To achieve the highest marks your research and analysis of the factors that influence the creation of a positive care environment must be of a high level. You need to analyse and explain at least three ways in which positive environments can be promoted in organisations through the development and implementation of positive policy and practice.

AO4 Legislation

To achieve the highest marks your evaluation of how legislation safeguards and promotes the rights of service users must be excellent. You need to be able to analyse and explain the responsibilities of organisations under relevant legislation. You must also show detailed knowledge of the methods of redress open to service users by providing clear explanations and analysis of at least three methods.

Unit test

1. What are care values and why are care values important when working with vulnerable service users?

2. Explain the concept of empowerment and provide an example of empowerment relevant to working with young children and an example relevant to working with older people

3. List three different types of consequence that could result from care workers failing to maintain confidentiality

4. Identify at least three different types of barrier to access to services

5. Explain some of the consequences of discrimination

6. What is the difference between anti-discriminatory practice and non-discrimination?

7. If you were researching the degree to which a particular care environment could be considered to be positive list at least four areas that you might focus on.

8. What laws protect people from discrimination on the basis of their religion?

9. What methods of redress are open to a service user who is dissatisfied with the quality of service that they receive?

10. Discuss the effectiveness of legislation in ensuring that service users' rights are maintained and that service users receive a high quality of service.

The answers to these questions are provided on page 157 of this book.

References and further reading

Adams, R. Dominelli. L., and Payne. M. (1998) *Social Work: Themes, Issues and Critical Debates* (Palgrave, Basingstoke)

Biestek , F. P. (1961) *The casework relationship* (London, Allen and Unwin)

Brammer, A. (2002) *Social Work Law*, (Harlow: Pearson)

Braye, S. (2003) *Social Work Law* (Harlow: Pearson)

Collins (1995) Dictionary of Social Work (Collins)

Cull, L. A. (2001) *The Law and Social Work* (Palgrave, Basingstoke)

Giddens, A. (1997) *Sociology*, 3rd ed. (Cambridge: Polity Press)

Katz, J . (1978) *White Awareness: Handbook for AntiRacism Training* (Massachuseths, USA:Greenfield)

Mandelstam, M. (1999) *Community Care Practice and the Law* (Jessica Kingsley, London)

Payne, M. (1991) *Modern Social Work Theory* (Macmillan, Basingstoke)

Roche, J. (eds) *Hunter Kane* (1996) Hunter Kane Management

Seligman, M. (1975) *Helplessness* (San Francisco: W. H. Freeman & Co.)

Shardlow, S. (1998) quoted in *Social Work: Themes, Issues and Critical Debates* (ed. Adams. R., Dominelli. L. & Payne. M.) (Palgrave, Basingstoke)

Thompson, N. (1997) *Anti-discriminatory Practice* (Macmillan, Basingstoke)

Thompson, N. (2000) *Understanding Social Work* (Palgrave, Basingstoke)

Thompson, N . (1993) *Anti-discriminatory Practice*, (Basingstoke and London: Macmillan)

Tuckman, B. (1965) *Development sequence in small groups* in Psycological Bulletin, vol. 63, No. 6

Relevant websites

Please see www.heinemann.co.uk/hotlinks (express code 3718s) for links to the following websites which may provide a source of updated information:

* Government legislation

* Learning matters

* Commission for Racial Equality

* General Social Care Council

* Equal Opportunities Commission

* British Association of Social Workers

* Council of Europe consultation paper on mental health and human rights

* Department of Health summary of human rights cases

* European Convention on Human Rights

* Disability Rights Commission

* Mobility and Inclusion

* Nursing & Midwifery Council

* Surestart

Answers to assessment questions

Unit 1

1a. (i) Later adulthood
   (ii) 5
   (iii) Middle adulthood
   (iv) There is a lack of viable eggs in the ovary that causes reduced levels of hormones and declining menstrual cycles eventually stopping completely. Sue cannot become pregnant again or bear any more children. This can be a relief or a sad time coinciding with the likelihood that grown-up children will start to move away. Sue may suffer from hot flushes, night sweats and changeable moods due to the menopause.

1b. (i) John may withdraw from many social activities as he feels ashamed and also cannot afford them due to a lower income. His self-esteem has lowered and his self-concept changed from positive to negative. This makes it harder to find a new job. He has lost status as the breadwinner and now depends on his wife's earnings. He often feels humiliated and depressed, as well as angry as losing of his job was not his fault. He gets emotionally drained from discussing job prospects that he shuns company and is short-tempered with his family.
   (ii) Husband being made redundant, shop is regularly vandalised, she is going through the menopause.
   (iii) Stress causes release of adrenaline, which raises blood pressure. Constant stress results in hypertension producing heart disease and strokes. Lack of sleep affects daily performance and lowered immunity can result in more disease. Depression is more common and suicide rate increases.

2a. (i) Divorce, bereavement, moving house or business and unemployment.

   (ii) Danger of being attacked – especially at night. Surgeries, clinics get robbed and vandalised; poor facilities in the neighbourhood, no incentive to work in rundown area, little interest in healthy living and can get better paid job elsewhere in pleasant surroundings.
   (iii) Stimulates and raises energy levels, outlet for feelings, gives her the 'feel-good' factor, makes new friends, puts worries in better perspective, improves resistance to disease, digestion, sleep, circulation and respiration. Provides a physical, emotional and social boost to life.
   (iv) Advantages – Almost instantaneous treatment, no waiting for a doctor's appointment; often cheaper than prescription charge and easily available. Disadvantages – May have harmful side effects unknown to purchaser; may not be the most appropriate medicine for the illness; No control over purchase so abuse can occur readily.

2b. (i) More road accidents due to lack of adequate safe play facilities; poorer health and education, less likely to achieve physical, emotional, social and intellectual potential.
   (ii) It is safer to belong to a gang than to be outside of the gang and risk harassment or bullying; individuals feel braver within gangs. Leaving a gang causes ridicule, taunting and bullying. Gang activities tend to be exciting and risky.
   (iii) Self-esteem is the way in which you value or feel about yourself.
   (iv) Self-esteem enables you to disagree with others; provides self-confidence and the ability to cope with difficulties. A person is liked by others and therefore popular with peers. Generally speaking, an individual with high self-esteem is happier and more content.

3a. (i) Adolescence

(ii) Infancy

(iii) Sarah will feel physically and emotionally drained at the end of the day. After some time, she may be fitter and healthier than before. She may feel younger; having younger people living in her home providing that Melanie gives Sarah some of her time. Sarah may feel as if she has no privacy and this may make her feel depressed.

(iv) During adolescence, friendships become the most important relationships even over family. It is important that Melanie still has those relationships for her emotional and psychological well-being. She will be able to trust her friends with secrets and confidences.

3b. (i) This is a disorder caused by a fault in the hereditary make-up of an individual.

(ii) Genes can be dominant or recessive; a dominant gene responsible for a fault will pass on the condition to any individual who receives the gene. The affected gene often miscodes a particular protein thus affecting every cell in the body. Where this is an important enzyme for metabolism, the condition can be severe. A recessive gene will only pass on the fault when it is present with another recessive gene for the same fault, but miscodes the protein in exactly the same way, just tending to miss generations.

(iii) Smoking, occupation, air quality/pollution

(iv) Smoking is very harmful to health; raises blood pressure causing hypertension, heart disease and strokes; narrows the arteries and releases lipids into the bloodstream thereby causing reduced blood flow and poor oxygenation to vital organs; tars are carcinogenic, cancers of the mouth, tongue, lungs, stomach, bowel and bladder are common. Nicotine is addictive, so more and more cigarettes are taken with increasingly poor health. Smokers are more likely to get respiratory infections that last longer. Pregnant mothers have smaller babies, increased risks of stillbirth or premature birth. Children from smoking families do less well at school.

(v) At various times, scientists have proclaimed that the qualities of the environment surrounding individuals were more important influences on human characteristics than inherited or genetic influences. At other times, scientists argued for the importance of genetic influences over environmental ones. This continuous argument is known as the nature versue. nurture debate. Nowadays we believe that characteristics arise from both influences inextricably linked.

4a. (i) Local people will not buy more expensive fresh vegetables that they have to spend time preparing when tinned and frozen goods are available. Sue had a lot of wasted vegetables as a result and finally had to stop stocking them.

(ii) Generally processed food contains more sugar, salt and hidden fat than fresh food. It has to have preservatives added and because the food has been cooked at high temperatures destroying natural vitamins, these must be added too. There is little fibre in processed food so the 'feel full' factor is removed and hunger soon returns.

(iii) Recent research has shown that smoking only one cigarette each day has a serious effect on women's fertility. Foetuses carried by smoking mothers tend to be small for dates and suffer from more respiratory difficulties during pregnancy. There are more miscarriages and stillbirths in smokers than non-smokers and infants and children tend to be smaller than their peers, more prone to chest infections and perform less well academically.

(iv) Children on the estate are likely to have orthodontal problems, decayed teeth and pain. This is likely because they have no regular dental check-ups, no dental treatment, no orthodontal service and do not consume the recommended daily allowance of fresh fruit and vegetables. As self- esteem is low on the estate, it is possible that oral hygiene is carried out under poor supervision, this completes the loop for more dental problems in the future.

Unit 2

1. The eyes, face, posture, muscle tension, movement, gesture (with arms and hands), touch (hands), proximity (position of the body), orientation (use of face position).

2. Verbal: using a clear calm voice, speaking using normal tone and volume, using effective listening skills, using questions in order to negotiate.
   Non-verbal: relaxed or calm body language, varied eye contact, keeping arms at side, keeping hands open, avoiding tense muscles, avoiding postures or gestures that might suggest anger or fear.

3. Keeping head at the same height as the child's head, maintaining eye contact, increased use of smiling in order to create a safe friendly encounter, speaking in a soft voice, varying tone and pitch of voice to create interest and attention, using leading questions to try to influence the child.

4. Preparing a checklist of issues about care values in order to focus the interview; Preparing a series of open questions; preparing appropriate probes and prompts that you can use to focus the interview; rehearsing your interview with another person before doing the real interview.

5. Using communication skills to learn about the beliefs, life and needs of service users; building a supportive relationship involving understanding, warmth and sincerity; respecting and valuing diversity, showing respect for others; maintaining the dignity of others when providing physical support or care; providing choice, supporting service user independence; maintaining confidentiality; praising children's achievement.

6. Use of open questions, probes and prompts; using active listening skills or using the communication cycle effectively; building a supportive relationship with the person; using appropriate non-verbal behaviour to show interest and involvement with the person; using appropriate language and body language in order to convey respect and value for the person.

7. Observing the behaviour of the service user, or possibly asking the service user how they feel. If a person is receiving respect and value they are likely to reflect respect and value back to the people working with them. If service users appear relaxed and confident when communicating with care workers this behaviour may indicate the meeting of emotional needs.

8. Emotional barriers, language barriers (including signed languages), cultural barriers, sensory barriers (hearing and vision) environmental barriers such as background noise poor lighting lack of privacy.

9. Understanding cultural differences is very important because misunderstandings, stereotyping or discrimination can result from making the assumption that everybody uses language or body language in exactly the same way. Learning to understand what an individual intends to communicate is critically important in order for active listening to work effectively and in order to build a supportive relationship. Understanding cultural differences is essential for the transmission of care values.

10a. Service users have legal rights that are established through Acts of Parliament such as the Disability Discrimination Act (1995). Acts of Parliament influence the design of national minimum standards, and the policies and procedures that employers design. In addition to legal rights service users may be perceived to have more general, moral rights associated with care values. Formal codes of practice such as the GSCC code of practice provide a basis for defining care values.

10b. Without identified rights it would be difficult to ensure that service users received a reasonable standard or quality of care service. Without identifiable rights service users would have no basis for challenging or complaining about poor quality services. Without rights and responsibilities it would be difficult to ensure that service users emotional, social, and self-esteem needs were met. Without rights service users might be increasingly vulnerable to neglect, abuse or exploitation by others.

Unit 3

1. Values are beliefs that identify 'something that is valued' or 'valuable' in a situation. Values can influence what people do and the choices and decisions that they make on a day-to-day basis within care. Care values may influence the way in which workers provide care. Care values are part of what is needed to provide quality and empowering care.

2. Empowering services aim to enable the service user to make choices and take control of his or her life, the opposite of empowerment is dependency where the staff have the power and the service user is dependent upon them. Empowering services for young people will stress the provision of learning opportunities so that children can develop self-confidence and self-esteem. Empowering services for older people will seek to enable older people to maintain personal decision-making and retain self-esteem. Direct payments may enable some older people to control the services that they receive.

3. Service users' security or safety could be put at risk if details of their property or behaviour are shared with an appropriate people. Service users could lose trust and confidence in care workers if personal information is made available without consent. A service user's self-esteem could be threatened by the sharing of personal information. A service user may feel disempowered if they cannot control the way personal information is used. Service users have legal rights to confidentiality defined in the Data Protection Act together with rights specified within National Minimum Standards by the CSCI.

4. Discrimination, communication barriers, organisational barriers, emotional barriers, geographical barriers

5. Disempowerment, increased vulnerability, emotional stress and poorer physical or mental health, loss of confidence or failure to grow up as a confident person, loss of self-esteem, exclusion from social groups, failure to develop an effective identity.

6. Non-discrimination involves not damaging other people by providing some people with a better quality of service than others. Antidiscrimination involves actively identifying and challenging discriminatory behaviour - in yourself and others or in systems within a work setting.

7. The quality of communication skills; the accessibility and clarity of the organisation's policies and procedures; the training opportunities available to staff; the application of care values including the GSCC code of practice, the valuing of diversity and promotion of equality and the maintenance of confidentiality.

8. The Employment Equality Religion and Belief Regulations 2003 provide a legal right to protection from discrimination within the field of employment. Some limited rights are provided by the Race Relations Acts.

9. Every service must have a complaints procedure, where a local authority has purchased the service the local authority's complaints procedure may also be accessed. A civil action for negligence can be taken, complaints that allege maladministration can be taken to the ombudsman. Commissions including the Commission for Social Care Inspection will hear complaints relevant to their role. Special courts called tribunals are involved in hearing certain kinds of complaint or appeal.

10. Legislation provides a framework that influences the design of policies and procedures that will be used as an organisational level to guide staff. Legislation also provides a framework for redress where service users can evidence a breach of their rights. Legislation cannot by itself control the moment by moment actions and decisions of care workers. Care values guide the moment by moment decisions that workers make. Legislation is therefore only part of what is needed in order to ensure that service users rights are maintained and that high quality services are delivered.

Glossary

Act of Parliament known as primary or statute law. Contains powers, duties and responsibilities

active listening involves more than hearing, it also involves using the communication cycle and being able to demonstrate what you have understood when you listen to another person.

adolescence the life stage from 8–18 years and the total of the physical, emotional, social and intellectual changes taking place in this life stage.

advocacy arguing a case for another. In law, an advocate argues a legal case. In care work, an advocate tries to understand and argue from a service user's perspective.

anti-discriminatory practice professional practice that challenges both discrimination and the assumptions that may result in discrimination.

assertiveness the skill of negotiating for your own needs whilst respecting the needs of others.

autonomy having independence and control over local or personal issues. In the context of care work, autonomy implies control of decisions over daily living activities.

axillary hair hair growing in the armpits.

babbling a pre-language stage of making meaningless sounds that may help in developing language at a later date.

bereavement and loss a process of transition, or coping with change, following a loss. This may be loss of a loved one, a skill or part of the body such as a limb. The process involves phases of shock, searching, using defences, denial, anger and guilt before final reconstruction is possible.

bill a statute law in draft form that goes through the House of Parliament, House of Lords and Royal Assent before it becomes an Act of Parliament.

bonding making an emotional attachment to a person.

buffering absorbing shock to protect people.

Care Standards Act 2000 an Act of Parliament that established the National Care Standards Commission.

care value base a series of principles that guide care practice. These principles were originally identified in National Vocational Qualifications but can also be identified in codes of practice.

centile charts normal ranges of measurements of large numbers of infants or children at different ages.

cephalo-caudal development development that takes place from the head downwards towards the tail (or legs).

code of practice guidance document making recommendations for practice. This does not have the force of an Act of Parliament but still needs to be incorporated into health and social care practice.

cognitive development forming the mental processes of understanding and knowing.

Commission for Social Care Inspection (CSCI) the inspection authority for care services that has taken over from the National Care Standards Commission and the Social Services Inspectorate.

communication barriers blocks which prevent communication. Examples might include blocks which prevent people from receiving a message, making sense of a message or understanding a message.

communication cycle the process of building an understanding of what another person is communicating.

concept a term used to classify, predict and explain physical and social reality. Concepts are probably dependent on experience of events and are useful to simplify experience and enable others to share.

Concrete operations the third stage in Piaget's theory of intellectual development. In this stage, children are unable to cope with abstract things but can solve logical problems, providing that they can see or sense the objects they are working with.

contagion the transfer of disease from one person to another by contact.

culture the collection of values, norms, customs and behaviours that make a group distinct from others. Many cultures have values linked to religious beliefs. Our culture may be one of the biggest influences in our lives.

Data Protection Act 1998 provides people with legal rights with respect to the confidentiality of information.

dementia a range of illnesses involving the degeneration or wasting of the brain. It is not part of the normal ageing process.

depression loss of social and emotional functioning. Many people experience depression at some time in their lives.

development Increase in skills, abilities or capacities relevant to physical, social, emotional or intellectual development.

duties defined in law with the word 'shall'. Local authority and social workers must carry these out.

educational/behavioural approach or model of health promotion a model that emphasises information giving to promote better knowledge and understanding of health matters so that individuals or groups can adopt healthier lifestyles.

embryo the first 8 weeks of human infant development in the uterus.

emotional development a process of forming the feelings that individuals have in association with relationships.

empowerment being given power. Not being dependent on others – making choices and taking control of own life decisions. Empowerment is the opposite of dependency.

environment the surroundings that people function in, such as air and water qualities, housing, landscape, crime, noise, etc.

Equal Opportunities Commission a commission that has the duty of monitoring gender equality issues in the United Kingdom.

ethics the term used to describe moral principles in action and to refer to the behaviour of social workers and other professionals towards service users and carers.

European Union formed in 1993 of member states with common foreign and security policies and with a political and economic focus.

fertilisation the union of a nucleus from the father's sperm with the nucleus of the mother's egg or ovum.

foetus the technical term for a baby in the uterus from the 8th week until birth.

formal operations the final stage in Piaget's theory of intellectual development. People at this stage can think abstractly.

funnelling a system for organising questions so that closed questions are always 'led up to', using general open questions to prepare the respondent.

gender the differences between males and females based on cultural or social expectations.

genetics the study of inheritance.

group a collection of individuals linked by common characteristics.

group maintenance the social needs of group members when they are working. Maintenance activities create an appropriate social atmosphere to enable members to work effectively.

group task the work or activities that a group of people have come together to do.

group values help to explain and define group norms of behaviour. (See **values**).

growth increase in physical size or complexity, getting taller or heavier.

GSCC code of practice a code that prescribes key principles to guide the professional conduct of care workers.

health the extent to which an individual or group is able, on the one hand, to realise aspirations and satisfy needs, and on the other hand, to change or cope with the environment. (WHO)

health education involves trying to influence or direct a change of attitude or behaviour in people as a result of giving information about health.

health promotion the process of enabling people to increase control over and to improve their health.

holistic health physical, social and mental well-being.

identity the understanding of self and life in relation to other people and society; how an individual person identifies him or herself. Social identity might focus on social group membership; personal identity might focus on a description of personality.

ill health or disability.

impairment damage to or loss of a physical function of the body.

income money that an individual or household receives from work or other sources.

independence being able to function without being dependent on others.

law set of rules made by Parliament that is enforceable by the courts and regulates the behaviour and responsibilities of individuals and public bodies.

lifestyle choice the way in which people choose to live their lives.

marginalise to treat as insignificant.

Maslow's hierarchy the psychologist Abraham Maslow's description of human needs as belonging to the following categories: physical, safety, love and belonging, self-esteem and self-actualisation. Care should not only cover physical and safety needs.

medical approach to health promotion using medical science to prevent disease.

menarche the onset of menstruation.

menopause the gradual cessation of menstruation and fertility.

milestones of development significant events taking place at certain, average periods of time, used for monitoring progress.

motor development the coordination of muscles to enable complicated movements to occur.

National Minimum Standards a set of requirements that forms the basis for inspection of care services. There are different sets of criteria for different services.

nature – nurture debate a long-standing debate on whether inheritance (nature) or environment (nurture) is most important in making people what they are. The modern view is that nature and nurture cannot be meaningfully separated.

neonate a newborn infant.

norm recognised standards of measurement.

norms patterns of behaviour that are followed by the members of a particular society, family or group.

noxious harmful

object permanence the understanding that objects exist whether they can be seen or not.

paediatrician a doctor who treats children and their illnesses.

palliative something used to relieve pain or anxiety.

PCS model a model developed by Neil Thompson (2001: Unit 2) to explain the different levels on which discrimination may operate and the levels on which anti-discriminatory practice needs to operate .

peer group a group of people who share common characteristics or circumstances and feel themselves to be like one another.

person-centred care care that places 'the person' at the centre of decision-making and activities, thereby valuing the individual 'personhood' of service users.

Piaget (see **concrete operations, formal operations, pre-operational, sensorimotor**).

poverty having insufficient resources to participate fully in society. Usually, but not always, measured in economic terms as a percentage of the mean or average of a benchmark e.g. average wage. Being in poverty is currently considered to be where income is less than 60% of average wage.

powers indicated by the word 'may' in an Act of Parliament. This means the local authority has a choice of whether to implement or not. Powers can change to become duties. An example is the Direct Payment Scheme, which started as a power or 'enabling piece of legislation' and it is now a compulsory duty for all local authorities to have one (and has been since 2003).

pre-operational the second stage of Piaget's theory of intellectual development. Infants in this stage cannot reason logically.

presbyopia long-sightedness developing in most people from the mid-forties onwards.

primary socialisation the socialisation that takes place in early childhood, in which the language, norms and values of the society the child has been born into are acquired.

primitive reflexes temporary reflexes occurring in the newborn, replaced after a few months with learned responses.

puberty the physical changes taking place in adolescence.

Race Relations Act 1976 amended 2000 an Act of Parliament which makes discrimination on the basis of race illegal.

redress to remedy or put right something that is wrong.

Registrar-General's social classification a method of dividing the population along the lines of class or occupation.

rights and responsibilities social values result in rights for people – but rights have boundaries. Rights are balanced with responsibilities.

role the behaviour adopted by individuals when they are interacting in social situations.

secondary socialisation the process by which we learn the norms, values and behaviour that makes us a member of a particular group. We learn the roles we are expected to play as a group member.

self-actualisation the highest level of development in Maslow's hierarchy. It means fulfilling your potential and everything you need to achieve.

self-concept the use of many concepts to describe, understand and perhaps, predict what you are like – an understanding of self.

self-confidence being assured of the ability to achieve something or cope with circumstances. Self-confidence may influence and be influenced by self-esteem.

self-esteem how well or badly individuals feel about themselves. Self-esteem is likely to influence how we relate to other people and how confident we are. High self-esteem may help a person to feel happy and confident. Low self-esteem may lead to depression and unhappiness.

self-image how a person views him or herself.

sensori-motor the first stage of Piaget's theory of intellectual development. Infants learn to co-ordinate their muscle movements in relation to things that they sense.

Sex Discrimination Act (1975) (amended 1986) an act of Parliament designed to make discrimination on the basis of a person's gender illegal.

social class see Registrar-General's social classification.

social development a focus on the way groups may influence relationship patterns within a culture.

social exclusion being excluded from opportunity – people with fewer life chances become less economically prosperous than the majority of people.

social networks when people who are linked together provide help and support in times of need.

social support networks partners, friends, family, relatives and members of community groups who provide a source of support for own self-esteem.

socialisation the process by which we learn the norms, values and behaviour that makes us a member of a particular group – learning to become 'social' or a social member of a group.

societal approach or model of health promotion concentrates on changing society to improve the health of the population rather than the individual.

speech community people who share the same rules, behaviours and expectations about the way a language is used.

stereotype a fixed way of thinking that involves generalisations and expectations about an issue or a group of people.

supportive relationship an encounter between people that conveys warmth, understanding and sincerity.

values beliefs about what is good or bad, right or wrong, worthless or worth striving for. Values relate to a judgment made about the merit, worth or importance of a particular action, attitude, behaviour, person or situation.

vulnerability being at risk of some kind of harm – not being protected from risk and harm.

zygote an alternative technical name for a fertilised egg.

Index

 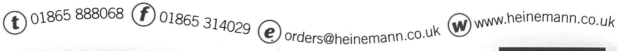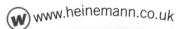